Digital Marketing For Dummies®

C000245188

Ways to Use the Internet for Marketing

Internet Service	Use for Marketing	
E-mail	**As a user:** Strive to be polite and positive. Create a signature file with marketing content for the end of your e-mail messages.	**As an Internet publisher:** Standardise key e-mail practices within your company. Use your Web site to offer relevant e-mail addresses for customer use; then carefully manage the (possibly large) number of e-mails you receive.
E-mail Lists	**As a user:** Join mailing lists that contain information relevant to Internet marketing or to your industry.	**As an Internet publisher:** Create an e-mail list as a relatively simple and inexpensive way to build a strong feeling of community within your customer base.
Message Boards	**As a user:** Join communities that concern your industry area. Seek out Web site-based discussion groups specific to your interest or industry.	**As an Internet publisher:** Offer a message board facility if it is appropriate to your business. Allow open, but moderated, dialogue between your customers and your company to develop a relationship and community feel. This way you can respond to any problems before they grow.
Blogging	**As a user:** Enter the blogosphere and check out the sites that are relevant to your business. Start with Blog search engines such as http://blogsearch.google.com/ to find your first sites and then follow the links.	**As an Internet Publisher:** Set up your own blog about your company or your industry and keep it up to date. Post relevant information and give your subscribers a reason to keep coming back, such as 'inside' information on new product development or statistics and research on your industry.
Paid Search	**As a user:** Pay attention to adverts that appear for other companies in your industry when you use search engines. See what keywords they come up for and the wording of their adverts.	**As an Internet Publisher:** Use this book to determine your paid search strategy. It is the single biggest advertising market online and has a proven track record of delivering results. If you don't use it your competitors will.
World Wide Web	**As a user:** Become an expert Web searcher for information on your industry and your competitors. Create bookmark files of key sites.	**As an Internet Publisher:** Start with a simple Web presence site to allow Web surfers to find basic information about your business online. Then expand with marketing-related content and news. Move to sales support and e-commerce if appropriate.

For Dummies: Bestselling Book Series for Beginners

Digital Marketing For Dummies®

Cheat Sheet

Key Digital Marketing Terms

3G. Or third generation, the name for the enhanced data communication services on mobile phones. The birth of the technology led to the setting up of mobile operator 3 in the UK.

Blogging. The act of creating a Web Log – A personal online Web space where users can put their thoughts and anything else they want.

Cookie. A small text file on the user's PC that identifies the user's browser and hence, the user so they are 'recognised' when they re-visit a site.

CPA (Cost Per Action). A metric for measuring the effectiveness of an Internet advertising campaign. Take the total cost of the campaign and divide it by the number of desired responses (actions).

CPC (Cost Per Click). One way to price Internet advertising. In the CPC model, the advertiser pays when a customer clicks an online ad.

CPM (Cost Per Thousand). The standard unit for buying or selling Internet advertising. To figure out what it costs to reach each individual viewer of an ad, divide the CPM rate by 1,000.

CTR (Clickthrough Rate). The percentage of viewers of a link who then click on it.

FAQ (Frequently Asked Questions). A document provided by many Web sites (and sometimes e-mail lists) with general information.

HTML (HyperText Markup Language). The code, placed in special markers called *tags* that is added to a text document to make it function as a Web page.

Hyperlink. Links in online marketing campaigns that take the reader to the next step in a process.

IE (Internet Explorer). The most popular Web browser in the world.

ISP (Internet Service Provider). A company that provides dial-up or other kinds of access to the Internet to individuals and businesses.

JPEG (Joint Photographic Experts Group). A standard for compressed pictures, widely used on the Web.

Keyword. A word or phrase that customers type into a search engine to find a service or product.

Podcasting. Making audio or video files available over RSS to consumers for viewing or listening on mobile devices.

ROI (Return On Investment). The percentage of profit or avoided costs generated by an expenditure.

RSS (Really Simple Syndication). A technology that allows people to receive constantly updated content without having to revisit a Web site.

SEO (Search Engine Optimisation). The process of making a site and its content highly relevant for both search engines and searchers.

SMS (Short Message Service). The most widely available service on mobile phones other than voice. Often known as texting, it permits the sending of short messages between mobile phones, other handheld devices, and even landline telephones.

Spam. Unsolicited commercial e-mail.

TLD (Top-Level Domain). The three letters at the end of an Internet domain name that denote the type of organization that owns the Web site.

URL (Uniform Resource Locator). The technical name for a Web address. For example `http://theinteractivezone.blogspot.com`. The URL allows you to locate services via the Internet.

WAP or Wireless Application Protocol. An open international standard for applications that use wireless communication. The main function of WAP is to provide access to the Internet from mobile phones.

Web 2.0. A collective name given to new technologies and consumer trends online including blogs, social networks, RSS, and podcasting.

WWW (World Wide Web). The number one vehicle for digital marketing efforts. (Also, `www.` is commonly found as a prefix to Web site names such as `www.yourcompany.com`.)

For Dummies: Bestselling Book Series for Beginners

Digital Marketing

FOR

DUMMIES®

Digital Marketing

FOR

DUMMIES®

by Ben Carter, Gregory Brooks,
Frank Catalano, and Bud Smith

John Wiley & Sons, Ltd

Digital Marketing For Dummies®

Published by
John Wiley & Sons, Ltd
The Atrium
Southern Gate
Chichester
West Sussex
PO19 8SQ
England

E-mail (for orders and customer service enquires): cs-books@wiley.co.uk

Visit our Home Page on www.wiley.com

For general information on our other products and services, please contact our Customer Care Department within the U.S. at 800-762-2974, outside the U.S. at 317-572-3993, or fax 317-572-4002.

For technical support, please visit www.wiley.com/techsupport.

Wiley also publishes its books in a variety of electronic formats. Some content that appears in print may not be available in electronic books.

British Library Cataloguing in Publication Data: A catalogue record for this book is available from the British Library

ISBN: 978-0-470-05793-3

Printed and bound in Great Britain by Bell & Bain Ltd., Glasgow

10 9 8 7 6 5 4 3 2 1

WILEY

About the Authors

Ben Carter runs his own digital agency helping famous and not so famous brands launch marketing initiatives to capitalise on the changing media landscape and ever-changing consumer behaviour.

Current clients of Ben Carter & Associates include npower and AOL, and the company has also provided consultancy services for several major UK-based blue-chip companies. Before setting up BCA, Ben worked as a business journalist for eight years, covering the UK's media and marketing sectors and most recently was News Editor of *Marketing* magazine. He has also freelanced for a number of national newspapers including *The Times* and *The Guardian* and is used regularly as a commentator on the booming digital economy by different media, including the BBC, *The Independent,* and CNN.

Greg Brooks is a freelance journalist who has written for a number of broadcasters, newspapers, and magazines including Channel 4, *The Guardian*, *Marketing*, *New Media Age,* and *Marketing Direct*. He has also carried out corporate ghostwriting and consultancy duties for a number of blue-chip clients around the globe. As part of his role as an industry commentator, he has spoken to organisations such as the BBC about how to communicate with consumers and journalists using interactive channels.

Frank Catalano is a veteran marketing consultant and analyst. He's the principal of Catalano Consulting, a strategic marketing firm advising Internet and technology companies. His consulting assignments include stints as Managing Director for PC Data's Internet Monitoring Division, VP Marketing for McGraw-Hill Home Interactive, VP Marketing for iCopyright, and VP Marketing for Apex Computer. He also was a marketing manager for Egghead Software and for the Apple Programmers and Developers Association. When not consulting, Frank provides tech industry analysis and commentary for KCPQ-TV Fox Seattle and is the author of the long-running Byte Me columns for *Seattle Weekly* and others. His essays and short fiction about technology have appeared in a wide variety of print and broadcast media, including ClickZ, Omni, Inside Multimedia, and Analog.

Bud Smith's experience is split between the technical and marketing sides of the computer and Internet industries. Bud was a short-order cook before starting in the computer industry at age 21. He was a data entry supervisor, programmer, and technical writer before working as a competitive analyst and QuickTime marketing manager at Apple Computer. He has been a full-time writer and has joined Frank in several consulting projects. Bud is currently Director of Marketing at AllPublish, a venture-funded Silicon Valley startup. Bud's writing experience is all on the nonfiction side and includes computer and medical articles as well as a dozen computer books.

Dedication

This book is dedicated to Imogen and Ruth for their love, patience, and support in all of our endeavours.

Authors' Acknowledgements

We would like to thank Alison Yates (Commissioning Editor) and Simon Bell (Development Editor) at Wiley for their tireless work and support in helping us produce this book. It's thanks to them that this book is now in print.

We would also like to thank our network of contacts for their support in helping us make this book become a reality. Special thanks to our technical editor, Stephen Small, for ensuring that we weren't too far off track with our comments and suggestions. All mistakes are, of course, our own.

Publisher's Acknowledgements

We're proud of this book; please send us your comments through our Dummies online registration form located at www.dummies.com/register/.

Some of the people who helped bring this book to market include the following:

Acquisitions, Editorial, and Media Development

Development Editor: Simon Bell

Commissioning Editor: Alison Yates

Copy Editor: Kate O'Leary

Technical Editor: Dr Stephen Small, marketing copywriter and communications consultant: www.top-copywriting.com

Executive Editor: Jason Dunne

Executive Project Editor: Martin Tribe

Cartoons: Ed McLachlan

Composition Services

Project Coordinator: Jennifer Theriot

Layout and Graphics: Claudia Bell, Carl Byers, Stephanie D. Jumper, Laura Pence, Rashell Smith

Proofreader: Susan Moritz

Indexer: Techbooks

Brand Reviewer: Jennifer Bingham

Wiley Bicentennial Logo: Richard J. Pacifico

Publishing and Editorial for Consumer Dummies

> **Diane Graves Steele,** Vice President and Publisher, Consumer Dummies
>
> **Joyce Pepple,** Acquisitions Director, Consumer Dummies
>
> **Kristin A. Cocks,** Product Development Director, Consumer Dummies
>
> **Michael Spring,** Vice President and Publisher, Travel
>
> **Kelly Regan,** Editorial Director, Travel

Publishing for Technology Dummies

> **Andy Cummings,** Vice President and Publisher, Dummies Technology/General User

Composition Services

> **Gerry Fahey,** Vice President of Production Services
>
> **Debbie Stailey,** Director of Composition Services

Contents at a Glance

Table of Contents

Introduction

*T*he Internet is the subject of great excitement these days – and of great anxiety. Businesses have wonderful new opportunities to grow and to extend their relationships with customers – and new types of competitors that may take those customers away. This book will help you make sure that the Internet is your friend.

Marketing, broadly defined, is everything that happens from the initial idea for a product or service until it is created, tested, sold, updated, repriced, promoted, and eventually retired from inventory. Marketing differs from sales in that marketing responds to customer needs and creates demand for a product or service; sales fulfills that demand. However, this book is not a marketing primer; for that, see *Marketing For Dummies,* by Craig Smith and Alexander Hiam (Wiley). The job of this book is to tell you and show you how to market your products and services effectively on the Internet.

About This Book

If you've ever surfed the Web, you've no doubt stumbled across a great deal of marketing content; a large part of this book is therefore devoted to marketing on the Web. But in this book we also show you that the online world is much more than the Web. Online services, Usenet newsgroups, e-mail, personal organisers with Net connections, even cell phones are all part of the Internet's reach and are all potentially useful for your Internet marketing strategy.

We, the authors of this book, have many years of marketing and Internet experience, and we draw on all of it to tell you how to best use each and every one of these Internet services – and how to prioritise and combine your efforts to create the most effective Net presence possible.

Conventions Used in This Book

Our *conventions* are standard ways of structuring specific types of information that you find in this book, such as steps and instructions. (One example of the use of a convention is the use of italics for the word *convention* when it appeared in the second sentence of this paragraph; when you see a term in italics, a definition of it may soon be following.) Here are the major conventions for this book:

✔ Things that you, the reader, are asked to type, as well as specific instructions that you need to follow in a set of numbered steps, are shown in **bold.**

✔ New terms are printed in *italics*.

✔ Information used in specific ways is formatted in a specific typeface. This book uses a special typeface for URLs (Uniform Resource Locators), which are the addresses used to specify the location of Web pages and other Internet resources. For example, the URL for the *For Dummies* site is as follows:

`http://www.dummies.com`

✔ In most of this book, we omit the `http://` from Web addresses because you don't actually have to type that part of the Web address into your Web browser.

✔ Related, brief pieces of information are displayed in bulleted lists, such as the bulleted list that you're reading right now.

✔ Right-clicking means clicking something on-screen while using the right mouse button. (That's right, mouse button as in "the mouse button on the same side of the mouse as your right hand," not "the mouse button that isn't the wrong one.") If you are left-handed or for some other reason have changed your mouse settings, you may need to use a different mouse button to achieve the effect of right-clicking something. Also, right-clicking doesn't have a direct equivalent on the Macintosh, which has only a single button on the mouse. For the Macintosh, the commands you choose by right-clicking in Windows are usually available via program menus.

How This Book Is Organised

To make finding things in this book easier for you, we divide it into parts that separate chapters into easily located, related groups. Here's a quick guide to the parts in this book.

Part 1: Getting Started with Digital Marketing

You need to know a few basics to use the digital world effectively for marketing. For example, you need to know what Internet services are available for you to deliver your marketing messages; just as important, you need to know who's out there in the online world for you to reach with your marketing effort.

Ever wonder why some companies have a great URL (online address) that's easy to remember, and others don't? In Part I we tell you how to get the right URL for your online marketing work.

The Internet is a place not only for you to do marketing but also to find information for all your marketing planning, both online and offline. (We use the term *offline* to mean everything that isn't online, such as all your traditional marketing efforts.) As soon as you know who's there and how to reach them, you're ready to plan your online marketing effort. We give you a step-by-step description of how to create just such a plan.

Part II: Marketing on the World Wide Web

Part II is your tour – we think it's a tour de force – of how to establish an effective presence on the most popular Internet service of all, the one that's captured imaginations (and investments) around the world, the World Wide Web. In four easy-to-follow chapters, we tell you how to build your own Web presence, either as a DIY project or working with other professionals, whether employees of your company or hired consultants. After reading this part, you'll know just how to get what you want from your Web marketing effort.

Part III: Marketing with Search

Search engines have become the most important way by which Internet users find content and information online. This helps to make them by far the most valuable digital advertising tool available, so in this part we guide you through the pros and cons of search and give you a guide to how to implement your own search marketing strategy.

Part IV: Even More Digital Marketing

This part takes you over the finish line to knowing all the angles in digital marketing. Usenet newsgroups and other discussion groups can be a big help or give your marketing efforts a big hurt. Chat and online services are two more ways to learn from your (potential) customers and to get the message out.

Internet advertising is a whole other realm of communication. As Web marketers, we've learned a great deal about what works and what doesn't. And public relations is free (except for all the work you do); we show you how to use PR effectively on the Net.

In this part we also discuss the impact of Web 2.0, the self-publishing blog phenomenon, and the explosion of social networking and video sharing which has been ushered in by MySpace and YouTube. We also offer tips on how to make these new arenas work for marketers.

Part V: The Part of Tens

The chapters in the Part of Tens are fun but have serious information about things to do in Internet marketing, things not to do, and pointers to some of the best *offline* resources to use in creating your online marketing presence.

The Digital Marketing For Dummies Internet Directory

The different design of the pages used for this part tells you that something else is going on here. This part consists of a directory of Internet resources to help you in your online marketing efforts. Each entry in the directory gives you an address and a quick description of a site or service that offers valuable information for the online marketer.

Icons Used in This Book

You're ready to begin using this book, but let us quickly tell you one last thing. This book uses icons, or little pictures, to flag things that don't quite fit into the flow of things. The *For Dummies* books use a standard set of icons that flag these little digressions, such as the following:

This icon is just a friendly reminder to do something.

This icon is a friendly reminder *not* to do something.

This icon points out nerdy technical material that you may want to skip.

This icon points out a tip or provides a bit of useful information.

Where to Go from Here

Where you go from here depends entirely on what you want from this book. If you're new to the whole idea of setting up a marketing-based website, you need to check out the essentials of planning and preparation in Part I. If you want the inside track on making even a basic Web site the most effective marketing tool it can be, turn to Part II. The crucial importance of search engines to digital marketing is covered in Part III, and Part IV gives you the information you need to know to get your marketing message across on a range of platforms.

Part I
Getting Started with Digital Marketing

'How's the written plan coming, John?'

In this part . . .

The digital – or *online* – world is a whole new arena for marketing, one with many opportunities – but also with its own history and rules. Use this part to become familiar with using Internet resources effectively, learn more about who's online, and find out how to start extending your marketing efforts to reach this new audience.

Chapter 1

Getting Net-Savvy

. . . .

. . . .

*T*he Internet is a relatively new phenomenon; only 30 years have elapsed since it was first invented and it was used for business for the first time in the early 1990s. Marketing is old – 'the second-oldest profession', as some of us would have it. Guess which topic is more misunderstood – the Internet or marketing?

The answer to that question is 'marketing'. Marketing can mean anything from pure public relations to all the stuff you do in running a company. We use a broad definition because we think marketing is vitally important.

Marketing, in our definition, is part of just about everything you do in creating a product. Identifying something that people might want to buy is a marketing activity, even if the person coming up with the idea is an engineer, salesperson, executive, or secretary. (A six-word description of how to get rich is: 'Find a need and fill it'. Doing so's the first step in marketing.)

So you've identified a need and want to fill it. Creating a specific definition of your product or service is also a marketing activity. Product development people might then take the ball and run with it for a while, creating a prototype of the product or service. But deciding when the product or service is acceptable and ready to sell is marketing, too.

The marketing department then sets the initial price and hands the whole thing to the sales department. Sales's job is to sell; marketing tracks the progress of sales and tweaks the product and price for maximum profit. Promotions, public relations, and packaging are also part of the marketing effort.

The Internet versus the Web

In many cases, people use terms such as the *online world, Internet digital,* and *World Wide Web* more or less interchangeably. Doing so's okay and reflects some interesting realities about the Internet. (Okay, you got us already: When we say 'the Internet' we mean the whole thing – the Web, e-mail, traditional online services such as AOL, Yahoo! and MSN, and all else that depends on being wired or wireless – as is increasingly the case. Basically the online world is anything that you can connect to with your computer, or with a smaller device such as a Palm handheld organiser or a mobile phone and a modem.)

At present, the World Wide Web is the most exciting place on the Internet, and your company or product Web site should be both the starting point and the lynchpin of your digital marketing effort. However, you need to use other Internet services such as e-mail and online advertising in its various formats to complement and support your Web presence. So don't be confused when you see terms such as *Internet, Web digital,* and *online services* all used more or less interchangeably; they're just different parts of the online jigsaw that everyone is trying to put to work for themselves.

Marketing also influences areas that don't directly involve business. Politics has been revolutionised – for better or worse – by marketing-type practices. Job-hunting is increasingly understood to mean marketing yourself. Even non-profit organisations hire specialists to help them identify and reach target markets of donors and recipients of aid and services.

Companies vary widely in what areas they call 'marketing' and what they call product development, engineering, or something else, and that situation's fine with us. Our point is not to say that marketing should take over everything in a company, but to point out that marketing either determines or affects almost everything a company does. If you care about making something – anything – happen in this big, wide, wonderful world of ours, you care about marketing.

In this chapter, we introduce the Internet and how it fits the needs of marketers (which means just about all businesspeople). *Hint:* You've probably never thought of some aspects of the Internet the way we do, so be ready to discover something. We then justify the need for marketing on the Internet – so you can tell your boss why you're suddenly spending so much time surfing the Web – and show you how to find the market for your products or services online. We finish by telling you how to use digital marketing resources.

Marketing on the Internet

What is the Internet? Well, the Internet's a big mess – a mix of good and bad ideas, shaken, stirred, half-baked, and served buffet-style. More seriously, the

Internet means many things to many people, but luckily we can give you a simple answer as to what it really is.

The Internet is simply an *inter-network* (which is where we get the word 'Internet' from); that is, a way to connect many smaller computer networks and computers with one another. The reason people call it *the* Internet, and not just *an* internet, is that the Internet is the one network that connects most of the computers on Earth, so it deserves to be recognised as one specific thing. What makes all this connecting possible is that the Internet has a set of unifying standards. Though doing so is simplistic, you can think of the Internet as just a whole load of wires that carry messages that are compatible with each other.

Each different type of content that goes over the Internet is called an Internet *service*; e-mail is one Internet service, and the Web is another. An Internet service meets agreed-on, public standards so that any computer on the Internet can access the particular service, using any of a variety of available software packages. These standards are based on *protocols*, each of which is like a language that the computers on the Internet speak when they want to transfer a particular kind of data. When people talk about the Internet today, they're not just talking about the underlying wiring; they're talking about the various Internet services and protocols that they use or have heard about.

One such Internet service is used to transfer any kind of file between computers. This service is known commonly as *FTP*, which stands for File Transfer Protocol. You can send text documents, computer programs, graphics, sound files – in fact, just about anything – with FTP. E-mail, which uses its own specific protocols, emerged as an early, text-only Internet service. The Web, another service with, again, its own protocol, became wildly popular by adding graphics to the mix. And Internet usage is growing even faster as people use small, wireless devices such as mobile phones and PDAs (Personal Digital Assistants) to communicate over the Internet. Expect to see more new Internet services, and lots of growth and change in existing ones, as the Web develops still further in the years to come.

Introducing the Web

The World Wide Web (or just *Web* for short) is the most talked-about online invention ever. Hyped beyond belief in the world press, and the force behind rags-to-riches stories like that of eBay, Amazon, and hundreds of other start-ups, the World Wide Web is one of the great business stories of all time.

Luckily, the hype does come with some real justification. As we explain in detail later in this chapter, the Web has billions of real users who collectively spend millions of hours a day surfing the Web around the world.

Using the Web is made possible by software programs called *Web browsers*, the runaway leader being Microsoft Internet Explorer – although others exist including Netscape Navigator, Firefox, and Safari. In this book, we show Internet Explorer in our screen shots because this browser's the most widely used.

From a marketer's point of view, the Web is best understood as a collection of shopping services, news sources, glossy company reports, and advertising collateral that can be accessed by a large and fast-growing group of unusually influential people. But the Web is a wild world. Side-by-side with the company and product information are college course materials, personal home pages known as blogs, that describe hobbies, children, and pets, political advertising, and anything else that you care to name. A glossy corporate home page is shown in Figure 1-1, and a personal home page is shown in Figure 1-2.

The Web is one of the best tools ever invented for marketing. Unlike television adverts, which force themselves on the viewer, Web sites are accessed only by users who *want* to see them – your message is reaching people who actually choose tosee it by logging onto your site or clicking on your advert. But to get people to stay with you, you need to make your site sticky – that is, interesting and relevant to the user so they 'stick around'.

Figure 1-1:
The
corporate
look of the
Web.

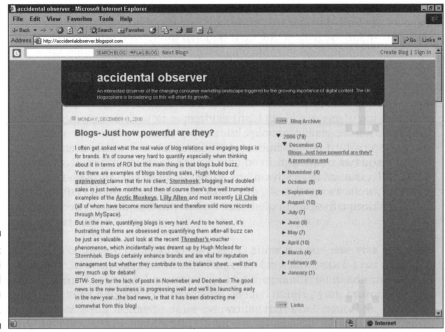

Figure 1-2:
The
personal
look of the
Web.

Shouting above the noise on the Web is impossible. You can't get in people's faces on the Web the way you can with a television or radio commercial or even a print ad; people can click the Back buttons on their browsers to leave a site even faster than they can turn the page of a magazine or find the TV remote control hidden in the crevices of their sofas. The trick is to put up a competent, easy-to-use Web site and then help the people who want to find you do so. (In Chapter 8 we show you how to get your site registered with the various search engines so that your site can be easily found. Chapter 2 covers using search engines in order to find marketing-related information on the Web.)

The Internet has now begun to live up to its hype about being the most important communication tool in the world. Finding Web pages that use either audio or video features to spice up the experience of the user is increasingly common. However, this tactic isn't right for everyone – a rock anthem playing over the home page of your online flower delivery company may not send out the right image.

To use the Web effectively, find the right mixture of information mixed with enough graphical eye candy to attract a reader to your business. Chapters 4 to 7 cover the ins and outs of building and publicising your marketing Web site.

E-mail and mail lists: Unsung online heroes

E-mail is one of the biggest reasons the Internet has become the success that it is today. The origins of the Internet are in the communication of information between different computers. A long time ago (during the 1980s), people had e-mail accounts with services, each with their own proprietary network and separate protocols. But people on each online service wanted to be able to send e-mail to friends and colleagues who used other services. To allow this interaction, the proprietary online services had to add *Internet gateways* (connections to the Internet) for e-mail to flow through from one person on one network to another person on another network. Businesses then connected their in-house e-mail systems to the Internet, and the Internet grew rapidly, setting the stage for the Web and other online resources.

Over the last ten years e-mail has evolved from a text-only format to one that is enriched with graphics, audio, and even video. *HTML mail* has now become the norm – although most companies will still offer their subscribers a text-only format. HTML mail is a message resembling a Web page, with graphics and formatted text, that can be viewed by most popular e-mail clients such as Microsoft Outlook, Yahoo! mail, and Hotmail. In both text and HTML forms, e-mail is still an important communications medium and a key part of online marketing.

Like real mail (or *snail mail* – the kind delivered (sometimes) by the Royal Mail), e-mail is a tempting channel for marketing. People have become used to getting advertising offers in their postal mail – though the disparaging terms *junk mail* or *spam* demonstrate what many people think of this kind of mailing. But e-mail, unlike much regular mail, feels very special to people; they seem to take their e-mail Inbox more personally than they do their postal mail. So when you're using e-mail for marketing to lots of people, proceed with caution, as we explain in detail in Chapters 12 and 13.

The most important things to remember when using e-mail for online marketing are two dos and a don't:

> ✔ **Do make sure that you and your company respond to all e-mail you receive.** We know managing your e-mail Inbox can be hard; and if you put an e-mail address on a popular Web site, you can easily get flooded with e-mail. But make sure that you don't ignore any contacts or prospective customers you bring in and that they receive quick and appropriate responses.

> ✔ **Do try to ensure that e-mail sent to people outside your company is positive and informative.** Every e-mail sent by anyone in your company is, at least in part, a marketing message.

> ✔ **Don't send unwanted e-mail, such as the mass e-mail *spam* that some companies send to prospective (that is, soon to be *ex*-prospective) customers.** Most recipients ignore spam e-mail; others respond aggressively, with angry notes or even *mail bombs*, automated mass mailings back to the sender that can choke the sender's mail system.

Most companies now have their own *mailing lists*, a set of e-mail addresses that have been collected or bought from third-party companies and represent people who are interested in receiving more information about specific companies, products, or services.

We describe the effective use of e-mail and creating, maintaining, and influencing a mail list in Chapters 12 and 13.

Online messageboards and forums: The threat and the promise

Thanks to the Internet, information can now be passed around the world at lightning speed. This –speed of communication is a great thing for marketers as they can talk to a massive audience from just one PC – but it also comes with some very real dangers.

Traditional marketing in the offline world is usually a pretty safe one-way experience. The company wants to say something, so they tell the consumer about it. Any response from the consumer is usually on a one-to-one level with the company. Any problems or arguments that arise between company and consumer are also on a one-to-one basis – unless the consumer calls the BBC's *Watchdog* TV programme, for example.

Enter the Internet and chatrooms and forums. Chatrooms and forums are online meeting places for people who have similar interests and, as such, they can provide a source of potential customers. Interacting with people in this environment, though, can be very useful but also very dangerous.

Here's an example of how a forum destroyed the reputation of one product. Kryptonite, a US company, produces and markets supposedly super-strong bike locks. In 2004, on a fairly popular bike forum called bikeforums.net, a consumer posted an article saying that he could break into his lock using a cunning device – a biro – and did anyone else know about the flaw?

Within minutes the message thread had been viewed by thousands; in hours hundreds of thousands had seen it; and then videos were posted online showing the locks being picked using a pen.

Kryptonite remained unmoved by the growing furore and did not respond to the forum postings, despite being aware of the problem and being urged by consumers and other forums to post online and reassure people – or to give an explanation. The company took over a week to respond – initiating a product recall – but by this time the damage was done. The story was picked up by CNN and other major news channels and made the pages of newspapers such as the *New York Times*, as well as fuelling a lawsuit brought by aggrieved customers.

The irony behind the whole story is that not only could some of the flak have been deflected if the company had used online forums to address the problems, but also the story itself was old, having been first published in a British bicycle magazine in 1992 and on USENET, a messageboard operating in the 1990s, at the same time.

This story provides a perfect example of how the immediacy of the Internet can destroy a brand as it gives new power to the consumer and new currency to information.

Online advertising

Online advertising is the extreme case of digital marketing, in that online advertising is usually intended to produce an immediate and easily measurable result. In many ways, the Internet is the ideal medium for advertising, and in other ways, this medium's the worst place for ads.

A plethora of different kinds of online advertising exist, ranging from traditional Jpg or Gif banner ads, which are horizontal strips of advertising placed across the top or bottom of a Web page to full 'bells and whistles' all singing and dancing video- and audio-rich media ads that can take over a whole Web page.

Rich media ads have risen in popularity over the past few years as Internet connection speeds have increased and digital marketing has become more sophisticated. These ad formats can vary hugely but all have the same principle in that they are high-impact and attract the eye of the user more readily than standard banner ads. See companies such as Tangozebra (`www.tangozebra.com`) and Eyeblaster (`www.eyeblaster.com`) for examples.

Other forms of online advertising include sponsorships, search marketing – which allows companies to bid on keywords in search engines to display their ads above competitors on the results page – affiliate marketing and pretty much anything else you can dream up. Above all, the Internet is a versatile medium.

The good news is that the impact of Internet ads, unlike any other kinds of ads, can be easily measured by how many people click the ad. A typical *click-through rate* on an Internet ad – the percentage of people who click the ad – is less than 1 per cent. You can roughly measure the cost of an Internet ad campaign by taking the total cost of running the ads and dividing by the number of times that users clicked the ad, which yields the *cost per click*. Less than 1 per cent is still more than, say, response rates to direct marketing; proof of how powerful online advertising can be – if done properly. See Chapters 9 to 11 for more on cost-per-click.

Cost per click captures only the actions of users who are so highly motivated by the ad that they stop what they're doing and click an ad that will take them somewhere else on the Internet. Harder to measure is the impact on people who don't click, but later take some positive action because they've been influenced by your ad – just like newspaper, magazine, TV, radio, billboard, and just about every other kind of advertising. This additional effect of Internet ads, sometimes referred to as *branding* or *brand awareness*, is much harder to measure (although companies do exist who claim to be able to accurately do so).

As an Internet marketer, you need to decide whether to promote your own ads, called *house ads*, within your own site and whether to allow others' ads on your site. You also have to decide when and how to advertise your products and services on other people's sites – Chapter 12 is all about Internet advertising.

Wireless access

Strictly speaking, wireless access includes portable computers and even desktop computers that connect to the Internet without wires. But in common usage, wireless access refers to small-screen devices that can access the Internet, especially Palm handheld organisers and mobile phones with WAP (Wireless Access Protocol) and 3G capability.

What do these wireless devices have in common? Here's a brief list:

- **Small screens.** A Palm system displays roughly 15 lines of about 40 characters each, less than one-fourth the text of a small laptop screen. A typical WAP phone displays about 4 lines of 12 characters each, far less than a Palm system and a 3G phone, and although able to show video and audio it is also constrained by the size of the screen.

- **Varying connection speeds.** Most wireless devices used to have slow connections, but that isn't the case now. Investment in wireless networks from mobile phone companies and also the development of wireless 'hotspots' have led to ease of access and fast data transfer – although some devices do still experience problems. Even so, most people only want to read an e-mail on the go anyway.

  ✔ **High utility.** People tend to find their Palm devices and mobile phones indispensable, taking them everywhere they go and trying to find new uses for them. The excitement level is much like the early days of PCs, with people interrupting meetings to beam new software from one Palm to another or look up a stock quotation on a WAP phone.

  ✔ **Widespread use.** Mobile phones are far more common than PCs and spreading fast – the UK holds more mobile phones than people. Handheld devices are also selling quickly and can easily be deployed throughout a company. The huge popularity of the Blackberry e-mail device is just one example of this technology.

You may ask, like any good marketer, what can wireless devices do for you? For most marketing purposes, you probably don't need to do anything just yet. You need to consider whether you can usefully and profitably deliver needed information to customers who use wireless access. Being the first on your block to jump into wireless information access may not be cost effective, but not being ready to move when the time is right may be even more of a problem. Get the other elements of your digital marketing strategy in place; then consider extending your domain to the wireless world.

Considering whether You Need to Market on the Internet

Because the Internet in general and the Web in particular have received so much hype, many companies have been swept up by a 'gold rush' mentality, spurring them to get on the Internet quickly, with the threat of otherwise missing out on the next big thing. The crash of technology companies' share prices in early 2000 showed that too many investors had moved in too fast, with too much money, trying to make money from the Internet. If you're wary of technological flashes in the pan (and given the demise of the 8-track tape, CB radios, and Betamax video players, maybe you should be), you can be excused for wondering whether you really need to market on the Internet.

In this book, we give you a lot of cautionary notes about how to avoid over-investing or foolishly investing in an online presence. A heavy investment in digital marketing isn't for everyone. However, we think that nearly all businesses should have a clearly defined online strategy, including goals, methods to use in meeting those goals, and ways to measure success.

Though businesses vary tremendously in how many online customers they have – for example, most potential computer buyers research prices and models online, but only a minority of all dog-food buyers do – the people online include most of the opinion-makers and trendsetters. Someone buying a can of soup made by your company may never see your Web site; but someone writing an article about trends in soup marketing is almost sure to try to look you up. (You do want your company to get mentioned in the press, right?) And increasingly, supermarket managers who make decisions about what food items to stock are starting their work by looking online, too. (And, of course, you want your company to be considered early in major buying decisions.)

So you need to market online. But just what is *marketing*? Marketing is the whole process of defining, promoting, and managing the sales of goods and services. The marketing cycle includes not only outbound communications such as advertising and public relations but also activities such as surveys, customer focus groups, demographic research, and so on that tell you what kinds of products to create and sell. This book shows you how to market your company, your products, and your services effectively using the Internet.

Marketing divides people up into groups called, strangely enough, *markets*. A market is a group of people who are conscious of themselves as a group and who communicate with one another on topics of shared interest that relate to your product. Gender and age groups are markets, as are people who share a profession, a nationality, or a specific role in a family – child, parent, or grandparent. An important part of digital marketing is knowing which markets you're trying to reach and where to find them online – this book helps you do just that.

Being online – especially having a decent-looking company Web site – is becoming as important as being in the phone book. If you want people to contact you at all, you'd better be listed. In Chapters 4 to 7, we explain the basics of creating a competent online presence cheaply, and we go into detail for people who want to go beyond simple *online presence* into proactive online marketing. But start by making sure that each product, service, or company that you're involved with has at least a basic, effective Internet marketing effort. The next section describes how to identify your target market as it exists on the Internet.

Finding Your Online Market

The online world has changed dramatically. By February 2006, over 10 million UK households were accessing the Internet via broadband, and most professional people in the UK have Internet access at work. (In general, the more purchasing power someone has, the more likely he or she is to be online.)

If you are doing marketing in the UK and you tell people that information they really want or need is available on your Web site, chances are that most of them can get to it if they want to. If you're selling goods and services to businesses, nearly all potential purchasers are likely to be online.

A few great sources for overall Internet data are OfCOM,– the communications regulator in the UK that can tell you the overall size of the market and other basic facts; IMRG, which can give you statistics on the amount of people shopping online and what they're buying; and organisations such as Jupiter Research and Forrester Research, which regularly carry out research into different market sectors. Some information is free, but the more detailed stuff will cost you. A very useful source of information for free is Alexa (www.alexa.com), an online service that gives you specific traffic information about Web sites such as reach, page views, and rank amongst other sites in its sector.

If you do your research properly you'll see that the online world is not the same as the offline world in the UK. In deciding how much time, energy, and money to spend on your digital marketing efforts, you really need to take some time to find out who's online and compare that to who you're trying to reach in your marketing efforts. Then you can size your online efforts to match your expected rewards.

Statistics are an attempt to capture a snapshot of current realities and can be accurate to within a few percentage points – or can be thoroughly biased, misrepresented, and misused. The statistics quoted here are the best freely available ones we could find. Projections are an attempt to *guesstimate* the future, and so are inherently unreliable unless you have Nostradamus on your team, or read tea leaves. We suggest that in your marketing planning for the online world, and indeed for all your marketing planning, you rely heavily on statistics and very lightly on projections.

People like to talk about how fast the online world is changing, but the results from many surveys of the online world are actually becoming increasingly consistent from one survey period to the next. Though the number of Internet users is growing rapidly, the characteristics of the user population – for example, the percentage of males versus females, types of professions represented, and so on – now change little in the six months between surveys. You can make decisions about your Internet presence today with relatively good confidence that the Internet population, though larger, will still look much the same by the time you implement your decisions.

Internet user profile

What does it mean to be online? This term can cover everything from being a light e-mail user, who may only look at Web sites such as the BBC and other 'trusted' sources, to a music downloading, MP3 ripping, podcast broadcasting eBayer, who only uses their MySpace URL on their business card and does all their Christmas shopping online.

Following are implications of the prevalence of Web use and other conclusions that can be drawn from available surveys of the online and offline worlds:

- **The online world is huge:** Working out exactly how big the online universe is isn't possible, but research company Nielsen//NetRatings puts it at around 475 million (home accessing users), with 36 million in the UK. That figure represents about 10 per cent of the entire world population and is growing all the time, especially with countries such as India and China coming online with increasing speed. Implication: The Internet has a large audience, but it doesn't reach everyone – although it is the best way to reach the most people.

- **The online world is English-language dominated.** According to Nielsen//NetRatings, the United States has 205 million home Internet users, representing about 40 per cent of all home Internet users as of May 2006. Japan is next with 68 million, followed by Germany with 50 million and then the UK with 36.5 million. Few figures are available for the emerging markets in the East but China is expected to become a major consumer of the Internet in the next five to ten years. Implication: Online efforts that are focused first on the English-language market will reach the most users and are more likely to get results.

- **The UK market is 12–18 months behind the US.** That the UK market follows the US market, but with a time delay of about 12–18 months, is a widely held belief. The closeness of this gap is due to the ease of business afforded by using (relatively) the same language and the similarity of the markets. A shared language can be very useful for spotting trends before they hit the UK, but beware merely transplanting US practices to the UK as doing so without adapting them for subtle UK nuances rarely works. Implication: The UK and Europe are closing the gap between them and the US, so be ready to market to more than just a UK audience if your business demands it.

- **The online world is young and affluent.** Statistics from research company Nielsen//NetRatings show that the majority of Internet-using households in the UK have an income greater than £30,000 a year, with 30 per cent earning more than £50,000 a year. The largest age group of online users are 35–49 year olds, who make up almost 30 per cent of the total UK online audience. Only 26 per cent of the UK online audience are over 50 years old. Implication: The Internet is a great place to reach a young and affluent audience that has money to spend on your products and services. More people are spending money online than ever. According to the Interactive Media in Retail Group (IMRG), online sales have grown 2000 per cent in the last six years and £80 billion of consumer spending is either on or influenced by the Internet. To put this statistic into perspective, the average weekly value of all consumer sales in the UK for one week in May 2006 was £4.7 billion according to the Office for National Statistics. Implication: The Internet is a good way to develop a new revenue stream, so research whether your products or services can be sold online.

Some facts and implications are obvious and their effects on your marketing strategies are easy to figure out. However, other conclusions may take longer to grasp. For example, in the offline world, older people tend to be richer than younger ones; the fact that the Web has both a younger-than-average population and a richer-than-average population implies that it must have a very high percentage of people who are both young *and* rich. (Maybe that means you can think about digitally marketing gold-plated skateboards – unfortunately, we doubt it.)

Working in the Online World

You picked up this book to help yourself do effective marketing work online. In this chapter, we provide an overview to help you get a handle on the online world, what the pieces are that make it up, who's in it, and how to start matching your marketing goals to it. Here are some lessons to carry forward as you use the rest of this book:

- **You have to be online.** No, not everyone is online, but the people who are online are your customers. If you're not reaching them, you can be sure that your competitors are. You don't have to wrench your business up by the roots and replant it on the Internet; but if you ignore the online world, you do so at your peril.

- **Start with the Web.** The Web is the ruler of the online world. Start your online efforts by planning now to create a Web site if you don't have one or to regularly update your site if you do.

- **Use the power of the Internet to your advantage.** Later chapters introduce you to search engines and search marketing, online advertising, e-mail advertising, blogs and communities, and many more channels to reach your consumers online. Use the detailed information in this book to consider each route separately and decide how best to use it.

- **Take a moderate approach.** *K.I.S.S.* should be your watchword. It stands for Keep It Short and Sweet. Online users want easy-to-navigate, fast-loading, up-to-date Web sites that look good on any device. They want product and reference information and don't want to work hard to get it. You don't have to bet your company on a big, fancy online presence; just be competent, accurate, informative, and up-to-date. The other chapters in this book show you how to create an effective digital marketing presence as quickly, easily, and cheaply as possible.

Chapter 2

Market Size Matters

In This Chapter

▶ Using Internet marketing resources

▶ Searching tips and tricks

▶ Finding your customers online

▶ Figuring out what the competition is doing

*O*ne of the biggest challenges facing marketers is learning about target markets for products and services. How large a market may there be for a product or service? Is the market growing or shrinking? What are the people in the market like – in terms of income, affiliations, and interests?

The Internet has revolutionised market research. A vast amount of information is available for little or no cost. Research companies that used to charge lots of money for basic information have been forced to adapt their strategies, digging out particularly hard-to-get data and analysing it in a way that is valuable for each customer.

Competitive information used to be among the hardest kind of information to get. Now companies tell you a great deal about themselves on their Web sites. And their customers post complaints and praise online, helping you learn their strengths and vulnerabilities – before your competitor does, if you're paying attention.

You're a step behind if you don't know how to get at the free and low-cost market information available on the Internet – and if you don't know how to use it appropriately. This chapter will get you where you need to go, fast.

See the *Digital Marketing For Dummies* Internet Directory in this book for pointers to market research sites such as Alexa, Hitwise, and others.

Using Internet Marketing Resources

Using the Internet for marketing research can be very rewarding but also very frustrating. Rewarding because a lot of great data is out there. Frustrating because the required information can be very hard to find: Either the data's not out there, or what you need is so hard to track down that you can't find it in the amount of time that you have. This frustration is exacerbated because, in the search for the specific information you need, you're likely to find excellent, current, detailed information that's *almost* what you need with no clues to help you take the one additional step needed for the exact information you just have to have.

The secret to solving this problem is found in the Nike slogan, 'Just Do It'. Diving into market research online gets you the facts you need, to the extent that they're out there, and lets you know what facts you need to find or develop from other information sources.

You can use Internet resources to meet some of the following key marketing information needs:

- **Market definition and segmentation.** If you're involved in creating a new product, ask yourself: For what market is your product or service intended? For an existing product that has a market, ask yourself: Do other related markets that may be more profitable exist? Online resources can help you with the key marketing activities of defining and *segmenting* your market – that is, identifying groups of customers who may be interested in your product.

- **Market trends and demographics.** Is your target market growing? Shrinking? Do demographic trends support your marketing plans? Or do demographic trends undermine what you thought was a great idea?

- **Assessment of the competition.** What activities are the competition up to – both online and in the offline world? You can find out about both of these areas of activity online. For instance, competitors often give loyal customers sneak previews of new products online.

- **Opportunities and *buzz*.** What new opportunities are coming up? Who's hot – or not? Plenty of news Web sites exist that can tell you what opportunities are just over the horizon. Figure 2-1 shows one example, ZDNet.

After you know where to look, you can fill much of your need for marketing information in all these areas online.

Use the Directory in this book as a starting point for creating your own list of top marketing resources.

After you find information sources for your industry, consider posting them on your Web site. Uh, why on earth would you hand such a tool to your competition? Because doing so will really impress your customers as well as relevant press and analysts. People are used to looking to market leaders in an industry for critical industry information; if you provide that information, you position yourself as a market leader. (And if you give people an e-mail address to which they can send corrections and updates, you'll hear of new info early – maybe even directly from your competitors!)

Though you may need only a modest online presence to match your offline competition's efforts, watch out for online-based competitors – either an established, well-known company that starts selling online or a new online-only venture. If you hear from your customers about new online-only competitors and start losing sales to this new competition, you need to go online urgently. To meet this kind of challenge, do everything in this book to bolster your online marketing presence.

Goals and costs of online searches

The main cost of most online searches is your time.

So have a clear goal in mind at the beginning of an online search and keep your eyes on the prize. Figure out what you want to know and how long you plan to spend trying to find out. Then, when that amount of time expires, stop and move on to Plan B – which may be phoning someone, sending an e-mail to a knowledgeable source, or even hiring a consultant to

investigate for you. Just don't allow yourself to spend hours searching for information, get distracted by a nice sports-related viral game, and find yourself wondering two hours later why you went online in the first place.

The mantra: Know your goal, set a time limit, get in, get out. If you haven't found what you want, reassess how critical the information is – or if a similar approximation will work just as well.

Building up your bookmarks

In marketing, you can't afford to be the last person to hear something – and being first gives you a big advantage over your competitors! As you search the Internet, build up a robust list of *bookmarks* (or *favourites*, as they're called in Internet Explorer) so that you can easily revisit valuable sites for new information. Spend some time making your bookmarks list a valuable resource. Here are some tips:

- ✓ **Create subject folders.** Don't make your bookmarks list a disorganised repository for all your personal and business interests. Create subject folders for areas of interest partners, the competition, demographics, marketing offline, marketing online, and more. Subject folders can make your future online searches much faster and more productive.

- ✓ **Create *frequency* folders.** Create folders for sites that you want to visit daily, weekly, monthly, and just occasionally. (Don't be afraid to put the same link in a subject folder and in a frequency folder.) With frequency folders, you can put your all-too-brief Web surfing time to the best use.

- ✓ **Prune early and often.** Trim your bookmarks list frequently. Get rid of any links that you haven't used lately and are unlikely to need again in the near future. (If you need a link in the *far* future, you can find it by searching again.) The less dead wood in your bookmarks, the more you use them.

- ✓ **Share your bookmarks.** One way to elevate the level of discussion among your colleagues is to give them the opportunity to be as well informed as you are. Send your bookmarks to them as an e-mail attachment and then show them how to bring your bookmarks into their own bookmarks list. If you have people working for you or with you on a project team, sharing bookmarks is a great way to get everyone on the same (Web) page.

✔ **Know how to use your browser well.** Whether you use Netscape Navigator, Internet Explorer, Firefox, or Safari, be aware that each has its own tricks for searching, managing bookmarks, retrieving previously visited links, and more. (Because searching is so important when using the Web for online marketing, we give you some tips and tricks for searching using each browser later in this chapter.) Pick the browser you like and use it intensively.

Try using social bookmarking sites such as `http://del.icio.us` (see Figure 2-2). Doing so allows you to share your favourite sites with a group of people and this technique is simple and quick to use.

Search tips and tricks

Do you ever watch a colleague working on a computer and feel your jaw drop as you watch the person do something in a few keystrokes that takes you 2 to 3 minutes of mousing around? As a marketer, you should be that kind of expert when it comes to Internet searching. Here's a few tips to help you get started.

Figure 2-2: Bookmarking sites help you share and manage your favourite sites.

Search engines are your best friends

Numerous search engines exist to help you navigate the Internet. The most well known in the UK are Google, Yahoo! Search, MSN Search, and Ask. Each search engine has its subtle nuances, but all are designed to connect users with the information they are searching for.

On the home page of each search engine you'll find a blank search box: This is your starting point.

Search engines will filter out words that are too common to search for, such as 'if', 'as', or 'it'. When you start a search, use the key phrases that apply to your question. If you want to find a company in London that produces toner cartridges, type in 'toner cartridges London' and hit the search button.

With so many Web pages out there, you'd need an eternity to sift through them all. Search engines do this sifting for you, but you still have to look through the results that they provide. Don't be daunted when Google tells you it has 200,000,000 matches for your search terms. Take a deep breath, look at the results on the first page or so and if you can't find what you want, go back and refine your search. Following this process is quicker than looking at every Web site on the list.

Try using different search engines with the same search. Each search engine uses different technology to provide results, so if you're having no luck with one maybe another will work better for you.

If you still can't find what you're looking for, try using some of the search engine's other features. Each is developing new services such as Local Search that may help you to narrow down your search. If you're using Google, you'll find these options under the 'more' link above the search box on the front page of the search engine.

Search engines also offer you the chance to refine your search through a series of options that can be applied to the results to narrow down what is returned to you. Use these options if you're still having no luck. On the Google UK service these options are found under the 'Advanced Search' option to the right of the search box on the front page of the search engine.

All search engines now offer 'toolbars', which can be downloaded and added to your browser window. These allow users to search the Internet from their browsers, without having to go to the search engine Web page. These tool-bars can be useful if you see something that interests you and you want more information immediately. Download the Google, Yahoo!, MSN, or Ask toolbars by typing the search engine's name, followed by the word 'toolbar' into a search engine and following the links.

If you operate in one particular sector of a market, or are looking for information in one sector, you can use a sector-specific search engine to help you find what you're looking for. Too many sector-specific search engines exist to list here but, again, if you type the name of the industry followed by 'search engine' into any search engine you'll be presented with plenty of options.

Search engines can find a lot more than just Web pages. You can also use them to find images, news stories, products, groups, and pretty much anything else you can think of. Each search engine is developing specific services to search for different types of information. Explore each one to see what they're offering – you may find one to help you.

Once you've found your information and have stored it on your PC, consider using the services of a Desktop search service to enable you to retrieve it quickly. These services are easily downloadable (and are often included on the toolbars mentioned earlier in this section) and can be found by typing 'desktop toolbar' into a search engine.

Wireless Net access

Searching the Internet is a high-bandwidth activity, best done with the fastest Internet connection and the biggest computer monitor you can get hold of. But you can use your wireless device to get a quick answer in between appointments or to really impress people you're meeting with (and those activities are all part of marketing, right?).

If you have a Pocket PC, Blackberry, Treo, or Palm device with a wireless modem, or even a 3G phone, you can access all the sites in this book's Directory as well. Here are a few nifty applications you should download and install for marketing use:

- **Instant messaging.** This communication medium allows you to keep in touch with friends and colleagues who use the same system. Instant messaging comes in many forms and is offered by companies including MSN, Yahoo!, AOL, and Google.

- **AvantGo.** Use the free AvantGo service to store and view favourite Web sites on your Palm computer. Whenever you synchronise your Palm with your desktop, new content will be synchronised automatically. AvantGo also provides for wireless browsing.

- **Any Microsoft Office product.** In today's connected world no reason exists for not being able to use every spare moment to catch up on e-mails or get on with that important Word document you need to finish. Many different office packages are available and you should definitely use one to ensure that you're using your time efficiently.

- **Multimap/Streetmap/Google Maps.** If you're in a hurry to get to a meeting but are not sure of the directions, applications like these can be very useful indeed. These applications provide you with a miniature map showing you exactly where you need to be – so you may never be late again.

- **Travel Tools.** Another vital service for today's busy executive, these tools give you loads of important information when you're travelling, including time tools, luggage lists, currency converters, and much more.

- **FT.com.** Available through AvantGo, *personal digital assistant* (PDA) service provided by the *Financial Times* enables you to download your choice of top stories and commentary from the *FT* onto your PDA and read it at a convenient time. Regarded as one of the best business newspapers in the world, the *FT*'s a great source of information for any level of business.

You can and should use all these same sources to become well informed from your normal work desk before a meeting. But having wireless access to them is quite a bit more convenient, and far more impressive, than doing the same thing from your desktop.

Following the experts

As you search for information online, think about the process in relation to planning your own Internet presence. People with a strong Internet presence are, to a certain extent, experts. However, because the online world is still relatively new, even the experts make lots of mistakes! Here are some of the potential pitfalls to online marketing and how they relate to your own planning:

- **Hard-to-find Web sites.** The Internet has no secret search engines or places to go where all the trendy people find sites easily. If you have trouble finding company or product information on the Web, lots of other people are having the same problem. Think about how you can make your own company and product information easy to find. Chapter 8 covers the details.

- **Slow-loading Web pages.** If you get frustrated waiting for someone's graphics-rich Web page to load, keep that fact in mind when you design your own Web site. If your site is too slow to load, people won't stick around to see it.

✔ **Missing information.** Often, people quickly find a site and then waste many minutes trying to find information that should be front and centre. For instance, many companies don't give their real-world address or a main switchboard phone number for people who want more information. Organise your site in such a way that it answers common informational needs, and at the very least provide numbers and addresses for more conventional methods of communication.

✔ **Unanswered criticism in forums and chat rooms.** You can find some of the most amazingly harsh criticism of companies in their own company-sponsored e-mail lists, in chat rooms online, and blogs – but even more amazing is the fact that it often goes unanswered. Think about how to respond effectively and constructively to online criticism of your company or product. Chapters 11 and 12 discuss this issue in more depth.

✔ **Unanswered registrations and e-mail.** Don't you hate it when you register at a Web site or send e-mail and never hear anything back? Visitors to your Web site won't like it if you do the same thing to them. Think about how to interact effectively with people who send you information and e-mail, and make sure that you respond to all e-mail messages and site registrations. Chapters 9 to 11 go into more detail on e-mail.

✔ **Privacy concerns.** Do you ever wonder what happens to that registration information you give online? So will people who register at your Web site. If they don't have a feeling of trust, they often enter false information. Think about how much information you ask people to give you online and how to tell them what you plan to do with it. Make sure you comply with privacy laws and data protection laws and let the user know about them. See Chapter 8 for more on privacy.

Sizing Up a Market

The biggest challenge in marketing may be identifying prospective customers for your existing and proposed products and services. To us, identifying customers is the key skill in marketing: Marketers typically don't build, sell, or physically deliver products, but we do make sure that the product is the right thing for one or more groups of customers, and we do size the target group to help build the financial model for a line of business or a company. We think sizing up a market is the most important activity in the entire life cycle of a company and the products and services that support it.

Identifying customer characteristics

The first step in sizing up a market is identifying your ideal customer: The type of person who'd be most likely to buy your product or service. For now, set aside the wide range of people who might buy your product, and concentrate on your ideal customer. Brainstorm with others inside and outside your company to identify this person. The first things you might look for are not strictly Internet-related:

- ✔ Is this person more likely to be male or female – or do you have that rarity, a truly gender-neutral product?

- ✔ What age is your ideal customer? Beware if the answer to this question is always 'the same age as me'.

- ✔ What is the profession of your ideal customer? This is a crucial question, because reaching people by their profession is relatively easy.

- ✔ Where does your ideal customer live? Pick one country. (In most cases, additional countries are separate marketing targets.)

- ✔ How much money does your ideal customer make? How well educated is he or she? Higher income and higher educational levels are related factors; consider income and education together and come up with a combined target that makes sense for both factors.

- ✔ What kinds of media does this person consume? Leave out the Internet for now; think about newspaper reading, magazine subscriptions, and TV and radio choices of your target customer. (Take your best shot initially; you can always fine-tune this later.)

- ✔ Can you guesstimate anything about your ideal customer's personality? Among the people of the same gender, age, profession, and media usage as your other ideal customers, what are the personal characteristics that differentiate people who'll be quick to buy your product or service from the rest? 'Smarter' or 'better read' are likely to be promising answers; 'plays more video games' or 'more likely to visit adult sites' are generally not. But be honest, at this step and throughout the exercise.

You can do a lot of fun things here to brainstorm: Ask questions of all your colleagues, call people, role play, free-associate, and so on. Include your non-marketing colleagues; they no doubt have valuable information you need.

Beware of the tendency to be inclusive – 'boys and girls will both love my product, and after all, adults are like grown-up kids, so let's include them, too'. You're trying to identify your *ideal* customer, not *every possible* customer.

The trick in identifying your ideal customer is to create the easiest initial problem for yourself: How to sell to the person who is most likely to love your product or service and to be quick to buy it. After you solve that problem, you can figure out how to reach people who are nearly ideal (one difference from your ideal customer), a bit less ideal (two differences), and so on.

Customer characteristics and the Internet

Notice that we didn't mention the Internet once in the previous section. (We can't keep that up, or we'll have to change the name of this book to *Random Musings For Dummies*, and that probably wouldn't sell as well.)

After you've identified the real-world habits of your ideal customer, consider his or her Internet habits as well. Include the following:

- ✔ Is this person likely to have Internet access at work? At home? Low- or high-speed (DSL, narrowband, modem, ISDN, satellite) connectivity? If you know the home country and income level of your target customer, you can get a pretty good idea of that customer's likely level of connectivity using the resources in this book's Directory.

- ✔ Is this person's professional group heavily online?

- ✔ What kind of Web sites is this person likely to visit for professional use? For personal use?

- ✔ What automated e-mail lists, discussion groups, chat rooms, forums, blogs, and social network groups might your ideal customer be part of?

- ✔ Is your target customer more or less likely to click a Web banner ad than most people? How about clicking a link embedded in an e-mail newsletter?

Don't get discouraged if the answers to the preceding questions lead you to believe that you can reach only a small number of your prospective customers over the Web. You need only a few. Product and service success these days is tremendously dependent on *buzz*, the online equivalent of word-of-mouth, and no better way exists to get buzz than through positive customer comments posted on the Internet. The small percentage of your potential customers who can be reached through any one Web site or e-mail newsletter will have a large impact on the rest.

Sizing up the competition

The Internet may well be the best tool ever for sizing up the competition. Take a 360-degree look at each of your competitors through the prism of the Internet before undertaking any serious product development or marketing effort.

Internet competitive research is so easy that you can even consider a broader range of potential competitors when you're doing your research. Start out, of course, with your direct competitors: Those who offer a product or service that is most nearly identical to yours.

After you've looked at direct competitors, though, you can broaden your search to include less direct competition – a new, affordably priced wine, for instance, may find itself competing for mindshare with a high-end, imported beer. And you can include 'psychographic competition'" (coining new phrases is what the Internet does best) – any product or service that is targeted at the same core customers as your offering.

In looking at a competitive set, include all your direct competitors, a couple of less-direct competitors, and a couple of 'psychographic competitors' (the term's growing on you, isn't it?), including one big-budget offering and one small, scrappy newcomer or niche product. By doing so, your thinking about the competition will cover a wide range of options on how to proceed.

Here are just a few of the many ways you can use the Internet to size up your competition:

- ✔ **Web-based product and company information.** The Web is the first place most people go to learn basic information about competitive products and companies. Figure 2-3 shows the products page for Dell, a company with many products, as an example of how a big company offers product information. Start your search with information on the Web and then use the contact information on a company's Web site to follow up by phone and to have more information mailed to you.

- ✔ **Web presence.** The quickest test of a company's or product group's competence is to check out its Web site. We get asked a lot for our opinions on Web sites, and one thing is certain: If the site doesn't look up to scratch, chances are that the company behind it won't be either. They say you should never judge a book by the cover, but when it comes to Web sites and marketing yourself online, first impressions count.

Figure 2-3:
The Dell
homepage
offers
product
information
in an easy-
to-use way

✔ **Search listing.** How many Web sites mention the competing product or service? By typing some key phrases into a search engine you can gauge how popular a certain product or service is. Listings rise to the top of the 'natural' search rankings when other Web sites link to them. Search engines use these links and measure the quality of the linking sites as well, to create their rankings – so in general terms the further up the list the Web site is, the better-known the company is.

✔ **E-mail lists.** Does a newsletter or e-mail list exist for competing products and services? If so, subscribe! You'll learn a tremendous amount of inside information and get a good overview of customers' attitudes. (See Chapter 11.)

✔ **Discussion groups, forums and chat rooms.** Sign up to these services that are frequented by your potential customers and competitors to find mentions of competing products, services, and companies. Can you connect the dots between what you know about the competition, what you can see of their Web presence, and how people 'talk' about them online? (See Chapter 12.)

- ✔ **Internet advertising.** Online adverts can be annoying when you don't need them, but finding a particular ad that you badly want to see for competitive purposes can also be difficult. Any time you see such an ad, make a copy of the screen immediately (see the Tip that follows) and then click the ad and make a copy of the page you end up at as well. Doing so will give you ideas – usually of what not to do — for your own offering. (See Chapter 13.)

- ✔ **Internet PR.** Use the press releases on a company's Web site to get a sense of the history of the product or service in question and of the company as a whole. This is a valuable source of information and another quick gauge of overall marketing competence. (See Chapter 14.)

To make a copy of the current screen on a Windows-based PC, just press the *Print Screen* button to copy the current screen image to the Windows Clipboard. Then open the *Windows Paint* application (by choosing *Start*, then *Programs*, then *Accessories*, then *Paint*) and paste the screen grab into Paint. You can then save it or print it from within Paint.

The good news is that you can learn a tremendous amount by doing all this research; the bad news is that no one else is going to want to read twenty or more pages of your notes. Summarise the results in a convenient chart, as described in Chapter 3.

Chapter 3

Your Digital Marketing Plan

....

....

*D*igital marketing reminds us of an old saying from the days when computers were first being used to automate business processes – no, not 'If it ain't broke, don't fix it'. The saying is 'Computerising a bad process doesn't make it a good process'. The upshot of this cliché was that you often had to fix your existing business processes before computerising them or you'd just end up with an expensive mess.

The same holds true of your digital marketing efforts. If you have a poor or incomplete marketing effort offline, then the likelihood is that you'll end up with a poor or incomplete marketing effort online.

Does poor performance mean that you can't do anything on the Internet until you fix every conceivable problem in your existing marketing effort? Not at all. But it does mean that you should keep your digital marketing efforts modest until your overall marketing effort is operating effectively. Remember, unless you're starting a Web-based business, the chances are that some of your customers will not be on the Internet. For most businesses, digital marketing is the tail; the rest of your marketing effort is the dog. The dog should wag the tail, not the tail wag the dog.

So, to mount an effective digital marketing effort you need to start with modest goals; meet those; add more ambitious goals; meet those; and so on. At each step in your marketing effort, think of marketing resources you wish you had in the offline world, such as white papers, business cases, data, press releases, Q & A (Question and Answer) documents, and others. By building your Internet marketing presence gradually, you give yourself the opportunity to budget for and develop traditional and Internet expectations together and reinforce one with the other.

This chapter tells you how to plan your overall digital marketing effort so that it succeeds the first time round. But whereas planning is vital for the longer term, the 'just do it' philosophy (also known as 'ready, fire, aim') has a long and honoured role on the Internet as well.

If you're really in a hurry to get something up and running, use Chapter 4 to start researching and securing your domain name, and Chapter 5 to create an initial Web site. This way, you'll cover yourself until you can complete and implement the more thorough planning process described in this chapter.

Assessing Your Current Marketing Efforts

The first step in creating an effective digital marketing strategy is to quickly assess your existing overall marketing effort. Nearly every traditional marketing resource you have can be used to help make people aware of what you're trying to do online, and almost every marketing document, ad, *white paper* (or research report), or other resource you have or create can be *repurposed* – modified and reformatted, but with the content left basically intact – for use on the Internet. So, knowing where you stand in the offline world is crucial to going online effectively.

Look at your current marketing effort for your company and for each part of what you sell – the products and services that are the reason for your company's existence. That way you can then decide how you want to represent yourself online.

Assessing your current company-level marketing efforts

To effectively market your company, you need to understand its strengths so that you can focus on them in marketing, and its weaknesses so that you can help alleviate them through new product development, third-party partnerships, and other efforts. Start the process of better understanding your company by asking yourself some basic questions:

- **What does your company sell?** List all the products and services that your company sells. (If you work for a really big company and you're taking only a small part of it online, restrict your answers to your division or product group.) Then come up with one short phrase that describes the majority of your product and service sales. Typical answers may be computer software or telephony services. That phrase will show you where to best direct your initial online marketing effort.

What's your role?

If you're part of a small company or organisation, you may be responsible for the company's strategy, products, services, public relations, and online presence. But in a medium-size or large company, you're more likely to be responsible for part of the picture: a division of the company, or a specific product or service.

So, unless you have total control, the likelihood is that you'll have to work with others to create an effective digital marketing strategy and merge it smoothly into the overall marketing efforts of the rest of the company. Even if you own only part of the picture, and even if some of the decisions we discuss here are likely to be made by others, go through all the steps in this chapter so that you can understand all the different roles and perspectives.

✔ **Who are your customers?** List your major customer groups. Your customers may include home-based professionals, middle managers, or golfers. If you know your customers well, you will no doubt already have a mental image of each type of customer, or even know one or more representatives of each type. Match up your major customer groups with the information about the demographics of the online world in Chapter 1 to identify those among your customers who are most likely to be online in large numbers.

✔ **What differentiates your company from other companies?** For instance, don't say that you're 'fast' unless your company is faster than your competitors in some measurable way. And don't say that you're 'customer-orientated' unless you have the customer feedback or customer service awards to prove that you're among the most customer-orientated companies in your area of business. 'Largest' is good – but largest in what market? Use the information in Chapter 2 to help you do a search of your competition online to identify your own advantages. Aim to end up with one or two differentiators for which you have good, solid backing.

Don't be surprised if you can't come up with much that makes your company stand out from the crowd; many companies, at certain points in their existence, don't really have strong qualities that differentiate them from the competition. But if you don't have even one outstanding quality at this point, take this as a warning signal that you're vulnerable to competitors who do differentiate – and when they do, it will be at your expense. If your company is SME Ltd, they'll tell customers they're 'faster than SME Ltd', 'more customer-orientated than SME Ltd', and, eventually, 'larger than SME Ltd'. Start thinking now about what differentiating qualities you want to develop.

A good example of the importance of differentiation is Apple Computer. Shortly after it was founded, Apple had the best-selling personal computer, the Apple II. When it lost that distinction to the IBM PC, Apple moved on to selling the easiest-to-use personal computer, the Macintosh. But when Microsoft Windows helped the PC close the ease-of-use gap, the Macintosh differentiation eroded. Lately the company has taken to selling the fastest personal computers – with its Mac Pro series – and the most stylish, with the iMac; whilst also establishing a dominant position in the digital music arena with the iPod digital music player and its accompanying software, iTunes. This new differentiation has led to Apple attracting big-spending, high-end customers, enabling the company to return to profitability.

Also assess your existing company marketing efforts. Gather together all your marketing collateral: your logo, stationery, press kits, catalogues, press releases, print ads, TV and radio commercials, annual reports, speeches by company officials, any Web pages you already have, and so on. Consider how you can use the text, graphics, and even audio and video clips from these resources in your Internet presence. Figure 3-1 shows the homepage of a multimedia company that uses several of these elements.

If your company's corporate ID really does need a makeover, your online efforts can be a key part of that change. Consider hiring an experienced consultant to help make a concerted push in this direction. Just don't try to revamp your brand in the online world only; until that overall company image makeover gathers steam, your online presence should reflect the image your company already has.

Figure 3-1:
EMAP's
homepage
pushes all
the media
buttons.

Making it so

One common mistake in the marketing process is to come up with differentiators for your company and products that you'd *like* to be true rather than ones that actually *are* true. So if you think of an adjective that describes how you'd *like* to be able to present your company or products, think about how you can 'make it so'. If you want to claim to be the 'most customer-focused', identify training programmes and practices that you can put in place to make your company the best at customer service; for instance, mobile phone operators now regularly use mystery callers to test their call centres to ensure that they are offering the best customer service. Or investigate ways to improve your product to make it the fastest or easiest to use;

look at the practices of your competitors who claim these differentiators now, and work out how you can meet and then beat them.

Changing what your company is doing to make its products more marketable is where marketing becomes a vital part of a company's overall business strategy and is why marketing is so important to companies (and why so many company CEOs come from the marketing side of the company). In taking the time to think through these issues and make much-needed changes to your products and services, you're making it possible to better market those same products and services in both the offline world and on the Internet.

Digital marketing at the company level

Many people who look for your business on the Internet are primarily interested in finding out where you're located, what business your company is in, how many employees you have, how much money you make (revenue), and how much you keep (profits). Having a competent, basic online presence at this company level is therefore critical.

Company marketing, whether online or offline, is somewhat vague and amorphous. Think of those 'brand image' advertising campaigns that you often see on TV for the world's biggest companies in sectors such as financial services or computing. These ads don't sell you anything, and you may not even ever buy anything directly from the company. They just lay the groundwork for the company's more targeted marketing efforts – boosting how their brand is perceived by the consumer.

The job of company-level marketing is to communicate the key attributes of your company and create a base of recognition with the customer for your more targeted, product-based marketing efforts. Such efforts also help market your company to potential investors. Figure 3-2 shows a Web page which describes the company precisely.

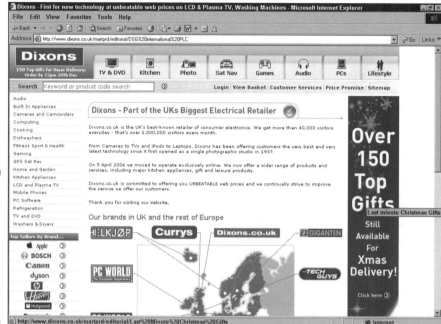

Figure 3-2:
The Dixons
digital
'About Us'
section
describes
the
company
perfectly.

Assessing current product marketing efforts

Your products can be physical things that people buy, or services, or a mix of the two. You may have packaged one or more services in a very product-like way by standardising what gets done, rates, duration, and so on. If you haven't already packaged your services, consider doing so. By packaging services in a product-like way, you make it easier for people who visit you online to compare your offerings to those of other companies.

In this book, we generally use the word 'products' to refer to products, services, and mixed product/service packages. If a concern or an idea specific to services is discussed, we point that out. In general, just think of your products as whatever the specific things are that people buy from you.

Now think about what differentiates each of your products or each service that you market as a product. If you think that your product is the best for its purpose, decide what 'best' means for your kind of product. List ways to back up your claim to be the best if someone challenges it. For instance, your product may be made of higher-quality materials, created by more experienced people, or used by customers who themselves have a reputation for doing good work. If your product is the cheapest, define the term more exactly as lowest purchase price, lowest cost of ownership over the product's lifetime, or some other aspect of low cost.

To gather evidence for your claims, use the Web and other online resources described in this book. The *Digital Marketing For Dummies* Internet Directory section of this book includes listings of not only Web sites but also discussion groups and other online resources that have valuable marketing and product information.

Rack your brain for product differentiators and work to back them up; undifferentiated products are not only vulnerable to competition, they're hard to make much profit from. Figure 3-3 shows a Web page for a product that doesn't mention competitors directly but instead shows off its differentiation.

Start your digital product marketing effort by assessing the existing marketing materials you have for the product, but don't feel too limited by them. You're more likely to have success in remaking the image of a product online than in remaking the image of a company. A company's image usually reflects some realities about the company's history, current practices, and personnel that are hard to change.

Figure 3-3:
And now for something completely differentiated – Sony's homepage.

Consider how to change your product's current image online. For example, you may be able to better emphasise the technical advantages of your product to the online audience than you've been able to manage offline because of the interactive nature of the Web. In marketing a lawnmower on the Internet, for example, you can include detailed photographs and explanations of what 'makes' your lawnmower so special more easily than in a typical print advertisement. If your online effort works, you can then consider how to change your offline marketing efforts.

Marketing your product on the Net

You can do a tremendous amount with product marketing on the Internet – ranging from launching a dedicated Web page to an entire Web site supported by efforts including e-mail, discussion groups, branded online services, and more. You can also decide whether to sell all or just a selection of your company's products online – see *Starting an Online Business All-in-One Desk Reference For Dummies,* by Shannon Belew and Joel Elad (Wiley), for details.

The Internet will also enable you to address the fuzzy line between products and services online, as we discuss in the 'Assessing current product marketing efforts' section, earlier in this chapter. Figure 3-4 shows an example of a digital music software company, marketing services as a product online.

Figure 3-4:
Just because your offering isn't physical, doesn't mean you can't package it as a product.

Is your traditional marketing sufficient?

As you look at your company and product marketing materials, you may notice that some marketing collateral that you'd like to have is missing. This discovery is normal; just about everyone can use a brand new or updated data sheet, marketing plan, Q & A, white paper, or what have you.

If you find that your overall marketing effort is lacking – if you can't identify strong company and product differentiators and see those reflected in a reasonable number of marketing materials for each of the audiences you need to reach – then you have a bigger problem than an online marketing effort alone can solve. The best way to jump-start online marketing is by borrowing logos, layouts, ad copy, and other resources from your existing marketing materials – if those are missing, then the online

marketing effort becomes much more expensive and difficult.

If this scenario sounds familiar, then you need to create an overall marketing plan now. *Marketing For Dummies* (Wiley) can be a real help. Then decide on either a physical-first or an online-first plan. If not many of your customers are online, then create a limited online presence to cover yourself while you build up your traditional marketing portfolio. But if many of your actual or prospective customers are online, consider developing a reasonably strong online presence first and then extending it to print, broadcast, and other media. In either case, working on your online marketing can be a catalyst for creating a strong overall marketing effort.

Net marketing for the one-man band

What if you're a *sole trader* – an independent consultant, author, or a freelancer? Do you need an online presence? As long as you keep it small-scale, then the answer may well be *yes*.

The practical benefit of having even a small scale Internet marketing presence is huge. Just having the ability to be found online by potential customers will benefit you, but you can also explain simply and clearly your product and service offering, rates, areas of expertise, and a host of other information that will bring in business. If you want to engage in some small scale Internet marketing why not try launching a blog or small Web page that you can highlight in your e-mail communication with customers? This way they can find out more information about your services or products and it will reassure them that you are on the ball.

If you're like most people working independently today, then you're probably already using the Internet for communications and research. If not, your first order of business is to get online. The easiest way to get online is by getting an account with an Internet Service Provider (ISP) such as BT allowing you to use broadband. Then consider getting a domain name for your business and a customised e-mail account, as described in Chapter 4.

For a small business, an online-first marketing effort may make total sense. As an independent, most of your marketing efforts so far have probably been informal, person-to-person efforts. You probably have at least some of the basics, such as business cards, stationery, and a fax number; but mass mailings, *Yellow Pages* advertising, and other small-business marketing tools are probably more than you need and beyond your meagre marketing budget.

If this is your situation, a modest online presence makes perfect sense. A small Web site describing you and listing some of your accomplishments serves as a seemingly external validator of your success and technical savvy for very little cost. Unless an unusually small number of your current and potential customers or clients are online, consider creating a simplified and scaled-down but professional-looking version of the business Web presence site described in detail in Chapter 5, and use other low-key online marketing efforts described in this book.

Matching Your Customer Base to the Online Community

You've looked at your existing marketing effort, probably finding a few holes in the process, and, we hope, getting some new ideas about what your company's image should be, how each of its products and services should be marketed, and what traditional marketing resources you need to develop. You're also probably pretty excited about creating or improving your online presence. Now take your first reality check.

The reality check is simply this: How many of your current and potential customers can be reached online? Use Chapter 1 to get a good idea about the big picture of who's online and discover how to research how many of your customers are online already. Unless your customer base includes groups that are online in high numbers, consider creating a modest initial online presence and then improving your traditional and digital marketing efforts in tandem.

You need to carefully research your customer base – which can mean anything from simply talking to all your own contacts in the industry about who you should be targeting, to commissioning a formal piece of research – to find out how many of your customers use the Internet. Ask your customers what they expect from you online and whether they're frustrated or disappointed with your lack of an online presence. Ask them what Web and other online resources they find useful and how they use them. Don't be surprised if what they want isn't cutting-edge technology but instead solid information about your company and industry that they can use in their work.

Here are some of the products and services that definitely require a strong Internet presence to reach their customer base adequately:

- ✔ **Computer products.** Absolutely anything having to do with computers must be represented on the Internet. Computer users and computer professionals want and expect to find computer-related products and services online.

- ✔ **Educational products.** Almost anything having to do with education is a good subject for an online effort. Not only are a large proportion of students online but so are many of their parents. Both students and parents are receptive to college, university, and private school recruitment, educational CD-ROMs, books, tapes, you name it. Figure 3-5 shows an online site for educational products.

- ✔ **Products marketed strongly to professionals.** Computer and educational professionals are the strongest professional presence online but are followed closely by other kinds of professionals. And although people often surf the Web aimlessly at work, they feel good about surfing sites that contain information or products helpful to them in their work.

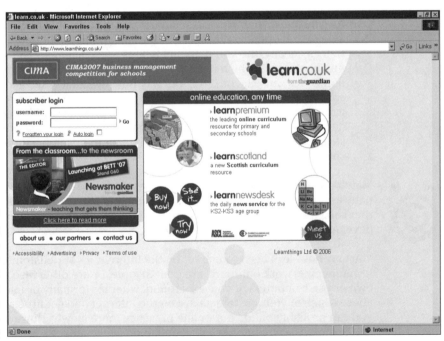

Figure 3-5:
Learn.co.uk, one of the largest education sites in the UK.

What about mobile?

The mobile market is like the World Wide Web was in the late-1990s: Everyone's talking about it but only a few million people so far are using it. And those few million people are split across multiple platforms: The Palm OS, the Symbian handheld platform, the Pocket PC platform, the BlackBerry, 3G, and Wireless Application Protocol (WAP)-enabled mobile phones.

Developing content for viewing on these platforms is hard because of the wide range of different development targets and the tiny size of the screens. For most businesses, the best idea is to market to the personal computer audience first and then size up the mobile market as it applies to your business.

> ✔ **Any product with a high-tech edge to it.** Having the latest high technology in your products is an important way to create highly differentiated (that is, highly profitable) products, and many people strongly associate high technology with the Internet. You need a forceful online presence to support your claim to be on the technical cutting edge, and to reach customers who are receptive to these kinds of claims.

> ✔ **Any business that uses a third-party reseller:** People now expect to be able to find opening times, schedules, locations, event details, prices, as well as, ideally, the ability to buy tickets and make reservations online. Any business in which it is advantageous to see what you are about – hotels, restaurants, or B & Bs, or any business that takes a lot of calls to answer very basic questions – needs a simple Web site, even if this is just to create a favourable impression and provide simple logistical details. By creating such a site you can also cut out the middle man, saving you commission money and helping to develop a direct relationship with your customers.

Match up your customer profile against who's online not only for your company as a whole but also for individual products and services. You may find that some products and services are better candidates than others for early development of your Internet presence.

You may have less need to market on the Internet if your customers are of lower income, work outdoors, are craftspeople, or are otherwise unlikely to own or use computers. If you ask around, whether formally or informally, about which of your customers are on the Internet and get little response, you can probably build your online presence more slowly. However, very few markets exist where not having an online presence makes sense.

What if my customer base is typically not online?

Maybe comparing your customer base to the online community described in Chapter 1 shows that not many of your customers are online, leading you to think that you don't need to do any marketing on the Internet at all. However, we can present three strong arguments against doing nothing.

Keeping your existing customers on board

Remember that almost any business has potential and current customers on the Internet, and that press, analysts, investors, and other influencers are heavy online users. But you aren't likely to impress these people with an Internet presence that's disproportionately large compared to your size in the physical world. What they do need to see is an up-to-date, simple, up-to-date, competent, up-to-date, complete, Internet presence. Did we mention that these people will think poorly of you if you don't keep your Internet presence up-to-date?

Impressing new customers

The second reason you need at least a basic online presence – no matter what business you're in – is that the online audience is growing all the time, with broadband penetration now at mass market levels. As your existing and potential customers get wired, you don't want their first cyberspace experience to be that of getting a bad impression of you from your hard-to-find, out-of-date, or even completely missing Web site. Take tiny steps onto the Internet today so that you can be ready to dive in fully tomorrow – before it's too late!

Guarding against the unpredictable

The third reason you need an Internet presence is the unpredictability of marketing in general and digital marketing in particular. Most companies to date have failed in their Internet objectives, whereas others have succeeded beyond their wildest dreams, and quite a bit of unpredictability remains as to who will and who won't do well. Keeping your initial effort modest reduces the risk of failure, but getting a presence online quickly improves the odds that you can build it into a big success.

What if my business is local?

How much should you invest in your online presence if you operate only in a limited geographic area? Internet users have access to a growing number of local sites or services such as Multimap (www.multimap.com), which pinpoints local resources. However, locally-based Internet sites (see Figure 3-6, for example) face heavy competition from the *Yellow Pages,* local newspapers, and word of mouth. Local businesses may have difficulty deciding how much effort to put into a new, globe-circling medium that can reach tens of millions of people, 99.99 per cent of whom are guaranteed not to be within driving distance of those businesses.

However, if you're in an area with high Internet usage, consider charging ahead. Size your effort to match a realistic estimate of the number of visits you're going to get from people who are locals and therefore potential customers. And take extra steps to publicise your online presence via local media and in Web sites, discussion groups, and so on that have a strong local flavour.

Figure 3-6:
Check out the homepage of this regional Web site for London (Thisis local london. co.uk).

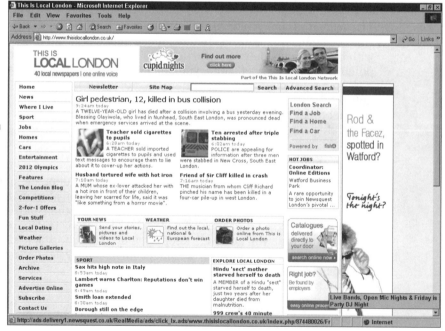

What if my business is global?

If your business is outside the UK or has customers sprinkled around a continent or the world, don't believe the hype: Study your local situation carefully before charging ahead. For instance, some of the world's biggest Internet companies have had their fingers badly burnt by opening large operations in China – only to find that most of the population is not online yet. This situation is now changing but the potential and reality are still some way apart – look before you leap.

The other special consideration for most non-UK-centric businesses is the language barrier. You may have several languages among your customers, but how many sites can you afford to build for each? Again, study the situation. You may find that one or two languages are spoken at least part of the time by your otherwise highly polyglot clientele. Consider translating key content into multiple languages but keeping your main site monolingual or bilingual. Specialists exist who offer such translation services and they're increasingly in demand as the Web opens up.

Assessing the Competition

A key step in deciding on how big a digital marketing effort you want to mount is to assess the online presence of your rivals. You have no doubt already encountered their online presence in several ways: visiting their Web sites; seeing their press releases, business cards, and other traditional marketing materials with pointers to their online presence; and hearing from your customers and colleagues what they've seen your competitors doing on the Internet. (If none of your direct competitors has an online presence, look at similar businesses that operate in a slightly different geographic area or business area.) Also take a look at the Net marketing presence of suppliers and customers, any industry or trade groups that your company is part of, and others who you work with. Use a search engine such as Google (www.google.co.uk) to find them.

Creating a comparison chart

Looking around and gathering impressions is invaluable to your effort, but comparing and contrasting their present efforts with your own is what will really help you. Doing so is not as hard as it sounds; just make a simple chart briefly describing key aspects of your competitors' online presence.

The best way to create such a chart is to restrict it to quantitative aspects: questions that can be answered by a yes or no, a number, or a short, factual phrase. Stay away from qualitative judgements, such as 'lousy' or 'slow' or 'beautiful', for now. Making objective decisions is most easily done when they are based on objective facts, and working through your findings with others is much easier if you initially stay away from value judgements and stick to 'just the facts'. An example comparison chart is shown in Figure 3-7.

Figure 3-7:
Map out a
competitive
comparison.

FEATURES	MAP CENTRAL	MAPS BY THE BEACH	OUTDOOR CLUB'S MAP NOOK
Web site	No	Yes	Yes- page on Outdoor Club's site
Active in newsgroups?	No	No	Yes (Outdoor Club, occasionally Map Nook)
Online mail list	No	Yes	Yes- for Outdoor Club, not Map Nook
Online service forums	CompuServe forum	No	AOL area for Outdoor Club
Web URL	x	www.beachmaps.com	www.outdoorclub.com/ mapnook
Number of Web pages	x	12	Dozens for Outdoor Club, one for Map Nook

Here's one way to create a comparison chart. Take a large piece of paper and create four columns – a narrower one for features of the online presence, and three wide ones for your top three competitors. (You may want to add more columns later, but start with three to help you focus.) Then create rows for key aspects of their online presence. The first few rows should be simple ones that you can fill out with ticks for yes, Xs for no, or a number or short phrase. Examples include Web site (yes/no), Active in discussion groups (yes/no), Has customer automated e-mail list for customers to subscribe to (yes/no), Online service area (yes/no).

The most important part of your online presence, and the most expensive part to develop, will almost certainly be your Web site. So go into some detail on your competitors' Web sites. Create rows for different aspects of the Web site: Web URL, Number of pages (estimate if the site is large), E-mail address for feedback, Sales locations listed, Online selling, Uses graphics, Uses multi-media, Has advertising.

Don't get caught up in a competition to have the biggest, most expensive Internet marketing presence. Chapters 5–7 discuss creating an appropriate Web presence for your company and its products and services.

Now create a new row and, for each competitor, list the major areas of that competitors' Web site. Areas may include About the Company, Products, News, Technical Support, and Feedback. If you're feeling energetic, put the number of Web pages in each area in parentheses after the area name.

Finally, create one more row for what you've been itching to write down the whole time: your opinions, or more formally, your *qualitative observations*. Note one or two pluses and one or two minuses that stick out for each competitor – things such as whether the site has complete descriptions of products, fast- or slow-loading pages, well-written text, and most vital of all, whether the site is up-to-date. Note whether a site has major categories missing or present compared to the others. You can also note whether the site is ugly or attractive – but don't be surprised if others disagree with this or any other qualitative assessment that you make. Don't feel that you have to write a lot about every competing Web site; if a site is competent but not spectacular, you may have nothing to say here.

If you're really concerned only about a specific product, you may still find performing the company-by-company comparison described in the previous few paragraphs very valuable; the company online presence often forms the base for the product online presence. You can easily use the same exercise for each product you want to market. Create categories that reflect the features and appropriate marketing resources for the kind of product you're interested in; then assess each competitor in those categories. You may find, as we have in the past, that some products have an entire site, e-mail contacts, mailing lists, and more, whereas a head-to-head competitor has only a single page and no contact information. Guess who's going to impress – and keep – customers more?

When you're finished, step back and take a look at the overall chart. Think about changing the comparative points for clarity or adding one or two competitors for completeness. Consider recopying your chart on a clean sheet of paper or recreating it in a word processor or spreadsheet program for neatness. Show the chart to a few colleagues and see whether they understand it.

Using your completed chart

At the end of this exercise, you probably have both bad news and some good news. The most likely bad news is that at least one of your competitors is doing much more on the Internet than you are. If you're like us, as digital consultants, seeing just how much your competitors are doing on the Internet can make you feel very nervous. As you consider the cost and effort to match or exceed your competitors' efforts in the online realm, you may find yourself in need of a stiff drink or the rest of the day off.

The likely good news is that the analysis you just did to create your chart gives you a tremendous amount of information about what your rivals are up to and some very good ideas for your own online presence. The areas (discussion groups, e-mail, and so on) of the Internet marketing universe that your competitors do (or don't) use, the size of their Web site, the areas they cover, and the overall impression their online presence gives are invaluable touchstones for you to use in planning your own effort. A chart like this is also a great motivator for getting the rest of your company to understand the importance of creating a presence on the Internet and getting management to approve the budget and resources you need to make it happen.

Sizing up your pure-play competitors

Take time to search the Web for Web-based competitors – competitors that complete most or all of their sales online. If you're a local plumber, then this detail isn't such a big concern; no one can fix a leaky sink over the Web (although several Web-only companies and search engines now can recommend and hire plumbers on a customer's behalf). But if you're a retailer, wholesaler, or consultant, you need to know just how much your current customers can accomplish without ever leaving their keyboard. Figure 3-8 shows the Web site of Amazon.com, the Web-based superstore that has posed a significant challenge to retail bookshops everywhere despite never having its own physical presence on the high street.

Figure 3-8: Still doing amazin' stuff at Amazon.com.

One way to find online sales sites is to search for keywords associated with online sales. A good keyword is the word *order.* If you use the + symbol to combine the category you're interested in with the word *order,* you're likely to find Web pages for online sales. For instance, if you use the search engines described in Chapter 2 to search for 'books + order', you're likely to get a link to the order page of Amazon.co.uk.

If you have significant online-based competition, people can browse, buy, and specify delivery options online, all without actually leaving their home or desk and all without giving you a second thought, or any chance for the business. Such competition will only grow in the years to come. Consider separately investigating and evaluating Web-based competitors. You may decide to launch an online sales effort yourself.

Sizing Your Digital Marketing Effort

If you've worked your way from the start of the chapter to this point, you've assessed your overall marketing effort; matched your customer base against who's online; and analysed what your competitors are doing online. This research, combined with the ongoing Internet hype we're all being subjected to, may well induce a certain degree of panic on your part.

The situation's not all bad, though. The Internet is still in its early days, and although more and more sites are being launched every day, millions of UK consumers have yet to discover the joys of the Web – so you still have plenty of time to get it right!

You may be too late to try to capitalise on the first round of Internet mania that has gripped the world's media over the last decade. You can, however, have the advantage of being able to benefit from the lessons learned as fortunes were made and, just as often, lost in the initial bubble of online enthusiasm. You may well be better off launching a sustainable and steadily growing Internet presence now than if you'd gone through the booms and busts that have occurred to date.

So now's the time to size the initial online presence that you want to achieve – the base from which you build in the years to come. Find the comparison chart you made in the previous section – if your research is a bit out-of-date, you may want to visit those sites again, or perhaps do another search for any other competitors. Remember that your competitors are the benchmark against which your customers, the trade press, and your management and shareholders or other investors measure you. Then make an initial decision as to where you want to be on the continuum of online innovation:

✔ **Innovator:** Perhaps you want to be an innovator online. This means that, compared to your competitors, your online presence is larger, more expensive, and has more smart features. As an innovator, some of your online efforts are expensive failures; others succeed so well as to get you noticed outside your industry and your traditional markets. You're the first in your sector to introduce selling over the Internet, and you work to increase your online sales even if they aren't initially very profitable. You spend significant amounts of money in the offline world to advertise your online presence, and you try to partner with other leaders.

✔ **Fast follower:** One smart way to play the innovation game is to be a *fast follower*. This means that you watch your competitors' efforts for good ideas and adopt them while avoiding expensive mistakes by letting others make them for you. If you do this following right, you spend less on marketing than your most aggressive competitors and, unlike them, every pound you spend counts. You keep a healthy balance between your Internet-based and traditional marketing efforts.

What if they're not online?

Throughout this book, we advise a conservative approach to building your online presence, mostly because we've seen so many overdone Web sites that were launched with incredible speed, enthusiasm, and expense and then quickly turned into liabilities because of poor initial design, poor usability, and infrequently updated content.

Another reason for a conservative approach is that getting going from a standing start takes time. If one or more of your competitors already have a complete, competent online presence – or, worse (for you), an exciting, innovative, technically excellent Web site and solid use of other Internet services – and you have little or no presence online, you need all the time and money you can muster just to catch up.

On the other hand, if your investigation of the competition reveals that your competitors are not online or that they have limited online presences, you may want to make a stronger initial effort – one that clearly *beats,* not just meets, the competition. Though the dot.com boom and bust occurred a few years ago, people continue to be fascinated by the ever growing online world. If you can make a concerted effort that results in online leadership, you benefit twice: once by the positive impression you make and again by the additional impression you make when you trumpet your Internet leadership in the offline world.

Don't bet the company on this kind of effort; your competitors can always surprise you with a sudden online makeover while you're working on your own, and the positive marketing impact you make with your Internet marketing effort still takes time and work to translate into sales. But business is often about taking chances, and the opportunity for Internet leadership within your business segment may be a chance worth taking.

✔ **Competitor:** Another reasonable approach is to create an online presence that is in the middle of the pack. You may occasionally do something innovative, but in most areas, you wait for solid evidence of success or failure before adding new directions to your online effort. Your expenditure is low; the new directions' impact high. Your traditional marketing efforts take priority over your Internet efforts.

✔ **Conservative:** You may well decide that your business needs are best met by having a minimal Internet presence for now, letting competitors take the lead and instead spending your marketing money in other areas.

Your position on this continuum of online innovation may or may not be tied to how innovative you are in other areas of your business. You don't necessarily need to be a top-flight innovator with your products to take a leadership position in your online presence. Do avoid causing confusion among your online visitors, though. If your overall company culture and marketing efforts typically take a conservative approach, don't suddenly go wild in your digital marketing approach. If you do decide to be innovative, do it in a lower-key way, with a classy overall design and without getting in customers' faces too much in the look or content of your site. Lead in the useful content and features of your site rather than in the use of advanced Internet technologies or whizzy design features.

Creating a Written Plan

Before investing the time and money to create and maintain your online presence, you need to create at least a brief written plan. Companies vary in how much they depend on such plans. Your company may require you to submit a highly structured, well-researched plan to justify your project to senior management before you can spend a single penny. Or you may be encouraged to just 'throw something up on the Internet and see what sticks'. If possible, take a middle course and write a relatively brief business case that covers at least the following elements:

✔ **Marketing assessment:** Quickly describe your current marketing goals and resources and the state of your current digital marketing effort relative to how many of your current and potential customers are on the Internet. Include any feedback you've received about your current Internet presence. This stuff should be lying around your office if you already went through the 'Assessing Your Current Marketing Efforts' section earlier in this chapter.

✔ **Competitive assessment:** One problem businesspeople have in working with the Internet is that they're often thinking about profit and loss while the more Internet-savvy are talking about hits per day and other technical measurements. A brief competitive assessment translates the online issues into terms that businesspeople can understand, such as who's ahead and who's behind. If you've already worked through the section 'Assessing the Competition' in this chapter and created the comparison chart suggested there, you're in business; if not, now's your chance to do so.

✔ **Goals:** Specify your goals for your initial online effort, framing them in terms of your customers' needs and competitive comparisons as much as possible. Use concrete terms such as the names of the major sections you plan to develop for your Web site, the specific online service forums you plan to monitor, any newsgroups you plan to create, and so on.

✔ **Resources:** Even if you're considering doing most or all of the work in-house, get bids from outside suppliers so that you can get a reality check on your internal estimates. Wherever you're using internal resources, consider what other work will be deferred or not done while employees are busy working on the company Internet presence. In many cases, you're best off planning to use external resources.

✔ **Budget:** List the budget items you've developed. Specify that digital marketing is a crucial enabling factor for your company's sales and relate the proposed Web investment and the number of people it is intended to reach to the rest of your company's marketing efforts. If about 10 per cent of your target audience is reachable via the Internet, for instance, you can build toward having about 10 per cent of your total marketing budget devoted to the Internet effort.

✔ **Timeframe:** Specify a timeframe for completing your initial online effort. Allow more time than you at first think necessary; the more work you expect to do in-house, the more generous you need to be with your schedule. Stage the effort to allow control by setting several smaller deadlines, rather than just one big one, and allow time for testing before you take the online resources you create public. Consider using a chart developed in a word-processing or spreadsheet program, or specialised project planning software such as Microsoft Project, to make deadlines and progress visible.

✔ **Create a detailed timeline:** Mark all the major milestones (specification approved, content created, design approved, coding completed, and so on) and all the internal review stages. If you are using in-house resources, get agreement from all the participants, and if senior, busy, people need to review, give them ample time to do so. Also involve key decision makers early in the design and specification process (that is, have them sign off on the specification and design mock-ups if possible).

Who owns your online presence?

The answer to this question: marketing. The IT people may be responsible for running your servers and providing you with reports – and you need them on your side, and no reason exists to alienate anyone involved in the overall online effort. But at the end of the day, the marketing department needs to be responsible for the look, feel, content, or other aspects of your online presence. Also, as we recommend throughout this book, you should consider outsourcing tasks such as the hosting anyway; controlling and reducing costs, and adding and removing services is much easier through an outside vendor than through people in your company.

If your company, division, or product group already has an online presence through the efforts of other departments besides marketing, then you may have to work with the other departments for now (and slowly bring them round to letting marketing call the shots). Your online presence has to be backed up by budget, of course, so start planning now how to have marketing pay most of the bills.

Even with marketing running the overall show, others in your company have to be part of your online presence whether you like it or not. Every e-mail message sent by an employee and (especially) every discussion group comment made by an employee using a company e-mail account are also marketing messages from your company. See Chapters 9–11 for information on how to get everyone on the same page to support – or at least not undermine – your company's online marketing messages.

It can be expensive and embarrassing to make major changes late in the day. Even if the big boss claims not to be interested in the design and is hands-off early on, you can bet he or she will have opinions about the precise shade of blue you've used later on. So insist, nicely, on their involvement and approval. In larger organisations, consider exactly who you want to be involved and what input or review you want from each. Smaller teams often work better in getting a job done, but you'll need to strike a balance between including key people only and letting everyone express an opinion on the site. Actually, they'll do that anyway when they see it, but you don't have to listen to everyone's opinion during the development.

✔ **Maintenance:** Your online effort doesn't end just because you finish the design and load the pages up to your Web server. As part of your plan, specify what your Internet presence requires in terms of ongoing maintenance and updates, including: responding to e-mail that arrives at your Web site; updating Web site content; and monitoring message boards and blogs. Don't be surprised if maintenance of your online presence ends up taking longer than you expected – if you don't prepare, it probably gets done poorly or not at all.

✔ **Next steps:** If someone in your organisation is pushing for a much bigger online presence, and that someone wants it fast, he or she may be disappointed when seeing your carefully staged, conservative plan. (In fact, if no one who sees your plan is disappointed in it, it may well be overambitious.) Here's where you can mollify any critics by pointing out what you can do in the future, after you've completed, deployed, and proven the value of your initial online efforts. (Don't be too overambitious here either, though; some day you may be called to account for what you have written.)

As you work on the plan, continue gathering information. Keep an eye out for changes in competitive efforts and in customer requests for an online presence. If your online presence is successful, you may receive a great deal of e-mail from potential and current customers – all of whom expect an answer. A smallish company or medium-sized product group may find itself receiving enough e-mail to require a full-time person just to respond to it. See Chapters 9 and 10 for information on how to manage the flow of e-mail, and don't put an e-mail address on your Web site until you're ready to respond to the messages you get.

After you create a plan, you have every right to be proud of yourself. You've done a lot of work and set the tone for your company's online presence for years to come. But you still have a few concerns to address:

✔ **Justifying the cost:** Even the senior manager who was initially most enthusiastic about going online may wince when she sees the budget. Marketing expenditures are always hard to justify; after all, they're expenses that don't immediately or measurably increase sales or decrease expenses. You'll be pressured to cut the budget or to do more internally and less with outside resources. Use the competitive assessment to defend the need for your online presence; if someone wants to cut expenditure, show exactly where your online presence suffers if you do so. To support using outside resources, point out that using an experienced, accountable supplier reduces risk.

You can justify your expenditure by posting your new Internet presence targets, using clear *metrics* – measurable items – such as number of sales or leads. If the site allows online selling, such targets are easier to quantify. If not, examples of metrics can include site visits, banner ad click–throughs, or new registrations. If you can measure any of these in terms of money earned, all the better. In other words, think of the whole cost-benefit impact that the site will have on the company as a whole and figure out a way to track each important element.

✔ **Riskiness:** As the old saying goes, 'making predictions is dangerous, especially when they concern the future'. Your plan is likely to be more optimistic and have more risk in it than you realise. An online development effort is somewhere between a major documentation effort and a software development effort in terms of the difficulty of predicting completion dates and the possibility of abject failure.

✔ **'But you said':** A problem that your plan may cause is a phenomenon we call 'But you said', after something that kids like to say to parents. The online efforts that you propose in this plan will likely be taken as firm promises rather than reasonable projections. If you try to modify your goals during the project, people may be disappointed and upset and question your character, integrity, and maybe even ancestry. Use some qualifiers in the plan, such as 'expect to', 'as resources allow', and 'as competitive comparisons indicate', to help manage this problem if it occurs.

When you complete your initial plan, don't show it to anyone. (If a group has worked on it, keep the plan within the group for a day or two.) Get a good night's sleep and then take another look at the plan. Trim it. Edit the plan so that it contains only the core elements needed to meet your customer and competitive goals. Delete or defer everything that's not critical to scoring an early success in the online world. Doing so reduces the amount of money you're asking for, greatly increases your chances of success, and thus increases the odds that management will trust you with more money later to expand your online presence as needed.

Creating a digital marketing plan makes more sense if the process is done while referring to an overall marketing plan. However, you may not have one, or your overall marketing plan may be out-of-date. If you need to have all your ducks in a row before proceeding, create or revise the overall marketing plan first; if getting going on your online presence is more important, create or revise the overall marketing plan after the digital marketing plan is done.

Implementing Your Digital Marketing Plan

If you've done most or all of the steps we suggest in this chapter to this point, congratulations! You're much better prepared to succeed online than many others who've just rushed in, and spent time and money without a clear plan or goals.

Should you start an Internet-based business?

In your planning process, or at the end when you show your plans to others who haven't worked on them, you may be asked whether selling online will be a part of your project. Online selling could be the future for your business, but this isn't really a marketing issue, even though one could say that online selling is best built on a base of successful online marketing.

Plan your online sales effort as a separate business with income, expenses, and (you hope) a profit. See *Starting and Running an Online Business For Dummies* by Dan Matthews and Greg Holden (Wiley) to get started with online sales.

The rest of this book shows you the nuts and bolts you need to implement each part of your digital marketing plan – designing and building your business Web site, using e-mail and automated e-mail lists, and more. Use this book and, if needed, other resources that focus on each element of your online presence.

If you're working with others to implement your digital marketing presence, ask them regularly for progress reports and for demonstrations of work in progress. Return the favour for them: Track your own and others' progress to quickly identify any elements that are exceeding the time or money allotted to them.

As you implement your Internet marketing plan, keep a record of the changes you make from it. You may find that the Web site, for instance, needs to be larger than you first expected; or the first time you actually see the prototype running on a Web browser, you may decide that the look and feel of it needs altering, thereby adding expense. You may also decide to cut back elsewhere to stay within budget. Keep a brief record of decisions you make, the reasons for them, and their impact on your schedule and budget. Such a record helps a great deal when you assess the overall success of your project and when you plan to revise your Internet marketing presence later. (The only thing constant in cyberspace is change!)

Part II
Marketing on the World Wide Web

'No-one in this company can change a video
— It's our brilliant young managing director
who's the technical wizard.'

In this part . . .

The hype around the World Wide Web has reached such dizzying levels that it obscures the fact that the Web is perhaps the single most important new marketing tool since the advent of television. In this part, we cut through the technical jargon and show you exactly how to create an easy-to-find, effective Web presence, whether you're doing all the work yourself or working with others.

Chapter 4

Mastering Your Domain

● ●

● ●

*T*his chapter is about the one piece of the Internet marketing puzzle that may affect your online presence more than anything else. This thing is your *domain name*.

Your domain name is the set of letters in the middle of your Web site's URL, and also (usually) the letters after the '@' symbol in your company-issued e-mail address. For instance, if you work at Big Company, your Web site URL is likely to be www.bigcompany.com (or *.co.uk*) and your e-mail address is likely to be yourname@bigcompany.com (or *.co.uk*) In this case, bigcompany.com (or *.co.uk*) is your company's domain name.

People use your domain name to reach you on various Internet services such as e-mail, FTP, and the Web, all described briefly in Chapter 1. A domain name is your identifier in cyberspace – kind of a cross between a company name, a business address, and a CB radio handle, if you're old enough to remember Citizens' Band radio.

Getting the right domain name is extremely important. The good news: You can register any available domain name quickly and for a small fee, as we describe later in this chapter. The bad news: Someone else may beat you to your ideal domain name, as we also explain later in this chapter.

If you're working in a company, or thinking of starting a company, that does-n't have a domain name yet, cancel your appointments, take your phone off the hook, and read this chapter immediately. If your company or other organ-isation already has a domain name, read this chapter anyway – you may need to change your domain name (including your e-mail addresses and Web URL) to a better one, add a secondary domain name for people who misspell your company name, or establish a new domain name for a product or service that you're working on. Thousands of new domain names are established every day. Time is of the essence.

It is also worth considering registering common industry terms to claim turf that competitors may also want. For example, if you run a holiday cottage letting business in Devon called 'Cute Cottages', as well as *cutecottages.com* and *cute-cottages.com* (and *.co.uk* of course) you may also want to register, if available, *devoncottages.com, devonholidayhomes.com,* and so on. You can then set up Web pages that redirect the user to your main site if anyone hits these. (You will need to be careful if these names reflect the names of existing business that just aren't as Web savvy as you, to avoid a legal wrangle when that business finally gets its act together and wants the domain.

But along with choosing a domain name, you may want to take a few extra minutes to think about who should provide the online access needed for your online marketing efforts. Do you want to stick with your current Internet Service Provider, or should you switch to someone better able to handle domain name registration, Web hosting, and more? The next section gives you the inside scoop.

Choosing an ISP for Digital Marketing

You probably already have Internet access in one form or another. You may use an *Internet Service Provider* (ISP), such as BT or Orange Broadband.

Choosing an ISP for online *access* is quite a bit different from choosing one for online *marketing*. All you need for Web surfing is a reliable connection to the Internet. If your ISP gets sold or goes out of business, you can just change to another one.

However, for online marketing, your needs are much greater. You need to choose a business that can do some or all of the following:

✓ **Register your domain name:** If you want to register your domain name yourself, see 'Discovering How Domain Names Work', later in this chapter. If you want your ISP to do it for you, pick an ISP that you can trust to do it right.

If you register your domain name through an ISP or online service, make absolutely sure that you end up as the legal owner of the domain name. Some unscrupulous ISPs (or 'free' domain name services) register 'your' domain name to themselves and then charge you whatever they can get for full ownership later, putting you at a real disadvantage in regard to this important piece of virtual real estate.

✔ **Receive and forward your e-mail:** You need an ISP or online service that can quickly and reliably receive and send your e-mail. (Your ISP receives all e-mail sent to you and then routes it to you.) Occasional mis-routings are inevitable, but regular blackouts, crashes, virus incidents, and wholesale losses of mail aren't.

✔ **Support you on the road:** You'll need access to all your online services from anywhere in the world. So an ISP that can provide connectivity through third-party deals, or even one with good coverage within the UK, is an advantage.

✔ **Host your Web site:** Your ISP needs to be able to host your Web site at reasonable rates. Carefully compare basic charges for business Web sites, per-hit (or bandwidth) charges for the number of visitors that you get to your Web site, and disk-space charges for storing the content of your Web site. Some providers hide high charges in these rates. You may also want to consider putting your Web site on a separate, specialised hosting service other than your ISP; we describe hosting services in the next chapter.

✔ **Give you support:** Although you can't expect your ISP to manage your online presence for you, you really need to be able to get someone on the phone to help you upgrade your online presence or troubleshoot problems.

✔ **Offer reliability:** Your ISP is your gateway to every customer online. If your ISP is experiencing problems your online presence will suffer. If you're selling online, connectivity problems mean that your shop-front is closed and you're losing business. Selecting an ISP that can provide continuous connectivity for your business is vital.

To find an ISP for online marketing, look for a major, nationwide provider that has been in the business long enough to get write-ups in major magazines. Search for those reviews online and compare carefully.

Try looking at sites such as www.ispreview.co.uk or www.broadband checker.co.uk to get an idea of what is available in your area. The *Digital Marketing For Dummies* Internet Directory in this book contains pointers to even more information.

For digital marketing, you also want an ISP that is technically savvy and thoroughly up-to-date. Among other things, an ISP should support a broad range of Internet applications and services, not just the Web and e-mail; if you can't even get access to services such as Instant Messaging (IM) you definitely can't use it for marketing.

A recent survey by UK broadband research company Point Topic found that the top 10 ISPs in the UK have 88 per cent of the market, so they're probably the best places to start when looking for a reliable ISP. Five of the biggest are BT, AOL, Orange, NTL, and Tiscali. The homepage for BT Retail is shown in Figure 4-1.

Figure 4-1:
BT Retail
is well
regarded as
a business
ISP.

Now (that is, before you start your digital marketing effort) is the time to switch to an ISP that can keep up with your Internet marketing needs, including your Web site. With all the competition out there, you should be able to lock in good rates for a package of services that meets your needs.

Though your ISP can be your best choice for hosting your Web site, a specialised Web-hosting provider may be a good choice as well. Consider investigating Web-hosting services if you expect to get a lot of visitors – thousands a week or more – to your Web site and if you need multiple e-mail addresses for your domain.

Discovering How Domain Names Work

Few businesspeople understand how domain names work. But that understanding is like being able to read a map of cyberspace – and with this knowledge, you can put your business, product, or service at a prominent spot on that map.

You're probably familiar with domain names of your regular e-mail correspondents and of Web sites that you frequently visit. But what if you're trying to find a company marketing site on the Web and you're not quite sure of the domain name? Of course, as we point out in Chapter 2, you can search using appropriate keywords. But even better, the right domain name can make a business much easier to find on the Web. A well-chosen domain name can further facilitate marketing communication by making your Web site address and your marketing e-mail address (maybe something like `sales@big company.co.uk`) much easier for people to remember.

Take a quick look at the Web URL in Figure 4-2 – which is the address of a personal Web page on the GeoCities Web site – and find the domain name in it. The URL has three parts:

- ✔ **Internet protocol name:** Each Internet service has its own special code, or *protocol,* for deciphering its messages. The World Wide Web uses *HyperText Transfer Protocol* (HTTP), usually seen on the Web as *http.* (In English, acronyms are usually in capital letters, but UNIX people – the originators of the Internet and many other important things in computing – tend to avoid them.) A colon and a double slash are used as separators, so the Internet protocol name always appears within a URL like this: *http://*

  Most browsers will now recognise that you need the *http://* prefix to reach Web pages and so have built in the capability to omit them and still reach the desired page, so you can just type in `www.dummies.co.uk` in the Address or Location text box.

- ✔ **Domain name:** The domain name identifies a particular Web site. The part of the domain name that you need to be most concerned about is the dot and three-letter code at the end – *.com*, *.org,* or *.net,* and so on, called the *top-level domain* (TLD) – and the group of letters just before the last full stop in the domain name, which in Figure 4-2 is geocities, called the second-level domain.

- ✔ **Subdirectory and filename:** The subdirectory and filename simply identify the particular file that the user wants. (If no specific filename is used, the Web server usually looks for a file named *index.htm* or *index.html* as the default.) If you've ever used MS-DOS or UNIX, you're very familiar with this kind of pathname and filename; on Windows and Macintosh, folders play the role of subdirectories, and the three-letter extension at the end of the filename is more or less hidden.

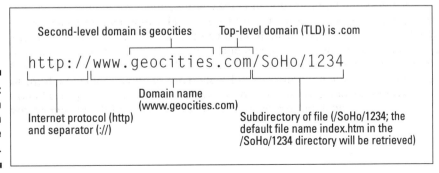

Figure 4-2: The domain name is in the middle of this URL.

Second-level domain is geocities   Top-level domain (TLD) is .com

`http://www.geocities.com/SoHo/1234`

Domain name (www.geocities.com)

Internet protocol (http) and separator (://)

Subdirectory of file (/SoHo/1234; the default file name index.htm in the /SoHo/1234 directory will be retrieved)

Breaking down domain names

The original role of a domain name is as a shared name for a group of machines connected to the Internet. Every machine on the Internet has a specific identifying number called an *IP address,* but people have trouble remembering long numbers. So machines can be assigned names as well; the names and the numbers that go with them are stored on an Internet server called a Domain Name Server, or DNS – initials you may recognise from setting up programs that access the Internet.

Domain names allow an organisation to take over for itself the job of naming all of its machines that are connected to the Internet. After an organisation receives a domain name of its own, it can also assign any name it wants to lower levels within that domain. For instance, an organisation with the domain name *bigcompany.com* can call machines that it owns *greg.big company.com, ben.bigcompany.com* and so on.

The confusing thing about domain names is that they're read backwards, not forwards, with the three-letter top-level domain, or TLD (such as *.co.uk* or *.com*) at the right end, the second-level domain just before it, and so on, as shown in Figure 4-2. A few years ago only a few TLDs existed, such as *.com, .net,* and *.org.* As the Internet grew a recognised need developed for more TLDs to support the growing number of sites and also specific industry sectors. Table 4-1 shows you a selection of those generic TLDs now available to use.

Table 4-1	Top-Level Domains (TLDs)
Top-level domain	*Meaning*
.com	Commercial organisations and businesses worldwide
.co.uk	Commercial organisations and businesses within the UK
.net	Used by business and also networks online
.org	Used by organisations, often charities and those not for profit
.gov	US government agencies (non-military)
.gov.uk	Used by UK government
.biz	Alternative business domain
.aero	Used by the aviation industry
.de, .fr	Country-level domains for countries outside the UK and the US. These do not use *.co.*

Cybersquatting

As more people come online domain names are becoming more important. This has led to *cybersquatting* – a practice whereby someone registers the domain name of your company and business and then attempts to get you to pay them to release it to you.

When developing the original AltaVista search engine (see Figure 4-3), Digital Equipment Corp. (DEC) didn't register the right domain name. In order to use AltaVista, users had to go to *altavista.digital.com*. Most people looking for the search engine didn't think of the *.digital* part. Eventually, Compaq acquired DEC and paid the owner of the name www.altavista.com $3 million for the domain name.

In the UK Apple faced a similar issue with the launch of iTunes. A company called Cyber Britain had already registered *iTunes.co.uk*. The owner of the domain name *iTunes.co.uk* claimed that he had legitimately registered the domain a month before Apple's trademark application was published in December 2000. This dispute was settled by Nominet UK, the domain registrar, who ruled that the domain had to be handed over to Apple.

Disputes like this are common and are now often settled by the World Intellectual Property Organisation (WIPO). In 2005 WIPO saw 1,456 cybersquatting cases filed with its Arbitration and Mediation Centre, a rise of 20 per cent on the previous year.

The most desirable online domain is still *.com,* as it has the longest heritage and that means a lot in an industry that is only ten years old. After *.com,* *.co.uk* is the best domain for a UK business and will be one of those uppermost in a user's mind when they're searching for the Web page of a UK company. Avoid using domains that have no obvious link with your business, such as *.aero* if you're a caterer or *.org* if you're a credit company as it is strongly associated with not-for-profit organisations. Using domains that have no link to your business will only confuse the user.

As far as online marketing is concerned, the most important part of a domain name is the second-level domain. The second-level domain is the middle part of a typical Web URL – for example, the *bigcompany* component of www.big company.com. The second-level domain that you choose needs to represent your company and organisation as well as possible within a few constraints:

- ✔ **No special characters:** Your domain name can contain only letters, numbers, and the dash character.

- ✔ **Not too long:** Your second-level domain shouldn't be too long because users need to remember it. Using http://www.thelongestdomain nameintheworldandthensomeandthensomemoreandmore.com won't do you any favours. The maximum number of characters is 63; 67 including the appropriate TLD. However, domain names this long are hard to remember, and people aren't used to them; they may think such a domain name strange. Try to stay under a 22-character limit.

> ✓ **Not already registered:** This part is tough. The combination of your second-level and top-level domains, such as *bigcompany.com, bigschool. edu,* or *bigcharity.org,* has to be new (not already registered). If it is already registered, you either have to induce the current name-holder to give it up or come up with a new name. (More on this subject later in this chapter.)

Domain name registering company Network Solutions has a Web page (www. networksolutions.com) allowing you to check any domain name you enter to make sure that it fits the rules in the preceding list.

The second-level domain of your choice, combined with the appropriate top-level domain, is what you register for your use on the Internet. The addition of the *www.* in front of this domain indicates that it is a page on the World Wide Web.

Figure 4-3:
The original
AltaVista
Technology
Web site.

The competition for domain names

According to research from Verisign, the registrar for the *.com, .org,* and *.net* domain names, there were 85.6 million domain names at the end of September 2005, a 29 per cent growth year on year.

The most recent statistics on domain registration show that over 52 million *.com* domains are now registered. In the UK, Nominet, which manages the *.uk* TLDs including *.co.uk, .org.uk,* and *.me.uk,* had over 5 million domains registered as of May 2006. The suffix *.com* is by far the most common top-level domain due to the US-centric nature of the Internet and also the heritage that the *.com* domain brings with it.

If you're part of a government agency or the military, please check out the policies that apply to your agency before registering a domain name. We don't want to get blamed for someone's online tax return getting sent to the wrong e-mail address.

In the US-centred online world, making clear that your business is outside of the US is a good thing. Using the appropriate country designation in your top-level domain (TLD) name is the best way to do this; in the UK's case this is *.co.uk*. Check here for a list of the domains that you can register throughout the world – `http://en.wikipedia.org/wiki/List_of_Internet_ top-level_domains`.

Because the *.com* domain is so widely used, many organisations that aren't really companies register and use the *.com* version of their domain name as well as the more appropriate version – country-specific or *.edu* or *.org* or whatever. If your domain name ends in something besides *.com* and you need to reach many of the non-cyber-savvy, consider registering the *.com* version as well.

A great deal of competition exists for desirable domain names. Although the initial land-rush for the best domains is pretty much over, battles still take place over prime spots in cyberspace, and you can't risk not staking your claim.

Why domain names are so important

A business consultant once said that the three keys to starting a business are location, location, and location. Your domain name is the location on the Internet to which all your e-mail and Web traffic comes. You're likely to print this name on business cards, stationery, and advertising, as well as hastily tell it to enquiring people in the lift.

Typically, when people use the Internet, they're trying to get information quickly. If they've heard of your company in the offline world, they're likely to try to guess your Web URL and enter it in their browsers. If you have the URL that they expect – *www.<a reasonable version of your company name> .com* – they may find it on the first or second try. If not, you have problems.

Having failed to find you quickly, Web surfers – also known as customers, investors, prospects, news reporters, industry analysts, and others – can do several things. More often than not, they just go surf somewhere else. Or they may try using a search engine to find you. But even if these people's search is successful (and especially if it's not), you've inconvenienced and annoyed people important to you by not having the 'right' domain name.

In many cases, figuring out a good domain name is easy: Your company name translates into an easy-to-guess second-level domain, the domain name that you want (your desired second-level domain and the appropriate top-level domain, such as *.com*) is available, and you're in business. Other times, identifying the appropriate unused domain name is much more difficult, especially if only one name is really a good fit and that name's taken.

The benefits of the right domain name are significant. With the right domain name, every time you advertise your company name or communicate it in any way, you effectively communicate your online location as well.

Check out `http://www.bcentral.co.uk/business-technology/your-company-website/choosing-a-domain-name.mspx` for more detailed info and advice on how to choose a domain name for your business. *Bcentral* is Microsoft's UK initiative to help small to medium-sized businesses in the online world, and is a handy resource.

Possible new domain names

Every now and again new TLD domain names are floated for specific industries or sectors. The original seven TLDs – *.com, .edu, .gov, .int, .mil, .net,* and *.org* – have since been added to by *.biz, .info, .name, .pro, .aero, .coop,* and *.museum*. No guarantee exists that these extensions to the list will stop here. In recent times the possibility of a *.xxx* domain for the adult industry has been floated, and more sector-specific domains are bound to be put forward in the future. Keep an eye out for these new domain names from time to time – even though the approval process is tortuously long – as you need to snap up any domain that may affect your marketing efforts. To check for details of proposed new domains, see the Internet Corporation for Assigned Names and Numbers Web site at `www.icann.org`. This site includes pointers to valuable information about the current domain name system as well as the proposed changes.

Significant numbers of these domains haven't been registered since the introduction of the new domains began in 2001 and 2002. Some such as *.museum* and *.info* have proved more popular than others, but for the relatively small cost of registering a domain name you need to cover all your marketing bases and if any particular TLD applies to your business, we'd recommend registering it to protect yourself from cybersquatters, as well as to mop up any online users who may try to access your site via that domain name.

Tuvalu for you?

The small Pacific island nation of Tuvalu has the country-level domain *.tv,* short for Tuvalu. An American company called dotTV www.tv, seeing the potential value in new URLs ending in *.tv,* licensed the top-level domain from the country for tens of millions of dollars. The company has had great success in reselling these domain names to media companies such as NBC, Sony, and others who want a *.tv* name, and this success means that people are likely to hear about these names and find them an easy-to-remember and credible alternative to the much more common *.com* suffix. Consider other top-level domains such as *.md* – the suffix of the former Soviet republic of Moldavia – but refrain from jumping on board the bandwagon until they become popular enough to catch on widely.

Choosing Your Domain Name(s)

With a little thought as to how people use domain names, you can understand why registering the domain name(s) that you need is so important. Consider registering the following kinds of domain names:

- ✔ **Ideal company domain name:** Figure out the ideal domain name for your organisation, as we describe in the following section, and register it if it's still available.

- ✔ **One or two close alternates:** If reasonable alternate domain names for your company – names that people may try – are available, consider registering them too. You can then set up your Web server to automatically redirect people who type in the alternate name to your main Web site.

- ✔ **Product and service domain names:** If you sell products or services that have gained wide awareness – anything a substantial number of current or future Web surfers may find interesting – register the domain name that's the best fit for each one soon, before someone else does. Do the same for products under development.

Domain name follies

The ideal domain name is the one that a savvy Internet user who knows your company's name would guess first when trying to find your company on the Web. This name's simply the closest translation that you can make of your company's name into a single word with no spaces, commas, full stops, or other punctuation.

Who registers domain names?

You may think that your business is too small or does not need to register a domain name. Surprise! According to Verisign 75 per cent of all domain name registrations are made by companies and 71 per cent of those in Europe felt strongly about the impact of the Internet on their business. The Small Office Home Office (SOHO) market is booming thanks to the advent of mass communication via the Internet. Table 4-2 also shows that the SOHO user is Web savvy, with a higher percentage of broadband connections than any other region. If you want your small business to succeed, you need to be one of these 'switched on' users.

As we mention earlier in this chapter, the only characters allowed in a domain name are letters, numbers, and dashes. However, we suggest avoiding the dash – remembering whether a domain name has a dash in it and where the dash goes can be difficult, and may cause potential visitors to miss your site. In choosing your domain name, stick to letters and numbers whenever possible.

For some examples, Table 4-2 lists ten top UK companies, the best domain names for them, alternates that would probably be worth registering, and their actual domain names.

Table 4-2	Domain Names of Top UK Companies		
Company name	*Ideal domain*	*Alternates to name*	*Actual domain registered*
Marks & Spencer	Marksandspencer.co.uk/Marksandspencer.com	MandS.com	marksandspencer.com
Boots	Boots.com/Boots.co.uk	Bootsthechemist.com	Boots.com
BHS	BHS.com/BHS.co.uk	BritishHomeStores.com	BHS.co.uk
Argos	Argos.co.uk/Argos.com	Argosonline.com	Argos.co.uk
WH Smith	WHSmith.co.uk/WHSmith.com	WHS.co.uk/Smiths.com	Whsmith.co.uk
Tesco	Tesco.co.uk/Tesco.com	Tescos.com/Tescos.co.uk	Tesco.com
Sainsbury's	Sainsburys.co.uk/Sainsburys.com	JSainsbury.com	Sainsburystoyou.com

Company name	Ideal domain	Alternates to name	Actual domain registered
HMV	HMV.co.uk/ HMV.com	Hismastersvoice. com	hmv.co.uk
Borders	Borders.com/ Borders.co.uk	Bordersbooks.com	Bordersstores.com
Dominos Pizza	Dominos.co.uk/ Dominos.com	Dominospizza.co.uk	Dominos.co.uk

Looking at Table 4-2, you may think, 'Well, those companies are all big and they no doubt have lots of lawyers working on getting the right domain names and rights.' But large companies can just as easily miss out on their domain names as small ones. We've already mentioned Apple earlier in this chapter as a company that almost missed out on the URL *iTunes.co.uk,* a massive mistake that was rectified through legal channels. The most recent addition to the domain name family is *.eu,* for sites within the European Union, and companies must be careful to ensure that they extend their existing domain name program to include these new domains if they're not to suffer the same fate as Apple.

Governments aren't immune to domain name confusion, either. The URL www.tendowningstreet.com gets you a little political message that the current resident probably doesn't want you to read, whilst www.white house.org gives you a parody of the official site for the US president (which is www.whitehouse.gov).

Good and bad domain names

You can see from the examples in the previous section how to pick the best domain name for your company: Find the word or short phrase, with no spaces or other punctuation, that best represents your company name. You simply translate your company name into a domain name. (The test of whether you have the right domain name is: Can someone who knows your company and regularly uses the Web guess your company's domain name on the first try?)

Not all companies come as close to the ideal domain names as most of the companies shown in Table 4-2. Also, many companies' names are difficult to render into a domain name. To view some examples relevant to your own business, use a search engine and search for other businesses in your category to see how well or poorly they've done in registering good domain names.

Should you make your product name a domain?

One interesting dilemma is whether you should make your product name a domain name. We don't think that you should use your main product's name as the domain name for the whole company unless the product is much more well known than the company (in which case, you may want to change your company name to match it!).

However, you may want to consider registering key product names as domain names in addition to your company name. You may eventually want to have a Web site dedicated to a product, or automatically reference people who enter your product name as a URL to your main company site. (For instance, if you enter `www.`

`itunes.co.uk` you'll automatically be taken to the relevant page on the main Apple Web site.)

Defensive reasons exist for registering your major product names as domain names as well. If you don't register your product names, your competitors may; other sites desperate for traffic, such as porn sites, may even have a go at it. And if you're trying to trademark your product names, registration is even more important. Someone else who wants to use the same name could use your failure to register the name as evidence that you were never serious about protecting the name in the first place.

For instance, looking up 'Bookshop' in Google and elsewhere, you can see some interesting examples of different approaches:

- ✔ **Amazon. URL `www.Amazon.co.uk`.** This is the most simple and direct approach and the one that works best if people know the name of your company already. Amazon has a trusted name online and is extremely well known, but as long as the person searching for your business knows your company name this will probably be their first guess.

- ✔ **Royal Institute of British Architects online book store. URL: `www.riba bookshops.com`.** Knowing that they're not as well known as Amazon, RIBA has identified that people searching for bookshops will not automatically type in 'RIBA' and find them. They've therefore tagged the subject onto their name to stand out in this sector. This handy if simple technique will work well with search engines, even if it won't necessarily be the first thought that comes into everyone's mind on entering a URL direct into the browser.

- ✔ **Amnesty Bookshops. URL: `http://hardy.amnesty.org.uk/give/ bookshops/`.** The UK branch of the International pressure group has used the *.org* suffix that is most associated with charities and not-for-profit groups and has also used the *.uk* suffix to show that it is the UK arm of the organisation. However it has also used a 'third-level' domain name in front of its main domain, Amnesty. We don't think anyone would naturally come direct to this page other than via a very specific search through a search engine or through other pages from the main Web site.

✔ **University of Liverpool School of Modern Languages – recommended bookshops.** URL: `http://www.liv.ac.uk/sml/ug/resources/ bookshops.htm`. The University has done all the right things in terms of flagging up that it is an educational institution using the *.ac* suffix. The *.uk* suffix gives it a location but then little hope exists of any student remembering the URL to get to their preferred reading lists. Again, a specific search engine keyword search will find this page or students will have to navigate through the main Web site.

Though we picked one very narrow category for these examples, any group of organisations is likely to have a similar range of easy-to-guess and hard-to-guess domain names. Just make sure that yours is in the easy-to-guess group!

Choosing a company domain name

Now's the time to choose your own domain name (or, if you already have one and you don't like it, to choose a new one). With new top-level domains such as *.eu* being added, and with millions of new domain names being registered every year, you need to get registered now. Follow these steps to choose a domain name:

1. **Sit down with a piece of paper or a blank document in your word processor and list all the possible domain names that fit your organisation.**

   Start with *.com* as the ending (top-level domain, or TLD for short) for your domain name if the name's your company. Also consider *.net* (which is often a popular 'back-up' to *.com*) and any new top-level domains such as *.biz*. As the UK has its own country-code TLD you can also use that – *.uk*. If you're part of a not-for-profit, educational, or government organisation, you can also use the appropriate TLD *(.org, .edu,* or *.gov).*

2. **Ask several friends and colleagues who use the Web what domain name they think your company should use.**

   Most people encounter domains as part of Web addresses (URLs), so ask some of them what Web address they think you should have. Experienced Web users try to guess Web addresses without consciously thinking about it, so you may want to even ask a few people to sit down in front of their browsers and try typing in the right URL for your company. Just hope your friends don't type in something like `www.<yourcompany> sucks.com`!

3. **Shorten your list to a few favourite candidates.**

   Include alternatives that aren't the best choice but that some people may try – for instance, a name with your company's acronym should be kept as an alternative if people usually think of your company by its full name. Also include any common misspellings of your company name if any exist.

When you have a good idea of the domains that you would like to register you should use the WHOIS online service to see if your domain names are available, and if not, who has registered them before you.

1. **Check if your domain name is already taken by using the free WHOIS service online.**

    Fire up your Web browser and go to `http://www.networksolutions.com/whois/index.jsp`. The page is shown in Figure 4-4.

2. **Enter the first domain name that you want to check; for instance, as a domain name for this book, we may try** *dmfd.com*.

3. **Press Enter.**

    The Network Solutions WHOIS domain name checker service tells you whether someone already has your domain name. If the name's still available, you're given the option of registering it there and then and adding in any other domain extensions that are available to register on your main domain, such as *.co.uk* or *.tv*. If the name's not available, you'll see a page with information about who has registered that domain already.

4. **Click the check box next to any domain names that you may want to use; then click Add selected domains to order.**

    Names you choose will be kept on a list on the Web page as you proceed. You're then given the chance to select to make your information private, meaning that nobody else can search your domain name on WHOIS and find your details.

5. **If your top choice or top few choices are taken, follow up with the domain name-holders and see whether any of them are willing to part with their domain name for a reasonable price or even for free.**

For the choices you like that are taken, try entering the domain name as a URL in your Web browser – add *www.* at the beginning and then the domain name – to see whether the domain name is in active use.

If the name's not in use, it may be easier to negotiate getting the domain name for yourself.

After you have compiled a list of choices that you like, print the list. Consult your colleagues and financial advisors – quickly, before the name gets taken – then come back to the Network Solutions Web site to register the name, as described later in this chapter.

If your first choice or a strong alternative is available, you're ready to take the next step and claim your domain name. If all the reasonable choices for your business are taken, consider using a variant on the name of your business. For example instead of *abcplumbing* (which is taken as we write this), consider *abcplumbers* (which is not). If you're really stuck, try inserting a dash – *abc-plumbing,* for instance.

Figure 4-4:
Network
Solutions
leads the
domain
name
charge.

You can also contact the current holder of the domain that you want to use and see whether the people who own it are willing to give up their rights to it. If the domain name is not in active use, they may be willing to let you have it.

Many domain names are held by domain-name brokers, speculators who reserve domain names that they don't need in hopes of selling them to a high bidder later. (Yes, this practice is common, and no, it's not a crime.) If such a person holds your domain name, you may have to pay him or her to get the rights to 'your' name, or consider another name.

Alternatively, you can use the domain name dispute resolution service offered by Internet Corporation for Assigned Names and Numbers (ICANN) – the not-for-profit corporation that has responsibility for Internet Protocol (IP) address space allocation, generic (gTLD), and country code (ccTLD) Top-Level Domain name system management. These services were originally per-formed under US government contract by the Internet Assigned Numbers Authority (IANA) and other entities. ICANN now performs the IANA function. To check out their dispute policy, go to http://www.icann.org/udrp/udrp.htm.

Starting out

As you get your virtual feet wet in cyberspace, you may decide to go ahead and start out with a Web site that exists in a subdirectory of someone else's domain or go for a simple ISP-hosted option. Here are a few dos and don'ts:

✔ **Don't use subdirectory services such as AOL and Yahoo! GeoCities.** Although these services are tempting as someone else sorts out all the technical aspects, from a marketing point of view they are a big no-no. The URL you'll receive will be something along the lines of `www.members.aol.com/yourbiz`. You are basically saying that you have no competence when it comes to online marketing and need someone to hold your hand at every step of the way – even if this image is true, plenty of other providers exist that won't create that impression.

✔ **Don't publicise a subdirectory URL too widely.** If you do put your Web site in a subdirectory of someone else's site, don't publicise your URL too widely; you'll just be publicising the fact that you haven't got your Web presence just right yet. Also, you're just making life more difficult for yourself later on when you do get your own domain name and need to publicise it.

✔ **Do get your own domain quickly.** Most ISPs help you quickly move your Web site to your own domain name and even register the domain name for you for a small fee. Then you can publicise your Web site freely.

✔ **Do use an ISP.** Almost every ISP in the UK offers you the opportunity to have Web space as part of their package and these have a slightly better reception than pure Web services. Try looking for some independent ones such as *clara.net* who are well regarded.

You can also consider suing the current holder of a domain name for rights to it. If you have a strong trademark claim to the name and the current holder doesn't, then you may be able to win – but suing is often a long, expensive, and uncertain venture. Threatening to sue a domain-name broker for this reason may drive the price down – or, if the broker believes that your claim is weak or is just stubborn, suing may drive the price up instead.

If your business is small and your desire to be accessible on the Internet is large, you may even consider changing your business name to one that translates well to an available domain name. ABC Tools may become London Tools (domain name *Londontools.com*) or Toys Aren't Us *(ToysArentUs.com)*. (Just kidding on the last one; you don't want anyone suing you.)

After all your efforts, you may just be stuck and end up having to use a less desirable name. If so, go ahead and get the less desirable name registered – before someone else takes that one too! – and take steps to make reaching your Web site by a link or by a search engine easy, as we describe in Chapter 5.

What if you're local?

For a local or regional business, the trouble with the World Wide Web is the 'World' part. Your Internet presence is held up to the same standard as the big boys, and your domain name must be available everywhere.

No one looking for a place to eat lunch cares whether a Sandy's Sandwich Shop is available in Colchester and a different business with the same name operates in Coventry. But desirable domain names for such a business, such as `www.sandys.com` and so on, are available only once. You can't have two businesses with the same domain name on the Web, no matter how unlikely these two businesses are to compete for customers in the real world.

A variety of ways exist, none of which is very appealing, to make your domain name localised. (Your customers expect to find you as `www.yourbiz.com` on the Web, and anything different from that is a hassle for them.) In the UK you can use the country-code extension *.uk* to differentiate yourself from overseas players with the same name. But the best name for your business ending in your country's top-level domain may be taken too!

A good approach is to work the name of your city or county into your domain name. A sandwich shop in Colchester. Essex can be `www.sandys colchester.com` to set it apart from its Coventry cousin. You'll have to repeatedly tell your customers about your domain name, though, for them to have any chance of remembering it.

Another technique is to rename your business with a title not already taken online. If you do decide to rename your business, carefully weigh up the benefits against any damage that may be done to it in the 'real' world.

Search engines are beginning to launch search services that are tailored by geography as well as name, so users can search for 'sandwich shops' in 'Colchester' rather than getting every sandwich shop in the world. No such distinction exists in domain names as yet, though. For now, locally orientated businesses will just need to be creative – and be ready to get a pound's worth of mileage out of a penny – when setting up their presence on the Internet.

Registering Your Domain Name(s)

After you identify an available domain name that you want, you need to register it. You can register the domain name yourself or hire someone to register it for you. Each approach has its own benefits and hazards.

Registering your domain name yourself

The good news is that you can register the domain name by filling out a form on the Web site of any number of domain name registration companies – search Google for a list. We'll use Network Solutions Web site as an example as it is probably the best known and oldest – www.networksolutions.com. The cost is as little as £20 a year.

Other registration services operate, but at the time of writing, Network Solutions is the biggest and, we believe, the best. Before proceeding, if you want to get a site up immediately, you need to get Domain Name Server (DNS) information from your ISP or Web-hosting provider. However, you don't have to have this information to register a name.

To decide what URL(s) you want to register, and to research their availability, see the preceding section on choosing a domain name. Then follow these steps to register your domain name:

1. **Open a Web browser and go to the Network Solutions Web site at www.networksolutions.com.**

   The Network Solutions homepage appears.

2. **Enter the domain name in the text entry box; then tick each of the boxes for the suffixes that you desire *.com, .net, .org, .tv, .co.uk*, and so on.**

3. **After you have the domain name and top-level domain right, click the Search button.**

   The Web Address Search Results Web page appears, as shown in Figure 4-5.

4. **Click to tick the box for each name that you want to register now.**

   You're getting ready to make a financial commitment here, so pay attention.

5. **Click Add selected domains to order.**

   You'll be offered the chance to make your details private for a fee – this means that anyone searching the WHOIS database on your domains will not see any information about you. This precaution isn't strictly necessary and we wouldn't bother with it. Click Continue when you've made your decision.

6. **You'll then be offered the add-on services offered by Network Solutions.**

   Choosing these add-ons is up to you but you'll be offered a full Web package, e-commerce site, e-mails, and a Web hosting package and right at the bottom (in tiny letters) it says *No thanks, I just want my domains.* Click this button.

NSI - Web Address Search Results - Microsoft Internet Explorer

File   Edit   View   Favorites   Tools   ″   Address 4AAAX0MNWFI3EFCFE4YVDUQQIV0?_requestid=972126   ⟳Go

NETWORK SOLUTIONS®
A VeriSign® Company

> HOME   > MAKE CHANGES   > PRODUCTS & SERVICES   > SITE MAP   > HELP

Web Address Search Results   > Back to Home Page

DOWNLOADING C I HOST FOR WEB HOSTING - 1000MB FOR ONLY $20!

Select the names you want

Congratulations! **acorpocracy.com** is available.

The name(s) below are available. Select the ones you want and click Continue. There are **no restrictions** on using .com, .net, or .org — anyone can register them.

☑ acorpocracy.com
☐ acorpocracy.net
☐ acorpocracy.org
☐ myacorpocracy.com
☐ eacorpocracy.com
☐ aboutacorpocracy.com
☐ acorpocracyonline.com

Registration Steps

→ Select Web Address(es)
• Choose services you want
• Review shopping cart
• Provide your information
• Payment & checkout

SPECIAL OFFER!

Get **20% off** when you select a one-page Web site and/or personalized e-mail with your domain name*

Special Offer 20%

Contains commands for working with the selected items.

Figure 4-5:
Web address search gets results.

7. **More add-ons will be offered in the form of forwarding traffic from other domains to your main one or adding search engine visibility**.

   Again, these are merely add-ons and you can change your mind later on and get most of the services from your ISP anyway. Make your decision and click the Continue button.

8. **You'll then be shown the different price options.**

   These vary depending on how long you want your domains for and the popularity of your chosen domains. You can choose to buy them for anywhere between 1 year and 100 years, the choice is up to you. Remember, you'll get the chance to renew any domains you use, so best treat the arrangement like a mortgage and go for a short fixed term of around three years; then if it all goes wrong, you haven't wasted too much money. After you've decided on this detail, click the Proceed to purchase button.

9. **You'll be asked to log in or create a new account and will be taken through the payment options (see Figure 4-6).**

   You need to provide your payment details at this point. *This is where you pay* – so make sure that you have everything in order before you click 'submit order'.

Well done, you have registered your domain name (see Figure 4-7)!

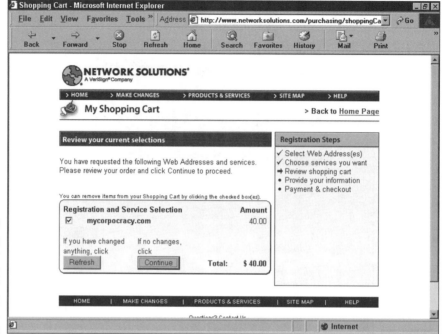

Figure 4-6:
Your
shopping
cart for your
domain
name.

Figure 4-7:
You're King
of the World
(Wide Web)!

Having an ISP or Web-hosting service register your domain name for you

If you don't want to register your domain name yourself through Network Solutions, as described in the previous section, you can get someone else to do it for you. Major ISPs and Web-hosting services offer domain-name registration as part of their range of services.

Reputable companies charge a small fee for taking care of domain registration, but not a lot more than the cost of the domain name itself as the service has become commoditised over the last few years. Watch out for any sneaky add-on services that they try to charge you for as well, though, and make sure that you only pay for what you want. A good Internet partner can have you up and running with a basic Web site very quickly for less than £100.

You can use a combination of methods to find a good ISP or Web-hosting service. First, make a clear, understandable list of your wants and needs, such as fast connections, e-mail services, Web consulting help, and so on. Pass this list around colleagues to make sure that you all agree on your goals.

Then look around. Talk to other businesspeople about their experiences. Check with people in your own industry, if they'll share the information. Use online resources such as search engines and Web sites – for example, www. ISPreview.co.uk – to arm yourself with information before you begin.

Then, talk to several potential providers. Watch out for some of the following possible pitfalls:

- ✔ **Overcharging you:** Some ISPs charge you a high monthly fee for a package of Internet services that includes your own domain name. Shop around for a reasonable price, and try to pay a low one-time set-up fee for your domain name and monthly fees for the rest of the service.

- ✔ **Ripping off your name:** Some unscrupulous Web-hosting services or ISPs have registered customers' domain names to *themselves,* not the customer. The ISP can then charge you to get your own domain name back if you ever stop using its Web-hosting service. Check the contract you sign with the ISP to make absolutely sure that you own the exclusive rights to your domain name.

- ✔ **Insufficient backup:** Your ISP or Web-hosting service should have backup hosting of your site using a different Internet connection in a different location to the main Web-hosting computer. That way, if a problem with the main host computer arises, support for your site can continue at the backup location while the problem at the main hosting site is resolved.

✔ **Going out of business:** You really don't want your ISP or Web-hosting service to go out of business; for the online marketer, this situation's like being a cowboy and having your horse shot out from under you. Try to ensure that your ISP will be around for a long time. (We discuss some of the general considerations of choosing an ISP in greater depth in the 'Choosing an ISP for Digital Marketing' section, earlier in this chapter.)

✔ **Confusing legal language:** You need to be able to clearly understand the terms of any contract that you sign regarding ISP and hosting services. In particular, make sure that the contract clearly states that you own your domain name and that you can transfer it to another ISP or Web-hosting service at any time.

Do all you can to avoid these potential problems. If you screen out potential service providers who can't reassure you on these issues, those that are left may well be a good choice for you.

Chapter 5

Planning Your Business Web Site

∙ ∙

In This Chapter

▶ Creating a simple and effective business Web site

▶ Deciding on your site's contents

▶ Designing a look and feel for your site

▶ Having someone else create your site

∙ ∙

A marketing-orientated business Web site is the meat and drink of the online marketing world: not too exciting, but satisfying and extremely sustaining. By creating and maintaining a straightforward business Web site, you can easily provide customers, press, and analysts with vital information about your company and products. If the initial effort is successful, your site can lay the groundwork for a larger online marketing effort, possibly including your first move into online sales.

You've probably seen a lot of advanced Web technology used in high-profile Web sites – technologies such as Flash and Dynamic HTML. These innovations are all good, if used properly, but they have little place in a marketing-orientated business Web site. You can create a basic business Web site without too much planning. You can even begin to construct the site while you're in the midst of the planning process. The idea here is to jump-start your online presence by getting a competent representation of your company up and running – fast.

In this chapter, we describe how to create the initial site yourself or by working with a few colleagues or consultants.

Although some companies and consultants advertise that they'll create a basic business Web site for you for as little as £200, many of these ads are teasers designed to get you to pick up the phone and begin a process that can lead to you spending big money. Although you can and should use consultants or specialist suppliers for larger Web efforts, developing and publishing the initial site yourself is sensible. After you get some hands-on experience, you can know what you're paying for when you hire a Web-design agency to expand your Web site later. If you do hire help for the initial Web site effort, use this chapter to do as much of the work as you can on your own, and to double-check the outsiders' advice so that you can make sure that you're getting your money's worth.

Guiding Principles for Business Sites

A basic business Web site is like a simple, glossy brochure that briefly describes your company and is a showcase for your products. It reassures people that you're a competent player who'll be around for a while and from whom they can buy with confidence. Your Web site also lets users move easily from picking up basic information to more active steps such as contacting you by writing to you, or sending you an e-mail. But watch this last option, because it can backfire on you; you can receive so many e-mails that you have trouble responding to all of them. See Chapter 10 for more on e-mails.

These underlying principles should guide your effort to create a basic business Web site:

- ✔ **Harmlessness:** The first words of the doctors' Hippocratic Oath are 'First, do no harm', and this dictum should be honoured by people doing marketing as well. Misspellings, poor grammar, and basic errors in your site's text harm your company's image of competence. Web pages with large graphics that download slowly, or that have been developed using advanced technologies that not everyone can use, irritate potential customers. Allowing people to send you e-mail that goes unanswered can cause lost sales. Be cautious and avoid problems.

- ✔ **Fast build:** Your initial Web site effort should develop quickly from the initial idea to a live site. If you can do all the work yourself and don't need anyone's approval, you may get the site up and running in two weeks. If you need to discuss certain aspects of your site in advance and you need approval of the final product at the end, you may need a month or two to complete the site. Keep the project time as short as possible. However, make sure that you have a long-term plan in mind of what the site will look like once launched and evolved. Think about content and other sections you may want to add so that when you do, you don't have to completely rebuild your Web site!

- ✔ **Cheap:** A basic Web site can be created in-house, with perhaps some outside help on the look and feel, and published on a Web server by your Internet Service Provider (ISP) or Web-hosting service for very little cost. Expect to spend a few weeks on creating the site, possibly £1,000 on a consultant for graphics and navigation help, and around £20 a month for an ISP to host the site on its server.

✔ **Effective:** Any marketing effort needs to support moving a prospective customer along the sales cycle. A basic Web site helps potential customers consider you as a possible supplier and encourages them to contact you in order to go further. (A Web site gets press, analysts, and investors to take you seriously, as well.)

✔ **Widely usable:** A basic Web site needs to be usable by anyone with an Internet connection and a Web browser; it should not contain any advanced Web technology that isn't supported by almost every available browser. That means no frames, no Flash, no Dynamic HTML – so no complicated animations or clever graphics. Keeping it simple makes your Web site easier to design and use.

✔ **Fits in on the Net:** Because of its origins among academics and scientists, the Internet has certain standards and practices that you ignore at your peril. (Until early in the 1990s, any commercial use of the Internet was forbidden, and even now, although it's dying out, some resistance to online commerce remains.) Respect the history of the medium by avoiding hype, overstatement, alarming layouts and graphics, and so on. A conservative or formulaic approach will serve you well until you develop a good feel for where you can have some fun.

Specifying Your Site Content

A basic business Web site is not something you should advertise or market heavily. The site is there for people to find when they're looking for information on the Web. Therefore the site's contents should be simple and easy to access, attractive but not exuberant. In footballing terms, the idea is that the position's early in the match, and you want to start things on a positive note by not being too gung ho in attack for the first quarter of the game.

A basic Web site will help you fulfil the first marketing-related function that any Web site must fulfil, that of a validator. 'Valid' means 'worthy', and a Web site functions as a validator by showing that you're worthy of doing business with. Validators do much of their work on a subconscious level, so the absence of key validators makes people feel uncomfortable, in ways that they find difficult to define but that operate very effectively in steering them clear of you. The powerful role of validators is why, as we mention in the 'Guiding Principles for Business Sites' section earlier in this chapter, ensuring your Web site is free of errors, technical barriers, and other irritants is important. (Would you send out salespeople who were poorly trained, ignorant of your products, and unable to speak the same language as your customers? Apply similar considerations to your Web site.)

A basic Web site has to meet fundamental information needs, but not much more than that. In fact, putting more information on it than is absolutely necessary is more likely to make your site difficult to navigate than to make it more useful. Avoid piling on a lot of content until you can also devote some time and energy to making your Web site easy to navigate.

If some of your planned material seems like a good idea but not strictly necessary, drop it (or, better still, put it on a list for later). Your final list of contents will vary depending on your company, your industry, and the available information resources you have at hand that can readily be repurposed for the Web. But most sites include the following:

- **About Us and contact information:** This information is vital, and many sites – even big ones that cost a lot to create and maintain – either don't include it at all or bury it. Remember your customers may well be looking on your Web site to find out what your company does/how it does it. Also make sure that you provide your company, address, main phone number, and fax number. (Don't include your e-mail address until after you read Chapter 10.) Make your contact information easily accessible, one link away from your homepage.

- **Where you do business:** If your geographic range is limited, make this fact clear up front. Be subtle and positive. On your homepage or contact information page, include a phrase like 'London's leading supplier of electrical services to business' or 'Western Europe's most innovative maker of widgets'. Help people who don't need to spend time on your Web site find that fact out quickly and in a positive context so that they leave happy, rather than annoyed.

- **Key people:** A brief list of key people, with a paragraph or so of descriptive information about each, can go far to make people comfortable with your company. (Some companies are reluctant to include this kind of information because they're afraid of attracting executive recruiters, but the benefits to your site's visitors outweigh this risk.) Don't include spouse-hobbies-and-kids stuff – just name, title, and a brief biography.

- **Key clients:** Though some companies are reluctant to include it for fear of attracting competitors, a list of key clients is a very strong validator of your success. List their names and a sentence or two about how they use your product or what you did for them. (Make sure that you ask your customers whether they mind this inclusion and whether they want you to include a link to their Web sites.) But don't include this kind of list until your customer list is at least a little bit impressive.

- **Products and services:** Include simple, brief descriptions of your products and services. You can also link to more detailed information, but put the simple descriptions in one place and make them easy to access; that way, prospects can scan descriptions quickly to decide whether to explore your site further.

✔ **Price:** Include specific price information if you can. Price can vary by sales channel, by location, by options, or by many other factors, so including specific prices can be difficult, but at least find some way to communicate the rough price range of your product. Describing the price paid in a few specific instances does nicely. People hate to 'turn off' customers, which may happen when you indicate your pricing structure, but encouraging people who can't afford your product to contact you (by not letting them know your price range) is not in anyone's interest.

✔ **Where and how to buy:** Tell people who visit your Web site where and how to buy your products and services. This kind of information is hidden or absent on all too many Web sites. If you have several sales channels, list each of them, along with a brief description of each channel that highlights its unique advantages. One excellent method is to set up an interactive area of a Web page that lets people enter their locations and then receive information about nearby sales outlets. If this feature involves too much work to handle right now, consider getting and publicising an 0800 number as a stand-by until you can design and implement an interactive Web capability.

✔ **Company, product, and service validators:** You put information that validates specific products and services, employees, or the company as a whole here. List positive descriptions of your company, people, products, and services from any reputable source, including analyst reports, the general press, the trade press, and individual customers from well-known companies or other organisations. Include any awards you've won. Like your company Web site itself, these validators let people know that your company is worth doing business with.

✔ **Company news:** People visit your Web site when they hear about your company in connection with offline events such as trade shows, product launches, and even that bit of legal action which seems to be never ending. You look clueless if you don't list a few basics: trade-show appearances, product launches, press releases, article mentions of your company, and so on. (Oh, you don't do many press releases? Now's the time to start! Read Chapter 14.) Figure 5-1 shows the news section of a well-designed Web site. Construct this section after you've cut your teeth on the others and then put some real time and energy into getting it right.

✔ **Industry news:** This detail is optional, but important. A great way to position your company as an industry leader is to put industry news on your site. The goals of such an area include educating your customers about your industry, validating your place in the industry, and getting repeat visitors by creating a 'must-read' news area for customers, analysts, and press. (You think your competitors won't be annoyed when everyone in your industry goes to your site for news? Especially when they find themselves doing it too!) Don't hold up your site launch in order to get this detail in, but seriously consider creating such an area as soon as you can.

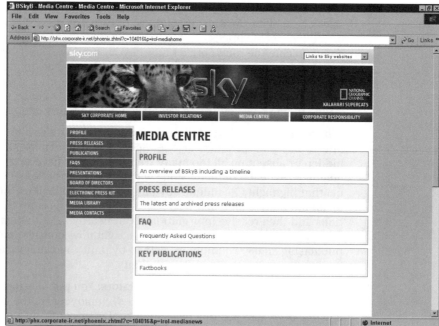

Figure 5-1:
Sky gets the
message
across
through
Sky.com.

If you don't want to develop your own news area, you can even link to a blog through one of the mainstream blogging tools like www.blogger. com. These self-publishing sites can be updated as regularly as you want and can be easily linked to your business Web site.

Creating a Look and Feel for Your Site

Most marketers that we know are very good with words – either in writing, public speaking, or both – and can create vivid pictures in listeners' minds. However, like many other people, most of them lack graphic-design skills.

Graphic design is the art of using visual elements to create a pleasing impression in the viewer's mind, and is a very important element in Web site design – to some of your Web site visitors, the most important element of all. Having a good design, or look and feel as it's called within the industry, is crucial to getting the right message across. Making a snap decision on the design of your site is wrong as it's probably one of the most vital decisions you may make when building your Web site.

Graphic design for the Web is a specialised art. Users view a company Web page in different-sized windows, using different-sized screens, with different colour capabilities, in all sorts of lighting conditions. Some users have custom settings to override the designer's choice of font, size, and text colours. Large graphics may make a page look strikingly attractive, yet take such a long time to download that they annoy and drive away users.

Using colour correctly on the Web is an art in and of itself. Colours and colour combinations that look attractive on one computer can look awful on another. In fact, out of the millions of shades of colour that a higher-end computer system can display, only 216 'browser-safe' colours exist that work well across most people's Web setups. If you use other colours, your site is likely to look awful to at least some of your visitors.

All these complexities and opportunities for error add up to a simple rule: Unless you have graphic-design experience and know, or are willing to learn, the details of Web-specific design, you need specialist help in designing the look and feel of your site. Here are a few possible sources of help:

- ✔ **Existing resources:** Your company may already have brand guidelines or a style guide based on its logo and marketing collateral, such as annual reports. Consider adapting this look for the Web, giving people who are familiar with your company in an offline context a comfortable feeling when they encounter your firm online.

- ✔ **Other well-designed sites:** Stealing the designs of other sites just isn't on. Looking at other sites, finding ones you like, and using the same *principles* as they do, however, is fine. (You're also free to avoid the practices of the sites that irritate you!)

- ✔ **Online advice:** Many sources of online advice on all aspects of Web page creation, including graphics, are available. Two good places to start are the World Wide Web Consortium at `www.w3.org` and `www.webreview.com`.

- ✔ **CD-ROM resources:** CD-ROMs with 'clip art' – professionally designed, non-copyrighted graphics optimised for online use – are available. You can pick up a few thousand buttons, backgrounds, icons, and other graphical elements for under £50 in many cases. An average person can achieve amazing effects with a little time and a good CD-ROM art collection.

- ✔ **Printed advice:** Many good books and articles describe how to create and deploy online graphics. Visit online bookshops such as Amazon.com (`www.amazon.co.uk`).

Outside help is an always available resource, and an especially good idea when creating your first site. Consider hiring a graphic designer to assist with the look of your Web site. Graphic designers who advertise on the Web are likely to have designed several sites they can refer you to as examples of their work. An example of one designer's Web presence is shown in Figure 5-2. If you need help finding a designer consider using a graphic design student; increasing numbers are available as the number of courses offering Web design grows. One of the best known is the University of Brighton (www.brighton.ac.uk).

Hiring a graphic designer is different from hiring a Web-design company. A Web-design company will construct your entire site for you; a graphic designer will just work on the look. For a basic site, which you want to do quickly and cheaply while learning as much as possible yourself, a graphic designer is preferable. You can get him or her involved early in the process, late, or even after your initial site is live.

Tell the designer who your expected visitors are, share any existing design elements that you have, and then let the designer work. Unlike a Web-design company, a graphic designer will need clear instructions on everything else about the site, including content and navigation. Expect to get a couple of alternatives and a quote for updating your site to include the design. (The designer may even offer to update your printed materials as well, improving consistency.)

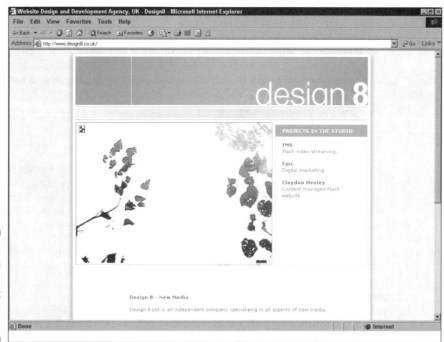

Figure 5-2:
Design 8
has a
simple but
effective
Web site.

At the end of the job, you should own the designer's work. This arrangement is called *work for hire* and is looked down upon by top professionals doing large jobs but is a fact of life for smaller jobs and for designers who haven't yet made a name for themselves. Avoid complicated intellectual property arrangements in which the designer retains rights to the design.

Having Your Site Done For You

Although creating your initial site yourself is a good idea, you may simply feel that you don't have the time or the expertise to do so. If you feel that way, get outside help.

The good news is that many individual consultants and Web-design agencies have sprung up to help companies create and maintain their Web sites. The bad news is that many, many ways exist to go wrong in hiring a digital agency.

But wait, we have more bad news! Having an external supplier or an individual do your Web site will probably save only a small amount of your time. A Web site is such an important reflection of your business that you should expect to be heavily involved with the project from start to finish.

The important steps in working with an outside supplier are setting up the engagement, managing the work, and following through when the work is done. Although these steps are the same for any general project, some specifics exist for a Web project that may surprise you.

Many of these steps apply to managing an internal Web project as well. Check these steps out even if you're doing the work yourself.

Getting engaged

Hiring an agency is often referred to as an 'engagement', and starting one may require more forethought than some marriages! Here are some simple rules that will help you get good results from a Web agency:

 ✔ **Find a site that has the elements you need.** Spend some time surfing Web sites, both inside and outside your own industry, to find a site that has most of the pieces you need. A clean and attractive front page, easy-to-find contact info, simple navigation, and brief, clear product descriptions are some of the elements you may be looking for. Figure 5-3, which incidentally is one of the authors' business Web sites, is a good example of a site with these elements.

✔ **Decide how many pages you want in your site.** Remember those sites you surfed in the previous step? See what the major areas are in some sites you like and count how many pages are in each area. Come up with a rough estimate of the number of pages in your site. *Hint:* The lower the number, the lower the cost and the greater the odds that your project will be a success.

✔ **Find several local agencies or consultants.** Even in this wired age, being able to meet with someone in person is a real benefit – especially for your initial project. Look at local business sites that you like and find out who created them. Talk to friends and colleagues to find specialists in your local area who have done good work. Check the *Yellow Pages* or the trade press for any local suppliers.

✔ **Set a budget.** Now that you have some idea of what you want and what other sites have cost in your local area, set an upper limit for your budget. Make sure that the figure you come up with is in line with the benefits you expect to get from your site. As a test, consider the impact that spending the same amount of money on radio advertising may have for you.

✔ **Hold a pitch.** Talk to the agencies you identified earlier. (Talking to more than one really helps, so don't rush this stage.) Get their ideas of what they think you need. Tell them what you're looking for and get a ballpark estimate as to timeframe and budget. *Hint:* Consider going to a marketing services intermediary like the AAR (www.aargroup.co.uk) or Haystack (www.thehaystackgroup.com) to help you find your digital agency.

✔ **Choose an agency.** Make an initial choice. Don't throw away the others' business cards until your first choice has shown you some good initial results!

Picking someone you believe you can trust is the most important part of engaging a specialist. You can always have your Web site made larger or flashier later, but the initial site simply needs to look good, be complete within a limited initial scope, and be delivered on time and on budget.

Make sure that you understand before engaging a firm whether it considers itself primarily a Web-programming company, a Web-design company, or a balance of both. Some agencies are excellent at creating the technical infra-structure of a site and making it work well but aren't adept at doing the graphics and copywriting. Others are excellent at look-and-feel but have little understanding of good Web site navigation or making things work 'under the hood'. The ideal firm is one with a good grasp of both aspects – or one that admits what its expertise isn't, allowing you to hire a freelancer to fill the gap.

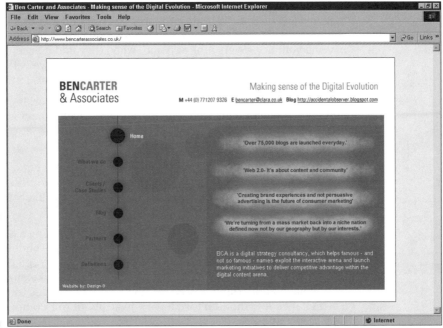

Figure 5-3:
BCA is an
uncompli-
cated Web
site with
clear aims.

As the focus moves away from building Web sites to what customers expect
from Web sites, a need exists for more strategic thinking. Agencies often can't
provide this strategy overview, so working with digital consultants (such as
the authors of this book, say) to get the bigger picture of where your Web site
will fit, what it will do, and how it will develop is useful.

Projecting your management style

Project management for Web sites has a lot in common with other projects,
but a few Web-specific techniques exist that you should be aware of in addition to your usual tactics. The main problem with a Web project is that
people react strongly to the look of a Web site – and if you wait until the end,
an influential person could send the whole project back to the beginning. So
clear up process hurdles early on to avoid hassle later.

✔ **Identify approvers.** Before you start, identify everyone who'll need to
approve the site before it can go live and be publicised. This list should
be short – and the people on it given status reports and updates at
every major step.

✔ **Image is everything!** People are likely to react first and foremost to the look and feel of your Web site – the way background colours, images, navigation elements, and layout work together. Get a mock-up early on, and have all your approvers look at it and, when they find it acceptable, initial it. Better still, get two or three mock-ups that you can live with, and let the approvers make their choice on which should go forward to the next step.

✔ **Make a first impression.** Have your agency create a working version of the first page of your Web site hosted on a development site. At this point, get everyone's final okay on the basic look of the site. Figure 5-4 shows the first page of a Web site we like.

The first page of a Web site commonly gets 20–25 per cent of all the page views for the site, so getting it right is important. Also, if the first page meets with everyone's approval, the rest of the site is likely to receive only minor comments.

✔ **Get skeleton text ready.** Next, fill out the site by creating a dummy page for each and every page on the site. Each dummy page should have the agreed-upon look and feel for the site plus a one-paragraph description of what will be on that specific page. You can use the skeleton to test overall navigation. Have people review the dummy pages too – providing a last chance for 'shouldn't we have a page about our company history?' type comments.

✔ **Fill in the blanks.** Now fill in the content of each page. (This task can often be spread among several people, who can 'borrow' content from your business plan and any brochures or other marketing materials you have.) If your site has several sections (news, products, and so on), each written by several people, make sure that each content section has a content 'lead' who is responsible for ensuring that the writing style and tone match across all of that section's pages.

If you don't already have an in-house copywriter then you need to consider hiring one who can rewrite your draft copy. Again, choosing the right copywriter is vital as the content of your site is imperative to getting the right message across to your customers!

✔ **Time for the testing.** After the site's dummy pages are filled in, set aside some time to test it. Have one person read through all the pages to make sure that they're consistent in how they present your company and its products. If there's a danger that your customers may stumble across it then consider hosting it on a development or a test server to iron out the tweaks. Also make sure that the Web site works with all the different browsers like Internet Explorer, Mozilla Firefox, and Safari. When you are happy, then do a 'soft launch' – put the site up on the Web, but don't publicise its existence until everyone who needs to approve of the site has had a chance to do so.

✔ **Go, go, go!** After the site's up and you're happy with it, get the word out. Put the URL on business cards, stationery, advertisements, and more. Ask for feedback from people you know and from site visitors as well.

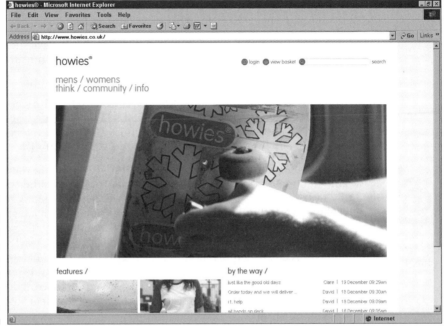

Figure 5-4:
Howies
uses its
Web site to
get its green
credentials
across.

This process crucially has many checkpoints, making it difficult for the project to get too far off-track without your knowing about it – and having a chance to fix the problem.

A caution about copyright

Getting wrapped up in the gorgeous graphics and clean navigation that a Web-site consultant develops for you is easy. But take a deep breath and – before making the new site live – ask the agency the difficult question, 'You do have the right to use all those design elements, don't you?'

A few inexperienced, rushed, or simply unscrupulous Web agencies have been known to copy graphic elements they like from existing Web sites and reuse them in sites they're creating, without permission. Doing so can violate the copyright of whoever created or owns the original site – and cause legal problems for you later.

In one case, a pioneering car Web site found that another car site was eerily similar – largely because most of the other site's design, graphics, and even text was identical to the pioneer's own. Lawyers quickly got involved.

Play it safe. Make sure that you get assurance from your agency, in writing, that all its design elements and text are either original or properly licensed.

Beating the wrap-up

Plan now for future updating of your Web site. The basic structure you've created should last for a long time. Work with your agency now to identify procedures for the following important tasks:

- ✔ **Updating content:** You should be able to update the site's content without the agency's help and to do this you will need to have access to a content management system, unless you want them involved as a checkpoint. Specify how content within a page will be updated.

  Content Management Systems (CMS) are important if you want to be able to update your Web site regularly and they should be considered if you are going to have a lot of text that will need changing regularly. Having CMS built in from the start will save you a lot of hassle and will mean that you can access/change your site very easily. There are lots of different CMS options but if you are a complete Web novice then you will need the simplest one. Known as *WYSIWYG* CMS (standing for 'What you see is what you get'), such a system will enable you to cut and paste copy into text boxes via a simple Web interface. You don't need to understand HTML to operate this, which is why it appeals to those who aren't Web wizards.

- ✔ **Adding pages:** Identify likely areas in which you may want to add a new page; the product area will need to be extended, for instance, if you launch a new product. Work out how long it should take to add a page from initial idea to launch, and who needs to be involved.

- ✔ **Revising the whole site:** At some point, you'll want to revise the whole site. Work out what might trigger that revision, and set up regular meetings with your agency – say, quarterly – to identify needed changes and to start the next major overhaul.

Don't be afraid to tell your agency that you may get other people involved for some or all of the work ahead; for your first agency to play a lesser role as the project develops, or even to have no role at all, is very common. Do let your consultants know about any expectations that weren't met, as well as the things you were happy about, and whether they can expect a good reference from you for future clients.

Making your site accessible

Make your site as accessible to as many people as possible. Avoid being in a situation where some of your customers can't use your site when they find it – you'll commit corporate suicide.

Lots of agencies will offer you an *analytics* service as part of the Web build project, in which they monitor how a test-base of users use and navigate the site. These 'test sessions' are crucial for you to identify any problems or pitfalls in the way the site has been designed and built. Better to spot flaws now rather than when the site goes live: Bad Web sites result in lost custom.

Also make sure that your site can be accessed and used by disabled people. Since 1999, the Disability Discrimination Act has put the onus on Web publishers to ensure that their sites have a basic level of accessibility. Ignore this advice at your peril: You could be breaking the law!

More information on accessibility guidelines and standards, which are endorsed by the UK government, can be found at the World Wide Web Consortium: www.w3.org.

Chapter 6

Marketing on Your Web Site

· ·

In This Chapter

▶ Using your Web site to market products or services

▶ Presenting marketing information on your site

▶ Including business-related news on your site

· ·

Although the World Wide Web is in its second decade, most people still don't realise just how powerful it can be as a marketing vehicle. Because the Web is still changing, using it effectively is an art that is still being perfected. But the same novelty factor that makes the Web difficult to use effectively also means that successful efforts are well rewarded. You can get a lot of positive attention and feedback if you do a good marketing job on your Web site.

In this chapter, you roll up your metaphorical sleeves and plunge into the nitty-gritty of the most important ways you can make marketing work on your Web site. If you follow the suggestions in this chapter, you should be able to move quickly to the top of the class in your digital marketing efforts.

Your Web Site as a Marketing Vehicle

Different businesses depend on different ways to get the word out about themselves, their products, or services. A consultant may depend on word of mouth, recommendation, and phone calls to business contacts to get new work. For the manager of a truckers' cafe, a billboard on an A road may be the lynchpin of marketing. For a used-car dealer, late-night television adverts and newspaper ads may reach the key buyers. Every business has one or more established method of advertising, and businesses that want to grow are always looking for new techniques to help them move forward.

The Internet and the Web will continue to be the fastest-growing and most important new marketing vehicle for most businesses over the next couple of decades. If you focus now on digital marketing, especially marketing over the Web, you'll be well-positioned to benefit from the growth in importance of the Internet in modern life. If you wait, your competitors will probably benefit from that growth rather than you. Now is the time to decide how to use your Web site as a marketing vehicle in the future.

Co-ordinating your Web site with your overall marketing plan

Starting your Web marketing effort is easy if you realise that the Web should fit tightly into your more traditional marketing efforts (we refer to traditional, non-online marketing efforts as *offline* marketing in this book). Every advertisement, direct mailing, and press release that you create can be used as a resource for your Web site. And every marketing-related event that you attend or participate in – each trade show, product launch, or news conference – can be reported on your Web site as well.

Your current marketing materials should feed into your Web site, and each marketing piece can be adapted for use on your site (See Figure 6.1 for an example of how a Web site can support a high profile marketing campaign). Your Web site in turn helps promote other activities, such as trade show appearances and public relations (PR) efforts. After you've been developing and expanding your site for a while, arrows pointing in the opposite direction also appear. Marketing events and seminars can be captured and put on your Web site as sound clips, movies, or even just as written reports. And new content you develop for your Web site can be recast as printed materials to reach those few people who don't have access to the Web.

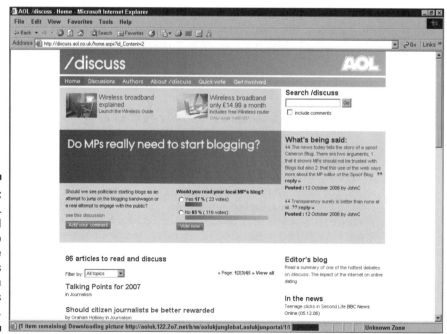

Figure 6-1:
AOL encouraged people to discuss the Internet's impact on their lives online.

Another concern is fitting your Web marketing effort into your company's other online efforts. You can predict your firm's online future by realising that nearly every division and department of your company will eventually have to be reflected online. Marketing goes online first but customer service and support, sales, recruitment, and other company functions will quickly go online as well. Here are some parts of a typical company that may be represented on a Web site:

- **Marketing department:** Marketing should be responsible for the overall Web site and most of its content. Marketing-related concerns and content include the overall look and feel of the Web site, company and contact information, product photographs, marketing material, descriptions and prices, information about where to buy products, and events the company is involved in. If you have any strong case studies then consider adding those along with customer testimonials as they can be very powerful.

- **Public relations:** This speciality within the marketing department deserves separate attention. PR should develop an area for press interest – if any group will depend on the Web for its first impression of you, the press will. PR need to put all their press releases on the Web site and may also want to put preview information and other useful material, such as photographs of key company personnel, for the press on a password-protected area of your Web site.

- **Sales department:** When your Web site captures visitor interest in your products or services, marketing and sales can work together to help deliver potential customers to the company's various sales channels. (You get a big boost in justifying your online marketing expenditures if you can show that your Web site is generating sales.)

- **Customer service and support:** Post customer service contact info and answers to common questions on the Web site. Online customer service is already very important and growing rapidly; companies can reduce expenses by making the customer part of the service and support solution. Use your Web site and other online resources to involve customers in finding solutions to their problems. Providing relevant customer information is a good way of cutting costs especially if you can provide the answers to common questions that may typically come into your call centre. Consider having a FAQ section.

- **Human resources:** Vacancies within your business can be posted on the Web site, with an e-mail address where CVs can be sent. A good-looking Web site helps your company attract top employees as well as customers. Marketing can help the human resources department get established on the Web site, but updating vacancies is HR's job.

- **Finance:** Your finance department needs to put your company's annual report or its equivalent on the Web site, or at least make ordering a copy of your report over the Web easy for interested parties. Finding your annual report online is very convenient for your customers, press, analysts, and others. However, annual reports are required to be honest, and in a bad sales year you may not want to post all the gory details on your Web site.

Out of all the departments that are involved, marketing should play the lead role in defining and developing the company World Wide Web site. But beware of the old saying, 'Too many cooks spoil the broth'. The Web site needs involvement from across departments, but one department, in this case marketing, has to be seen to take the lead and make all the tough decisions.

In addition to the preceding areas listed, other company materials may go online as well, but much of this other information should only appear on *intranets* – employee-only networks that often use Web browsers and servers to deliver information. An example is employee benefits information that the human resources department puts online for employees only.

Intranets aren't a direct concern of marketing, because customers don't access them. (Though one could argue that medium-sized and large companies need to market themselves to their employees, and divisions market themselves to other divisions, as well.)

A more interesting option, from a marketing point of view, is *extranets* – networks that link suppliers and customers. Though extranets may at first be used only for exchanging functional information such as order status, they can grow into marketing tools as well. If your company develops an extranet that includes customers, dealers, or others involved in the sales process, marketing can play a growing role in supplying and maintaining this content. One marketing option is to offer a bonus or loyalty scheme to your suppliers through the extranet, developed by the marketing department.

Web surfers frequently use bookmarks to return to Web sites and specific pages they like. Encourage your visitors to bookmark your homepage and also to bookmark Web pages within your site that have information about specific products and services. Make sure that the titles of those additional pages accurately reflect the information on them so that visitors can look at the title in their bookmark list and remember why they bookmarked the page in the first place.

Designing your Web marketing effort

Before you start or expand your Web marketing effort, you need to take a few initial steps. These steps can be formal efforts as part of a design process with storyboards and multiple levels of approvals, as described in Chapter 5, or – for smaller efforts – informal checkpoints that you keep in mind as you work on your own or with others.

The first step is to decide how you're going to separate company, product line, and product information. Each of your customers, plus suppliers, members of the press, and even your own employees, see your company through the lens of those products and services they use the most. This focus doesn't cause any problems for companies with one overwhelmingly important product or a single product line, but if you sell multiple products and services, the result may lead to a great deal of confusion.

The following are possible ways to handle Web site organisation for a company with multiple products and services:

- **Don't worry about organisation.** Simply throw marketing and other information for your products and services on your Web site in a disorganised fashion, with thorough coverage of some and little of others. (This Really Bad Idea actually seems to be the plan followed by too many sites.)

- **Separate the company and its products.** The homepage of your Web site needs to speak for your company or your brand and allow for easy access to company-level information. Your company homepage should also point to a separate area for products. Web surfers can check out company information and then *drill down* (link to pages with successively more specific information) to the product they're interested in. You can also have bookmarkable 'front pages', with a distinct URL, for your most popular products, which will make it easier for search engines to find your products. See Chapter 8 for more on optimising your site for search engines.

- **Separate the company's markets.** A more sophisticated approach is to structure your Web site around the different markets your company and its products serve. Because customers think of themselves in terms of their interests, not your products, organising your Web presence in this way is often the most intuitive for your customers. The Microsoft Web site is a good example of this method in use – it enables access by market, as shown in Figure 6-2. Creating a usable market-segmented Web site is hard to pull off, though, because you must include multiple paths to the same or similar information. Get experienced, professional design help before trying this approach.

 Given that your overriding goal must be always to think of the users' or customers' needs, this style of site is often a good idea, but it becomes almost essential if you have discrete audiences with very different needs. Perhaps one way to decide is to think about which pages will be used by which kinds of people and consider drawing a simple Venn diagram. If your circles barely, or don't, intersect, you need a site segmented by audience designed so they can 'triage' themselves on the homepage. If your circles largely overlap, then this kind of approach may just lead to another level of confusing navigation.

- **Use separate Web sites.** If you have products that have strong brand heritage, consider creating separate Web sites for those products. You can still put basic information on the company Web site, but the product site will be the home base for the real diehard users of the product. But beware, just because you're fascinated by your products doesn't mean that all customers are and dedicated product Web sites can be an expensive waste of money! Creating separate Web sites also adds in difficulty in design, coordination, and planning but on the plus-side, it can considerably increase the effectiveness of your overall Web presence.

From marketing online to selling online?

Because marketing is partly a sales-support activity, you need to prepare for the day – possibly not too far in the future – when you actually sell products or services on your Web site. Analysts are adjusting their estimates and forecasts upwards to accommodate massive growth in online sales of products and services. This percentage will only continue to grow. If you don't get your share of the online-sales pie, someone else will. So start thinking now about how your marketing efforts can be extended into sales efforts in the next few years.

One useful way to think of your Web site is as an online trade show or, if you don't do trade shows, a sales call or other customer interaction. Several of the lessons you learn in your face-to-face marketing interactions apply online as well. For instance, when you meet people in a professional context, you're usually trying to get them to do something: buy a large quantity of your product, write a positive article about your company, or feel good about their relationship with your company to put them in an upbeat frame of mind for a future pitch. Think about how to create these same effects in the minds of people who visit your Web site. Then identify the marketing materials that you use in various person-to-person situations and place this kind of high-priority information front and centre in your Web site.

Figure 6-2: Microsoft lets you in by product, by market, or by searching.

After you develop some idea of the overall structure of the marketing parts of your Web site, you're ready to identify some of the resources you can use on it. Follow these general steps:

1. **Make a list of all your marketing resources.**

   List all press releases, information sheets, sales brochures, ads, annual reports, and so on – even old ones. (Old resources may have information and themes that you can reuse.)

2. **For each marketing resource on your list, briefly describe what you may need to do to it before putting it on the Web.**

   'Reformat and convert to HTML' is the minimum that you need to do to each document. 'Update' is another common notation, because marketing documents need frequent updating – and putting outdated material on your Web site is worse than not putting up any information at all.

3. **Separate your resources into 'basic marketing' and 'news'.**

   Pieces that have a long lifespan, such as product brochures, can be thought of as basic marketing; pieces that have a short lifespan, such as press releases and events, are news. (We describe the difference more clearly in the 'Marketing Information on Your Site' section, later in this chapter, but take a stab at making the distinction now.)

4. **Give some thought as to what to do first; if your resources are limited, consider putting your company information and in-depth information for one major product online first as part of a test and then use the lessons learned to rapidly expand coverage.**

   You're likely to do a better job, and possibly even a faster job overall, by phasing your online marketing effort than by trying to hit every target simultaneously.

You may want to take this opportunity to review your marketing collateral with one question in mind: What does each piece urge the reader to do? You do have to be equally subtle and informative with your Web marketing effort; people quickly click away from obvious hype. But even on the Web, each piece of marketing needs to encourage the reader to take some action he or she wouldn't have taken otherwise. With luck, that action is a step in the direction of buying your product. Double-check your marketing collateral as you ready it for the Web.

Marketing Information on Your Site

In Chapter 5, we describe what to put on a basic business Web site, including descriptive and contact information for your company. Organising and creating a simple marketing-orientated site is easy. As your Web site gets larger and more complicated, information becomes harder to organise and update.

As your Web site gets more complete, you may spend an increasing amount of your Web-related time thinking about structure and usability, and less about specific bits of content.

As you expand your Web-based marketing effort, you may also run into specific concerns about each of the different kinds of information you put online. Based on our experience in both hands-on and consulting roles in this new medium, we can point out a few of the opportunities and pitfalls to help you be effective right from the start.

Understanding the vital role of press releases

Press releases are the most visible evidence of public relations on the Internet. Although they play an undeniable role in any online PR campaign you devise (as we discuss in detail in Chapter 14), should press releases have a role to play on your company Web site? Emphatically, yes.

Many journalists look down on press releases but their value is huge. However, guidelines exist to follow when compiling press releases; after all, what could be worse – or more likely to be misleading and self-serving – than company-written news?

Press releases are more notable by their absence on your Web site than by their presence. Site visitors expect Web site content to be updated frequently; press releases help accomplish that. Reporters working late into the night or at the weekend to finish a story will visit your company site for the latest news rather than call a PR contact.

Must Web writing be boring?

Try to avoid being boring, but remember that most writing for the Web does need to be fairly tame and matter-of-fact. Because people actively seek Web information themselves instead of passively receiving it, the World Wide Web has a tradition of honesty and directness that makes typical marketing hype seem misplaced. Think of Web writing as describing your company and product in a conversation to a business colleague, not as creating an extremely slow-moving TV advert. Adhere closely to the established tone of existing Web writing, at least until you gain enough experience to know when you can bend or break the rules.

Though the press releases are bound to reflect a positive point of view about your products, services, and company, you also have a strong motivation when writing the press release to explain the basic facts that people need to know in as clear, cogent, and understandable a manner as possible. Yes, a bias exists in press release writing, but at least that bias is what the reader expects – so don't go too over the top.

Many organisations prepare too few press releases – and don't post what they do distribute on their own Web site. Consider doing, and posting, a press release for every event of importance, including the following:

- Launching a product or service
- Relaunching a product or service
- Hosting or taking part in an industry event
- Entering into a partnership with others
- New senior appointments
- Agency/supplier appointments

Hitting targets, revenue, and other financial milestones are also good press-release topics.

Press releases are an underused yet vital tool in marketing in general and especially in marketing on Web sites. The concentrated effort that goes into creating and making sure that all the information is correct in a press release makes it something you can use and reuse online and in the offline world, as well. Follow these rules for using press releases on your Web site and you'll do a better job of getting all your marketing information online:

- **When in doubt, do a press release.** An important event has happened, and you want to announce it on your Web site. Writing a press release about the event is the best and easiest way to publicise it. If the subject's of general enough interest, you can distribute that press release through the newswires or your contacts in the press (as covered in Chapter 14) as well as posting it on your Web site. Remember that a press release must only be created when there is real news to announce as otherwise you will lose credibility with key journalists who get bombarded with hundreds of press releases every day.

- **Hit the Web instantly.** Press releases should be on your Web site at the same moment that they hit the wires. People who hear news about your company will immediately check your Web site for information; you look bad if the information isn't there.

✔ **Make press releases easy to find.** Put a prominent pointer to each new release on your Web site's homepage and then post the press release in an appropriate area on your Web site. Make sure that you send an electronic copy of the press release to people who may want to mention it on their own Web pages and blogs or otherwise make it known to others.

✔ **Link your press releases.** Your press release should include references to key business partners, customers, and others who have a role in the news, and you can include hyperlinks to their Web sites in the online, HTML version of your press release. This approach makes you look savvy and is often greatly appreciated by those you link to.

✔ **Do a careful job with the HTML.** Carefully converting a press release to HTML so that it looks good on a Web page takes only a modest amount of time and makes you look organised and professional. Set aside an hour or two to convert and review your press release before you send it out to the world and the rush to put it on the Web hits.

✔ **Create a text-only version.** You'll want a version of your press release that you can send out by e-mail; make that version available on your Web site along with the HTML version. Then visitors can e-mail the release to their contacts as well – doing your marketing for you for free.

✔ **Create a .PDF file.** Many people like the look of fully formatted documents (see Figures 6-3 and 6-4). The most popular way to reproduce this look on the Web is with an Adobe Acrobat Portable Document Format (.PDF) document.

✔ **Go beyond the release.** You can include additional information that links from the press release, providing more details. For example, an easy-to-create and valuable tool is a Frequently Asked Questions document (FAQ), a longstanding tradition for delivering technical information online that has been successfully adapted for online marketing. (FAQs are sometimes called Q&As, for Question and Answer documents, in traditional marketing jargon.) Link to product data sheets or any other information you can put online. Or be adventurous and include a sound or video clip from an analyst call or press conference.

✔ **Ask that others' press releases link to you.** After you earn people's gratitude by appropriately including them in your press releases and linking to their Web sites, ask for the same favour in return. When key partners, suppliers, or customers prepare press releases, ask them to acknowledge any role that your company played and to link from their HTML press release version on their Web site to your Web site.

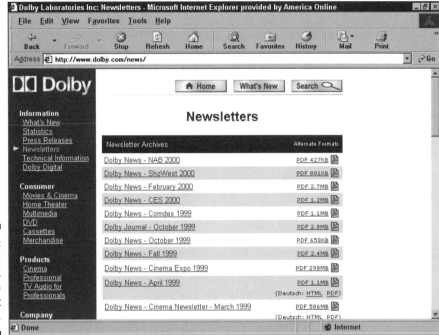

Figure 6-3:
Clicking a
.PDF link
brings up
the right
article.

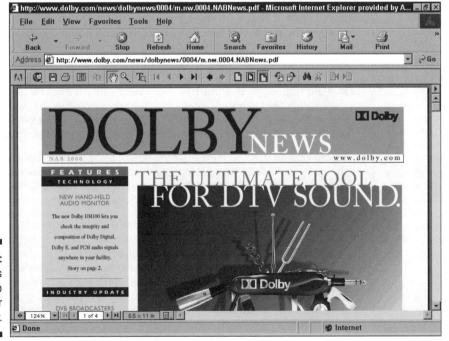

Figure 6-4:
.PDF files
show up
right in your
browser.

Many of the lessons you learn in creating and posting press releases apply to your other online efforts as well. Putting information up on your Web site fast; making it easy to find; linking to the Web sites of partners, suppliers, and customers; adding text-only and .PDF versions of files; and asking for mentions and links from others are all vital survival skills for online marketing. If you practise these skills as part of creating and posting press releases and then use your newfound skills 24/7, you'll go far in the online world.

Putting product information online

Many companies do a fairly good job of marketing online but don't give enough detail about the specific products and services that they sell. Your Web site isn't a success until you provide detailed information about whatever it is that you sell.

Here and elsewhere in the book we use the word *products* to refer to both products and services – partly for our convenience and yours, and partly because you probably need to package your services in product-like fashion to market them effectively over the Web.

Consider providing on your Web site the following information about each product your company sells:

- ✔ **Product name and functional description:** Don't forget to include a Web page devoted to the product, by name, and a brief functional description of what the product does. If all your previous marketing has been limited to a small audience that already understands what you do, via trade-specific publications, industry trade shows, and so on, you may be new to presenting yourself to an audience as diverse as that on the Web. Explain to people, in simple terms, what your product does – even if all the explanation accomplishes is to help them realise that they're not interested. Remember: People who know nothing about your company will be viewing your Web site, so keep the information simple.

- ✔ **Price:** People use the Web to comparison shop and find out how much things cost. Web design guru Jacob Neilsen lists not mentioning the price as one of the biggest mistakes on marketing or sales orientated Web sites.

- ✔ **Who uses the product:** Describe who uses your product and how. Go into some depth; allow your Web surfers – that is, your well-off, media-savvy, potential customers or influencers – to see themselves or someone they know as part of your customer base. Like the product's functional description, a description of who uses your product also helps your Web surfers know whether they should stick around for more information – or surf on.

✔ **System requirements:** Most products operate in a specific environment of other products and user activities. You can't run *Championship Manager* on an original BBC Computer, and you don't need a copper pot if you don't cook. Communicate, either subtly within other text or in a specific list, what kind of environment your product is used in, what other products need to be present for it to work effectively, and what skills the user needs to have to make it work.

✔ **Market position:** Everyone loves a winner, and if you can identify a customer group in which your product is number one, announce that fact loudly. 'Best-selling widget worldwide' is the best market position to have, but 'the leading widget for the UK brewing industry' is fine too. The markets in which you're number one are likely to be the most profitable for you anyway, so exploit your leadership position(s) on your Web site.

✔ **Customer information:** List big-name customers (with their permission, of course) or, if the numbers justify the claim, give a blanket customer description such as 'used by half of the FTSE 100'. Let the positive image and success of your customers reflect on you as well. For complicated or expensive products, create success stories that show how a specific customer used your product to solve a problem.

Make sure that you get customers' permission before including their names on your site, but don't worry much about being turned down; most customers love the attention. Ask for permission to use their logos on your site as a link: If you exchange links with them to their Web sites, everyone gets a boost.

✔ **Awards, accolades, and (positive) reviews:** Provide external validators (see Chapter 5) showing that your product is the best from some independent point of view. Any awards, positive feedback, or positive reviews that you can mention – or, better yet, link to on another Web site – go a long way toward helping people choose your product.

If you have a physical product or offer a service where the location/setting is important, include images.

Your product doesn't have to finish first in a review in order for that review to be worth mentioning on your Web site. In an average review, pull out any positive statement on a substantive aspect of your product and quote it. ('The easiest of the reviewed products to use' is probably worth quoting; 'the easiest to remove from its packaging material' probably isn't.) If you do finish first in a review, link to that review online if possible, even if it says some bad things about your product in between all the good ones. If you finish second or third, consider linking to the review, but surround the link with an explanation of the specific areas in which you're best or information about how you've improved the areas in which the reviewer found fault.

Don't be afraid to link

Linking strategies are an important part of overall Web site design. Link extensively within your Web site, of course; but what about links to other sites – don't they just send Web surfers elsewhere, never to return? Quite possibly, yes, so link to other sites only for a good reason. Web sites you should link to include press coverage or other sites that say good things about your company or product; sites of companies that are partners of yours; sites with industry information; or sites with information about products that are used with your own. These kinds of links not only help Web surfers find out more about your product in a broad sense but also keep them thinking of your product, as well – increasing the chances that they'll return to your site. Linking is becoming an increasingly important part of how users are navigating the Internet. As people spend longer online, they're actually limiting the amount of sites they're visiting to their favourite links and just a few others. So being linked and linking to are vital ways of building online awareness.

The underlying message in your product description and related information should be, 'No need to look any further; this widget is the one for you.'

If visitors to your Web site are looking to buy, be sure that your site tells them how. (See the 'Telling Web surfers where to buy' section, later in this chapter, for details.) Even if the people reading the information aren't looking to buy your type of product today, they may either make a purchase or be called on for a recommendation in the future. A distant recollection that comes out as a recommendation, even a low-key one like 'I heard Smith's Widgets are pretty good', can help you clinch a sale. Product information on your Web site can create just this kind of long-lasting positive impression.

Telling Web surfers where to buy

One of the most important but trickiest issues for marketing on your Web site is telling visitors how they can buy your products and services. Because the Web is global, everyone receives the same information simultaneously. However, because of legal restrictions in different places, language barriers, service and support concerns, or for many other reasons, you may not be able to sell the same way – or at all – to everyone who wants to buy.

The first step you can take to prevent problems is to make clear – on your Web site – any restrictions as to who can buy your product and how they can buy. Some limitations will be obvious: If you do interior-decoration consulting in London, you won't be expected to fly to Moscow to give a quote. But if you sell a product for one price in the UK and a higher price in Germany, think twice before providing pricing and ordering information on your Web site.

Just as an example, consider the issue of price information a bit further. Consider a mythical company that manufactures a high-end stereo system in the north-eastern United States and sells it only in the United States and the UK. This company charges a higher price in the UK because of shipping costs, lower volumes, and higher margins expected by the UK distribution channel. Now if this company puts the US price of its product on the Web, UK customers may start trying to get the product for the US price – perhaps by ordering over the phone, or perhaps by asking a US-based friend to buy for them and ship it over. UK distributors will then become upset by the pointed questions some of their customers will ask them and by the lost business caused by people trying to get around the standard distribution system. This is just one example of the potential problems that can occur when you give pricing information on your Web site. Yet giving customers at least a ballpark idea of your product's price is a necessary part of encouraging them to consider buying it, so what do you do?

To begin solving this problem for your own unique situation, review the kind of pricing information you give in existing marketing and sales materials, and study the ways you've previously handled the problems of pricing differences and availability restrictions. Think about how you can continue to support your current pricing and distribution arrangements – or consider how to change them if needed.

Here are the major options available for giving pricing and distribution information online:

- ✔ **'I know nothing.'** One approach is to give no how-to-buy or pricing information on your Web site. This is a poor choice, given the power of the Web to inspire sales, but a good way to defer problems until you've figured out how to avoid threatening existing sales or distribution channels by using one or more of the other approaches described here. Expect, though, to irritate – and lose – potential customers.

- ✔ **Give distributor information online.** A classy alternative to omitting how-to-buy information is to simply make your current distributor information available online so as to help your Web visitors reach their local sales outlet for your product. Giving distributor information online can be tricky; for instance, people based in one country may call another country, shopping for a cheaper price. You may need to consider clever alternatives such as having only information specific to a visitor's country show up in that visitor's browser.

- ✔ **Give a phone number for distributor information.** You can give a phone number for potential customers to call to find their nearest distributor. (Make sure that you employ and train the people in the position before posting the phone number!) This tactic is a nice, low-key way to support your existing sales channels and get the right pricing information to the right customers.

✔ **Give an e-mail address for distributor information.** You can give an e-mail address either in addition to, or instead of, a phone number. With e-mail, you have time to think before answering tough questions and you can reuse the contact information you get from the enquiries. You also don't have to pay extra staff to answer the e-mails unless you expect to be deluged.

✔ **Give a phone or fax number for ordering.** You can allow people to order directly from you, but don't upset your existing apple cart of sales arrangements without a lot of preparation first.

✔ **Support direct online sales.** Online selling is the logical end point of online marketing but is also a double-edged sword that has the potential to hurt more than it helps by upsetting your existing distribution arrangements, so make sure that you plan carefully!

You leave a very bad impression with potential customers if you don't handle phone calls and e-mail messages in a prompt and friendly manner.

Before you do anything that changes existing sales and distribution relationships, talk to people. Your existing sales channels no doubt know about e-commerce and have some thoughts or even fears about it; ask them what they think and what they would like to see you do. The two channels can work together but never surprise your offline sales channels with new developments online; talk to them first, and give them advance, written notice and time to respond before you implement any plans. Even if the only effect of your Web site is to increase overall sales volume without hurting anybody's interests, people need time to plan and staff for that development. If you do take steps that take business away from anyone, or increase sales for one channel but not others, more time and previous consultation is needed. Moving forward to help your Web visitors buy is very important; moving carefully is even more important.

News on Your Site

In Wonderland, the Red Queen tells Alice that reality is whatever she says it is. In just the same way, on your Web site, news is whatever you say it is. To be more specific, your Web visitors don't expect 'news' in the BBC sense on your Web site; they expect 'what's new' information about recent events that relate to your company and its products. But the tradition on Web sites is to call this part of the site 'news', so you need to have a 'news' area on your site.

Don't annoy your distributors

The first sentence of the Hippocratic Oath – First, do no harm – is one of the most important rules for digital marketing and a crucial principle when you give sales information online. Don't undermine your distributors, direct salespeople, and other sales channels by undercutting them with information about direct phone sales, access to other, cheaper distributors, or secure Web-based sales directly from your site.

But wait, you say: What if the online market is bigger and more profitable than the distribution channels I'm going to undercut? Then stop, take a deep breath, and study the problem carefully. Size the Internet market opportunity realistically, taking into account the experience of others and actual and potential competition. Last year, consumers spent over £8 billion on

the Internet alone and analysts are predicting that the Internet will soon overtake the High Street in the shopping stakes. This is, of course, all good news but remember that when you start out the online market for your products is still likely to be only a small percentage of your total market. Are you sure that, in going after this small slice, you won't undermine the rest of your sales pie? Review your legal obligations and, just as important, the impression you have left with your distributors, salespeople, and so on as to where they stand with you.

If you plan your move to online-supported or online-based sales carefully and make it with as little damage as possible to existing sales relationships, you'll be in the best position to come out ahead.

Possibly the most intriguing words in marketing any product are 'new' and 'free'. The Web is already free to use (after the Internet service provider gets paid), so you have that base covered. But the word we're concerned with here is 'new'. We believe that people visiting your homepage should see some piece of new information right up front, on the first screen of information they access, and that some brand-new information should appear there at least once a week. (The Microsoft homepage, shown in Figure 6-2 earlier in this chapter, is one of the many that follow this new information rule.) Seeing something new makes people stop and click their way into your site rather than just surf by, and it keeps them coming back regularly.

Figure 6-5 shows an example of news on a company's Web site. New information appears right on the first screen of the homepage and a news section is readily available. Use this approach or suffer from lack of public interest in your Web presence.

For a small business or one-man band, weekly updates may not be possible or warranted. Information should always be current, but that's not the same as providing updates every week if basic product offerings have not changed. You should ask yourself what the expected ROI on this kind of time investment may be.

Figure 6-5:
Intel's Web
site is a
good
example of
a company
putting
news on its
homepage.

So what kind of news should you put on your Web site? Earlier in this chapter, we emphasise the vital role of press releases in online marketing, but even we have to admit that not everything that happens relating to your company and products is worth a press release. Here are some of the things that you can put in the news section of your Web site:

- **Product developments:** Have you made any changes in your product – any at all? Anything 'new' or 'free' about your product? This is the place to put minor stuff such as slight revisions in software, new printings or editions of books, changes to the emission control system of a ride-on lawnmower, and so on. Your most devoted customers are often more interested in this kind of stuff than even your company's employees.

- **Trade shows:** Always let the world know your trade-show schedule well in advance. A month before the show, give details about what you'll be doing at the show; two weeks before, remind people that the show's coming right up. During and after the show, post any news generated on your Web site.

- **Other events:** Any event you participate in – a press conference, a trade group meeting, a university recruitment day – is worth mentioning on your Web site. (People who see you at these events will check your Web site to learn more about your company and will be pleased to see the event mentioned.)

- ✔ **Sales success:** Any significant new customers or increases in sales? Give ammunition to your fans out there – tell them how your business is growing.

- ✔ **Distribution changes:** Any new sales channels or expansions in your geographic reach? Other changes in how your products are sold and delivered? Again, even arcane stuff is interesting to somebody. Let people know how your distribution is expanding.

- ✔ **Executive changes:** Any senior new recruitments? Note them in the news section.

This list is hardly exhaustive; many other kinds of events appear in online news listings. Anything that seems significant to you in your work is grist for the mill. Key customers and suppliers may have as big a stake in your company as you do; include them in all the happenings. (But trumpet only the major news on the first page of your Web site; put the minor stories where your more dedicated Web surfers can find them.)

In each news item, try to include an action item for the reader and encourage the reader's involvement. Are there changes to a product? Tell people how to get the new one. Is a trade show coming up? Link to the trade show Web site or otherwise tell people how to attend. Did you clinch a big deal/win a new client? Remind people how to obtain your product themselves. You don't have to beat people over the head with your call to action, but do make sure that they are aware of it.

Whilst updates are crucial to making sure that your customers know that the site is being regularly updated, there's no point doing them if they are going to trail off as there's nothing worse than stumbling across a Web site that hasn't been updated in months. To avoid this, consider devising a realistic schedule and stick with it. Work out what you can realistically do and then commit to it.

Chapter 7

Getting the Most Out of Your Web Site

. . . .

In This Chapter

▶ Gathering information about visitors

▶ Improving your site

▶ Getting your Web site listed with the search engines

▶ Publicising your site

. . . .

*I*n Chapters 5 to 7, we show you how to build an affordable and effective Web presence quickly. To reach your goals in online marketing, however, you ultimately have to take your Web site further, but as the old maps used to say when showing unchartered waters, 'Danger! Here be dragons!' Wasting time and money is easy to do on badly planned Web efforts.

Luckily, you can build up to a winning Web presence that makes your existing customers happy and your prospective customers eager to become existing ones, at reasonable expense and within a relatively short timeframe. In this chapter, we highlight how to find out about who is visiting your site, point out some of the best ways to improve your site for future visitors, and show you how to help people find your Web site.

Gathering Information about Site Visitors

As soon as any new kind of Web marketing effort gets past the early stages you may start to wonder how to measure the effectiveness of the new medium. The broadcasting industry has BARB and Nielsen ratings to help advertisers discover who their ads reach and the Web also has powerful tools that allow you to know where your visitors go on your Web site, where they arrive from, and where they go to when they are finished.

The Web is now so important that you don't need to go to too much effort to justify having at least a low-cost, low-hassle Web presence for strictly defensive purposes – just a non-embarrassing Web billboard to prevent people from seeing you as road kill on the information superhighway. But as you start to invest more time, energy, and money into your Web site, you need to know something about the kinds of visitors you get.

At the lowest level, the easiest information to get from your Web server software or Internet Service Provider (ISP) is *hits* – the number of connections made to the Web server to receive HTML files, graphics files, or any other files on your Web site. However, hits are not always a good indicator of the number of actual unique visitors to your site as hits will register the same visitor returning for repeat visits. A myriad of companies can now provide counter software that you can use to chart how many hits you get to your site.

Techniques for gathering visitor information

You can use several different techniques for gathering information about your Web site visitors above and beyond hits, each of which could probably justify its own chapter in a book on the topic. But just to get you started, here are some methods for finding out about your site's visitors:

- ✔ **Reading site e-mail.** Just scanning the e-mail that comes into your site gives you some information about who's visiting and what their concerns are. (Of course, you should *answer* the e-mail too.) Consider printing a hundred or so e-mails, arranging them by category, writing a brief cover note and summary, and passing the whole stack around to marketing, sales, customer service, and other people in your company who may be interested in what your Web site visitors have to say about the site.

- ✔ **Visitor counters.** You can easily install software to count the number of visitors you get to each of your Web pages; your ISP may even offer this service for free or for a small fee. For access to counter software, just go to Google and type in 'free counter software' and choose from the many options listed. Good examples include `www.onestat.com/` and `www.statcounter.com/`.

  You can use a visible counter if you want others to see how many visitors you've had, or an invisible one if you want to keep the number to yourself. The information that counter software gives you is valuable feedback as to the amount of traffic you're getting on your Web site and which parts of your Web site draw the most attention. You can compare the number of hits and the cost of your site to the cost per thousand impressions that you pay for magazine ads to get a rough idea of whether your Web site pulls its weight.

✔ **Log analysis.** To get a better idea of who's coming to your site, whether they arrived there from an external link, a search engine, or a bookmark, how long they stay on your site, and the path they take through your site, you can use sophisticated logging capability in your Web server software and both software and human expertise to analyse the data. To check out software, again go to Google and type in 'log analysis' and look through the options. The results can help you understand what users value most on your Web site and will also show you if any navigational problems exist that are making navigating your site difficult.

It is also very useful to understand where visitors are leaving your site, so that you can make changes to any navigational problems that may spring up. This is particularly important if people are dropping out half way through a purchase.

✔ **On-site registration.** One good way to gather information about your Web site visitors is to ask them to register to use your site. If you ask them for their registration information, though, you need to give them something in return – for example, an industry survey of some sort, entry in a prize draw, additional information that cannot be accessed by non-members, or regular e-mail updates on changes in your Web site. (Different rewards get different kinds of people to register; try to get people who are current or likely customers.) Registration info is useful, but you have to remember that this tactic's biased toward whatever kind of person takes the time to register.

People are rightly becoming concerned about what happens to registration information that they enter on a Web site – they don't want it to be used to make them the target of e-mail spam, junk mail in their mailboxes, or phone solicitations. Many users give false information when registering, perhaps to avoid being the target of solicitors, or set up multiple e-mail accounts to sign up to different sites without having to read the follow-up e-mails. Reassure your visitors by telling them that you'll never rent or sell their information to anyone else (assuming that such an assurance is true; if it isn't, disclose what you will do with it so that you don't lose visitors' trust). Personal data in the UK is covered by the Data Protection Act. A good privacy statement – found at the bottom of any reputable Web site via a link – will reassure visitors that their information is safe. See this Web site for more information on what should be covered by the Data Protection Act: `http://www.ico.gov.uk/what_we_cover/data_ protection.aspx`. Figure 7-1 shows how a good privacy statement should be set out for visitors.

✔ **Surveys.** You can do on-site or e-mail surveys of visitors to your Web site. This tactic is much like registration, but with no ongoing relationship implied, so cash or its equivalent is a good reward. You can map survey data against log analysis data to get a pretty good idea of who's coming to visit your site. If you want only some people to respond to the survey – say, people within a certain geographic area – limit the reward or prize opportunity to people who fit your target. Everyone likes cash, so there may be less bias in the results of surveys with cash rewards than with other forms of information gathering.

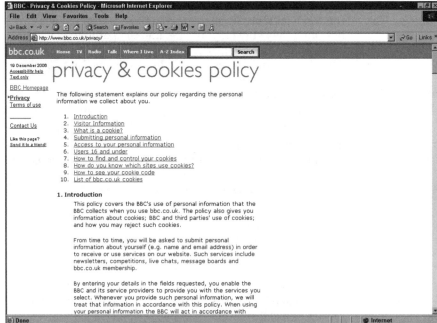

Figure 7-1:
The BBC
Web site
has a clear
and concise
statement
on privacy.

Unless you have a large online marketing group at your company already, you may want to consider choosing an Internet Service Provider, Web agency, or consultant who can provide some or all of these information-gathering services for you. Implementing and analysing these measurement techniques can be technically challenging, so find someone with lots of online experience, a degree in statistics, or both, who can help you determine who's coming to see you.

There are also a number of analytics companies such as Web Trends – www. webtrends.com – that provide user friendly software tools that require someone with technical knowledge to implement, but should allow a non-technical user to pull out reports and graphs on Web site usage. You can also check out Google's analytics product at http://www.google.com/analytics/.

Uses for visitor data

At some point in the process of planning and implementing your data-gathering effort, you need to ask yourself what you're going to do with the information you acquire. For example, if your Web site is giving you more impressions per pound than magazine advertising, and the impressions on the Web are reaching the same kind of people as the magazine, you may want to put more of your advertising and marketing budget into the Web site.

A special kind of opportunity for Web marketing is the ability to actually use the Web to maintain and improve your relationship with a specific customer – referred to as *one-to-one* marketing. One way to develop relationships in this way involves using a *cookie,* a data file that is stored on the site visitor's machine that records the visitor's activities on each visit to your Web site.

With a cookie file, you can access information about customer visits and track their online habits on your Web site. (Users can turn off cookie capability, but the majority don't do so as they don't realise how easy it is to do. You may want to ask users before creating the cookie file the first time.) Going further, you can actually modify the information you present to each of your Web visitors to fit that particular visitor's interests and habits based on their cookie. For example, imagine a homepage of a pet shop that shows three pictures, each a hyperlink: one of a dog, one of a cat, and one of a rat. Depending on which link the visitor clicks, you can offer information that interests the particular pet owner – clicking the dog, for example, may bring up an article on dog dental health. In addition, the site can include an ad for dog food alongside the dental health article and an Internet coupon for a pound off the next visit to the pet shop. In this way, the site can offer useful information that keeps visitors coming to the site, offer visitor-specific marketing information, and create visitor profiles that can be analysed by marketing to better assess who visits. If you're interested in fine-tuning your Web marketing effort in this way, ask your digital agency or your consultant to help.

Cookies, and other information gathered by Web sites, are a very sensitive area. The best rule if you're not certain how your visitors will react to cookies, registration, and other information-gathering techniques is to disclose, disclose, disclose. Does your site use cookies? Say so, and for what purpose. Do you ask for an e-mail address or other 'personally identifiable information'? Say exactly what you will, and won't, use this information for, and what other companies you work with (if any) may see it and do with it. Don't hide anything on the Internet – you'll be caught out.

Improving Your Site

Early in the existence of the Web, most people pulled out all the stops, creating large, attractive, highly interactive sites that cost huge amounts of money but did little to advance a company's interests in any measurable way. No reason actually existed for these big and clunky Web sites.

This Web site failure to promote companies' interests led, naturally enough, to a backlash. Many companies stopped investing in their Web sites altogether, and the Internet is littered with thousands of these 'dead' or barely breathing sites – they're rarely updated, uninteresting, and looking more and more stale with the passage of time.

Now, however, companies are starting to see real results from their Web investments. Companies that sell online are riding on the wave of the e-commerce boom; Web-based marketing and PR efforts are gathering steam and are starting to have a major impact in the offline world as well as simply making companies more famous in cyberspace.

As your own Web efforts start to have an impact, consider ways to improve your Web site – partly to meet or beat your competitors' improvements in their online presence, and partly to move toward more Web marketing or an initial effort at Web commerce.

Developing and improving your site into something really interesting and attractive brings in more visitors and results in a more effective online marketing push. Here are some of the techniques you can use to get there:

- ✔ **Improve navigation.** Also known as customer journey, this is one of the most neglected, and most important, concerns for your site. A clickable graphic with major site areas listed at the top or bottom of each Web page is one starting point. More advanced navigation approaches include a site map, table of contents information, and a search capability for users to find specific things within your site.

- ✔ **Streamline graphics.** Before broadband became widespread in the UK one of the single biggest irritants for many users of the Web was the slow speed with which pages load due to large graphics files. Whilst this is less of a problem with faster Internet connections, it is still a consideration if you don't want your site to appear cluttered. Reducing the size of the graphics files while maintaining or improving the attractiveness of the Web site is an ongoing challenge. Consider using tools such as Adobe Photoshop to help you reduce the size of graphics files, or find a graphic designer with Web experience to help.

- ✔ **Create valuable content.** Creating evolving content that users want to keep coming back for is a long-term win for your Web site. One approach is to maintain and update information for your industry area, which can be as simple as a good page of links to industry-related Web sites or as complex as an ongoing survey of customer attitudes. (Give away the top-line summaries, but keep the details for yourself!) Providing information for your industry segment sends the message that you're the leader.

- ✔ **Use other Internet services.** Too much online marketing starts and stops with the Web. Use other online services described in this book to create a comprehensive online marketing effort that makes your customers and potential customers feel part of your team. Use the information on opti-mising your Web site in Chapter 8 to be more visible to search engines, and remember – visibility is key.

- ✔ **Add multimedia.** When you add multimedia to your Web site, you also open yourself up to tech support questions from users who have trouble running it, and to complaints from users if a multimedia file takes a long

time to load. So set modest goals initially and make multimedia additions interesting and appropriate: a brief video clip of your CEO speaking; a 3D model or virtual reality object photograph of a product to show
what it really looks like or how it works. Figure 7-2 shows an example of
effective multimedia use on a Web site.

✔ **Make it interactive.** Today Web sites must be interactive. One popular
technique is to add a blog or message board that allows people to comment on your site. Many other sites create more ambitious interactive
effects such as taking over the whole screen to display information,
often through Java programs. You can make using your Web site much
more engaging this way, but you also make it more expensive to design,
maintain, and support, and many users object to having Web-based programs seemingly 'take over' their computer. Define your goals carefully
and identify your resources before going too far in this direction.

✔ **Create a channel for wireless access.** Wireless devices such as Palm OS
handhelds and 2.5 and 3G phones have little tiny screens and are natural
targets for focused marketing efforts. Wireless channels work best if you
have at least a couple of news items appearing on your site a day, and if
those items are short (again, the little tiny screens).

✔ **Add online sales.** The ultimate goal for many Web sites is to make
money through direct online sales. If online sales are an option for
you, start planning now for when and how to get there.

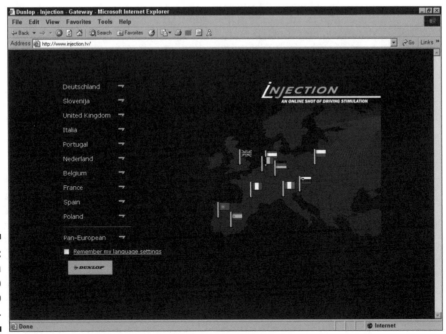

Figure 7-2:
Multimedia
jazzes up
your Web
site.

Getting Found with Search Engines

Your Web site doesn't do you any good if people can't find it. The single most important tool you have to make sure that people can find your site is to get a domain name that matches your company name as closely as possible, as described in Chapter 4. That way, anyone who knows your company name can easily guess your Web URL and visit your site.

However, you also want people to find your site when they know only a product name, or maybe just the kind of product or company they're looking for. Bringing these potential customers to your site is actually cheap, easy to accomplish, and easy to check up on. Web users who look for certain kinds of sites almost invariably use search engines – well over 80 per cent of Web users do so, according to several popular surveys, and search engine sites such as Yahoo!, MSN, and Google are among the most visited sites on the Web.

To understand how to make the search engines work to your advantage, you need to know how they work.

Getting the best out of search engines

Most search engines on the Web, and for other Internet services as well, use programs called *Web spiders* or *bots*. These programs open a Web page, read the contents, index them according to various criteria, store the results in a database, and then go on to the next Web page. The result is an indexed database of millions of Web pages.

When you query a search engine to do a search, the engine doesn't go out and start searching the Web – doing so would be way too slow. Instead, the engine accesses its database and provides you with the indexed sites that match your query.

If the information in the search engine database has become outdated since the last time the Web spider checked a site, you may get a different-than-expected Web page or an error message when you go to that Web site. Given the sheer size of the Web and other online resources, the database can easily get behind – one popular Web search engine says it needs two to four weeks to index a new site. However, the information that the search engine provides is accurate most of the time, and the search engines are very useful.

Most search engines enable you to register your site with them by simply entering your URL. The staff of the search site then point the site's spider your way so that it indexes your site sooner than if you were to wait for it to find you at random. The good news is that you don't *have* to register – the spider finds your site eventually.

Either way, with most search engines, the Web spider finds the keywords for your site and creates that entry in the search engine database. Web spiders, like real spiders, don't have much in the way of brains – they simply go out on the Web and index all the words in every Web page they find without knowing which words on a given Web page are the important ones. Some engines simply treat the first words they encounter as the most important; others use different weighting criteria. Your job: to make those first words count so that your site appears high on the 'hits list' when a search engine user enters keywords appropriate to your Web page.

The following steps suggest that you make some small changes to the HTML tags in your Web page. You can do this work yourself, if you know HTML or are willing to get your hands dirty (the changes are really pretty simple, and you can use a simple text editor to make them). Or you can find a colleague or consultant who knows how to use HTML to make the changes for you. For an introduction to common HTML commands, see *Creating Web Pages For Dummies,* 7th Edition, by Bud E. Smith and Arthur Bebak, *HTML 4 For Dummies,* 5th Edition, by Ed Tittel and Mary Burmeister, or *HTML 4 For Dummies Quick Reference,* 2nd Edition, by Deborah and Eric Ray, all from Wiley.

Here's how to make it easier for Web search engines to bring the right kinds of users to your Web page.

1. **Modify your homepage's title for 'findability'.**

   Every Web page can have a title that appears at the top of the Web browser window and that is also used by search engines and other Web tools to find appropriate Web pages. The title can include your company name, area of business, product names, or any keywords by which you would like to be found.

2. **Add meta tags to your homepage for 'findability'.**

   The meta tag is an HTML command that allows search engines to more easily find your site. Add the following meta tags between the <HEAD> and </HEAD> tags of your Web pages, with your own information inside the quotation marks in the content= areas:

   ```
   <META name="description" content="Dummies Consulting
           does marketing consulting for high-technology
           companies.">
   <META name="keywords" content="online marketing,
           online, marketing, high technology, Web,
           Internet, dummies, geniuses, veeblefetzer">
   ```

Most of the HTML editing software available includes features for adding meta tags. See the documentation for your Web page editing tool to find out how to add HTML tags directly.

A Web page, shown in Source mode with a summary and meta tags useful for searchability, is shown in Figure 7-3. You can view the source HTML document in Microsoft Internet Explorer by choosing View➪Source.

Some companies have gone to extremes in their meta tag content and have used rival company and product names as keywords. The idea is that someone searching for a specific product will be directed by a search engine to the Web site for the competing product instead. This practice is not only bad business but also may incur legal liability; several lawsuits have been filed over this issue.

Always include one odd, new word in the meta tag for keywords so that you can test whether each search engine has added your newly updated Web page yet. In the example in these steps, we use the word *veeblefetzer*.

3. **Upload your modified page to your Web server so that it is available on the Web.**

4. **Go to the major search engines and tell them whatever they need to know to list or re-examine your Web site.**

   Here are the URLs for submitting your site with some of the most important search engines:

   - Google: `http://www.google.com/addurl/`

   - Yahoo!: `https://siteexplorer.search.yahoo.com/submit`

   - MSN: `http://search.msn.co.uk/docs/submit.aspx?FORM=WSDD2`

   As you add your URL, check the search site for information on how long the search engine takes to index new sites. Expect not to see your site listed for at least one week and as long as four weeks.

5. **Use your test keyword to test each search engine weekly and see whether your site has been added yet.**

   As soon as your page shows up, test that search engine with several different kinds of search terms that customers are likely to use to find Web pages like yours. See whether your Web page shows up in the listings. If your page is among the top ten hits for crucial keywords that relate to your business, good job! If not, modify your meta tags, adding the needed keywords, and try again.

If your Web page doesn't show up near the top, use the View Source command in your Web browser to inspect the Web pages that do show up first. Take a look at the meta tags in those pages and see what keywords to use to make your own site rise to the top.

6. **When you're happy with the performance of the search engines on your Web pages, ask some colleagues and customers to try searching for businesses and products like yours – and tell you the results.**

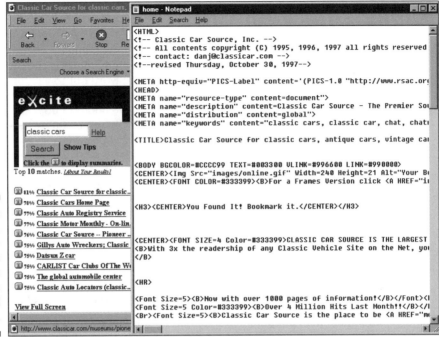

Figure 7-3:
A search
for 'classic
cars' finds
a site with
'classic
cars' all
over it.

This whole process is a lot of work but is vital. Your Web site is most likely the cornerstone of your entire online presence, and people who are interested in companies and products like yours must be able to find your site.

If you really want to make yourself accessible, consider listing the specific Web pages for each of your key products and services with Yahoo! and the various other search engines. That way, people go straight to the exact Web page they need to get the product or service they want – from you, not from someone else.

Many people test a new Web site by uploading it to their Web server, making it available on the Web, and simply not telling more than a few people where it is. This kind of testing allows you to see how features such as CGI scripts (if your webmaster uses them) work under 'live' conditions and allows you to test how long your Web pages take to download across the Internet. This test works well, but only for a few days, because if any links to the page exist, search engines find it. To protect your test site or secret site, don't link to it, take it down after a couple of days, password-protect it, or move it frequently to different Web page addresses.

Publicising Your Site

One of the most talked-about topics in Web publishing is publicising your Web site. A difference exists, though, between publicising your Web site to people who are looking for it and putting the word out to vast masses of Web surfers through banner ads, aggressive linking campaigns, and spam. You *do* want to get the word out to your customers and potential customers, which means that you want to include your URL on business cards and press releases and also make your site easy to find via the various search engines, as we describe in the 'Getting Found with Search Engines' section, earlier in this chapter. However, you *don't* necessarily want to spend a lot of time and money – having your Web banner ad displayed on popular sites can cost thousands of pounds – trying to get random Web surfers to stop by your site. Here are some of the common myths of why you should widely publicise your Web site:

✔ **To get more visitors.** Getting more visitors to your Web site sounds okay, but is pointless if the people who visit aren't potential customers for your products. Getting randomly selected people to – in most cases, briefly – browse your Web site probably doesn't do them or you much good.

✔ **To show people you're online.** This was a good reason ten years ago when being online meant you were technically savvy. However, these days a company *not* being online is news, and the online public is not likely to be impressed by the simple fact that you have a Web site.

✔ **To let people know your URL.** How much work does it take to remember the Yahoo!, Google, or BBC URL? None at all. If you know the company name, you know the URL. If your company has an easy-to-guess URL, you don't need to help people remember it; if not, read Chapter 4 and go and get one.

Developing an effective publicity strategy

Okay, so you should never publicise your Web site, right?

No, not publicising at all is going too far. Here are the steps to take in deciding how to appropriately publicise your Web site:

1. **Determine what you want from your Web visitors.**

   Web sites are hard to perfect because they must meet the needs of several different groups, including customers, potential customers, press, financial analysts, and even employees. What do you want people in each group to take away from their visit to your Web site? Put the answer in the form, 'With my Web site, I want to increase their likelihood to . . .' and include one primary goal for each group. Then analyse your Web site to make sure that it accomplishes your stated goal for people from each group.

2. Develop a Web site you're proud of.

Sure, you can start out with a bare-bones, cover-your-assets Web presence for people to find when needed, but that situation's different to trying to actively bring people to it. Until you've made your Web site really worthwhile, don't make extra efforts to bring it to people's attention.

3. Figure out where your customers are.

Don't put a banner ad on MSN for thousands of pounds and attract random Web surfers. Instead, work out where your potential customers are and publicise your site there. For instance, if you're selling organic produce online, try to exchange links with food-orientated sites. And consider using search marketing to display ads every time someone searches for organic recipes, for example. (For more on Internet advertising, see Chapter 12.)

4. Aim initial publicity at some customers.

Decide on some initial efforts to draw people from among your targeted groups – your potential customers, trade press from within your industry, and any other group you really want to visit your site. These efforts can include a print mailing, an e-mailing, a targeted press release, or other means.

5. Measure the results.

Carefully compare who visits your site before you make a publicity effort and then again after the blitz using the techniques we describe in the 'Gathering Information about Site Visitors' section, earlier in this chapter. You can get a quick idea about who's seeing your publicity by asking people from within your company whether they've seen it. But also do a more detailed analysis of the number of visits you get and whether your desired results – visits by people from certain kinds of companies, viewings of specific Web pages, registrations for information, downloads of specific files – are being achieved.

If you follow this process, you'll do the right kind of publicity and get good results that you can not only be proud of but also cost-justify thoroughly.

In the radio industry, the conventional wisdom is to not advertise a new format for a radio station – for example, a change from news to talk or from rock to rap – until a few weeks after the change. The reason is that radio listeners may sample a changed station once and then not come back unless they really like what they hear – and just after a change, glitches may still occur in the on-air experience for on-air talent and production staff, and therefore for the listeners. In keeping with this guideline, many radio stations make sure that they're firing on all cylinders before publicising their new format. Consider following a similar strategy in publicising your Web site.

Expanding your publicity efforts

When you've developed a Web site that you're proud of – that is, one that has at least basic company, product, and service information, tells visitors how to buy whatever it is you sell, is easily found by anyone using a major search engine, and is one of the better sites, or even the best site, among your direct competitors – then you're ready to milk it for all it's worth. Doing so means embarking on some real publicity work, both in the offline world and online.

Two factors influence the amount of benefit you get from visits to your Web site. These factors can be expressed as two questions: How impressive is your Web site? and What sales impact do you get out of visits to it?

The more impressive your Web site and the more sales impact you get out of Web site visits, the more publicity you want to do. Figure 7-4 expresses this idea roughly in a conceptual graphic form.

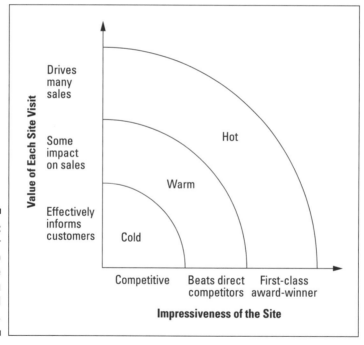

Figure 7-4:
The hotter your Web site, the more you should publicise it.

The idea behind this graph is that the more impact your Web site has on sales and the more impressive your site is, the 'hotter' it is and the more deserving of publicity. A really hot site – one that is a first-class, award-winning site and that drives a significant portion of sales for one or more of your products or services – should get a substantial part of your total company publicity effort. If your site does somewhat less, publicise somewhat less. Here's how we see the publicity effort:

- ✔ **Cold.** Your site neither stands out on the Web nor has much impact on sales. (The vast majority of company Web sites live here, and in many cases, that situation's okay.) Make your site findable, as described earlier in this chapter. Add your Web site URL to business cards and company stationery to give an impression of being technologically up-to-date and to remind your regular customers to visit you online. Make sure that your Web URL is in all e-mail signature files.

- ✔ **Warm.** Your site beats competitors and noticeably increases sales. Push to get the URL on printed company materials and include it in any broadcast ads that you do. Add your URL to any freebies you give away – soft toys or stress-relieving devices, for example. Start doing press releases when you make major changes to the site or reach visitor or sales milestones related to it.

- ✔ **Hot.** Your site is first class or wins awards and drives many sales. Pay for carefully targeted Internet ads to pull in traffic; issue regular press releases about awards, sales, and additions; advertise the site directly in the offline world; start developing online sales capability.

You can fine-tune your efforts based on the strengths and weaknesses of your site's impact. For instance, if your site isn't all that impressive but still drives many sales, put all your effort into targeted publicity among likely buyers, but don't waste money trumpeting your site outside those groups. Or if your site is award winning but has little direct impact on sales, advertise it in a low-key way to broad audiences; your site's a real plus to your company's image but not a real plus to revenues. In either case, consider ways to increase the site's impact.

The vast majority of Web sites live in the 'cold' zone and don't merit an active, costly publicity effort by themselves. Promotional costs related to this kind of competitive but low-key Web effort should be incidental. Only when you invest more in your Web site and see results from that investment do you need to step up the publicity effort.

Part III
Marketing with Search

'Shh — he's searching'

In this part . . .

Search engines have become the most important way by which Internet users find content and information online. Not only that, but they are also by far the most valuable digital advertising tool available, so in this part we guide you through the pros and cons of search and give you a guide to how to implement your own search marketing strategy.

Chapter 8

Optimising Your Web Site for Search Engines

Search engines are the number one way for Internet users to find information they are searching for. The Internet carries so much information that these engines have become indispensable in the process of finding content and as such they can make the difference between your Web site succeeding and failing.

Building and maintaining a Web site that features high in the listings on a search engine results page is not an exact science, although guidelines exist that you can follow to ensure that you get listed somewhere. But the art of boosting your profile in the natural listings of the search engine is sometimes seen as a 'smoke and mirrors' exercise by traditional media agencies.

The Power of Search

An entire industry has sprung up alongside the *Search Engine Optimisation* (SEO) business. The size of the industry is hard to gauge as no exact measurements exist to show the money being spent, unlike with paid search services. If you take into account the fact that paid search – which we talk about more in Chapter 10 – was worth over £750m in the UK in 2005, then you can estimate that the SEO industry may be worth a comparable figure as the two services often go hand in hand. Without either, your Web site may be missing a trick.

Getting to grips with how search engines work

To understand how to fully optimise your Web site so that it features as high as possible in the rankings of search engines, you need to understand how search engines work.

A few years ago only a couple of types of search engine existed. The first consisted of human-powered directories, where you had to submit your own listing and description of your site and an automated search would only look through those sites that had been submitted. These have now been largely replaced by the *crawler, bot,* or *spider* based search engines such as that operated by Google. These engines use software agents known as 'crawlers', 'bots', or 'spiders' that are sent out onto the Web and automatically read a Web site and its meta tags – see Chapter 7 for details on meta tags – and follow the links from that site before returning the information to the central database where it is stored. This central database is then interrogated every time a search is made. These crawlers return to pages every now and again to see if any information has changed. A page ranking is determined by the relevance of the meta tag information to the request and also by the quality and number of links that link to that page. Every search engine has a slightly different *algorithm* – a complex step-by-step method – to determine its page ranking, so SEO can become a very complicated art as you can gain a good ranking on one engine, which will not necessarily guarantee you the same result on another.

As we are not all Stephen Hawking it would be foolish for an individual to sit down and try to work out the different search engines' algorithms. Instead you can follow a few simple steps to ensure that your Web site is optimised to a decent level. We outline these in the 'Do's and Don'ts of SEO' section, later in this chapter.

Understanding what SEO is

SEO specifically relates to how your Web site is read and ranked by search engine spiders. Unfortunately, talking about the mechanics without having to go into some technical detail is pretty difficult, but we try to keep it as simple as possible.

SEO falls under the banner of *search engine marketing,* which encompasses anything that you do to help attract customers to your Web site through search engines. This process can involve a myriad of different techniques and processes from paid search – which we cover in Chapter 10 – to Web site design – which we cover in Chapters 5 to 7. The combination of all these different techniques forms your search marketing strategy.

SEO is a mixture of a number of different skills and nobody apart from the real experts can be great at all of them. Even then, the experts can sometimes get SEO wrong – as we demonstrate again later in this chapter (see the sidebar 'When SEO all goes wrong').

Using SEO on your site

Good SEO should begin before you have even built your site. Planning out your site so that it is as relevant and accessible as possible will help you to maintain a good ranking in search engine lists. Once you've decided upon the format and layout, you need to ensure that the build of your Web site makes it as accessible as possible. The World Wide Web Consortium carries a list of guidelines that will help you to ensure that your Web site is accessible as it can be. Try this link for some handy hints and tips: `http://www.w3.org/WAI/guid-tech`.

Thinking logically, a badly designed site will be hard for a user to navigate and the same will be true for the search engine spiders that collect information and rank your site. Having a clear structure, with relevant content and easy navigation will help you to improve your site visibility to search engines, which can only benefit your Web site.

A good technique to see if your site is already well designed, or if you have not built your site yet and want to see what works, is to look at sites of competitors to see how well theirs work. Note things such as:

- Speed of page loading
- Ease of navigation
- Whether links point to relevant information
- What information they give on their homepages

If you've used a search engine to find the sites under a common keyword, then also take notice of their rankings in the results and try to work out the link between the sites with good design and their ranking in the search results. Finally, it is important to remember that when you're designing your site, creating a site that is eye-catching, uses the latest Flash technology and whizzy graphics is all well and good, but the search engine spiders won't be able to appreciate them. These spiders are cold, calculating little creatures that simply apply their logic to your site to give it a ranking and then move on to the next one. So although focusing on your customers when designing a site is good, keeping one eye on the spiders is also worthwhile.

Some techniques that you should look at include *link building,* which means getting other relevant sites to link to your site so that its relevancy in the search listings improves. You can link up through deals with other sites, link exchanges, or through an SEO company that will organise link building for you. But beware of the pitfalls listed in the 'Don'ts' part of the 'Do's and Don'ts of SEO' section, later in this chapter.

If you haven't already built your Web site by the time you're reading this section, then you can build accessibility into it right from the start, which will improve the number of users that visit your site and in turn increase your search ranking.

Finally, you can also use online PR as part of your SEO campaign. This approach works by identifying target keywords about your company that can be distributed in a press release format through online news services. If these stories are then published online and linked to your site you will gain traffic. The stories can also be talked about by people who read them, who may then comment on them and also link to your Web site, all increasing your relevancy in the eyes of the search engines. We deal with more issues surrounding online PR in Chapter 13.

However you choose to approach SEO, you need to have a firm understanding of the skills that are needed, whether you undertake it yourself or bring in a specialist to help you.

Do's and don'ts of SEO

SEO can be a dangerous world and guidelines and rules are widely available online to help you navigate what has turned into a complicated minefield for most.

Your goal in using SEO is to pull in as many customers as possible to your site, getting as many links to your site as possible, and designing the best possible site for users and spiders alike, all with the aim of getting a good search engine ranking in the results under relevant keyword terms.

However, and this point is crucial, using SEO does not mean that you should undertake practices that trick users or spiders into thinking that your site is something that it is not just to get them through the door or improve your ranking. Doing so will without a doubt result in you being de-listed from the search index of a search engine. This de-listing is the SEO equivalent of football's red card and comes with a nasty stigma – see 'When SEO all goes wrong', later in this chapter.

Now, although SEO has nothing to do with wizards or witches, good SEO practices are known as *white hat* practices and bad ones as *black hat* practices. To further complicate matters, a continual argument rages between the two groups as to what constitutes unethical SEO. The very nature of SEO is to try to rise up the rankings and black hatters argue that this process should be by any means necessary as any kind of SEO is an attempt to manipulate the rankings. You can see their point – based firmly on the Laws of the Jungle – but we strongly advise you to avoid black hat practices as they're frowned upon by search engines and will result in getting you kicked off the index if you are found out.

The following sections function as checklists to help you decide what is white hat and what is black hat practice.

White hat practices

The following practices are the ones regarded by the industry as fair and ethical:

- ✔ **On each page use a unique and relevant title and name.** This way spiders can easily read the page and its content.

- ✔ **Keep the content as relevant as possible.** When spiders read the page the terminology found should be relevant to the subject of the page. Make the content what a user would expect to find after searching on specific keywords.

- ✔ **Remember that content is king in SEO.** Add as much content as possible to your site, but don't copy it from elsewhere, as doing so is frowned upon. Make sure as far as possible that you create your own unique content.

- ✔ **Make sure that your meta tags are relevant to your site and specific page content.** Avoid excessive repetition of words and over the top punctuation such as exclamation marks. If you repeat keywords a search engine may believe that you're attempting to fool it and its users.

- ✔ **Set up your site so that spiders can trawl through your pages easily.** If you set up your site to allow search engine spiders to trawl the site they will be able to automatically update your site in their listings when you make changes, saving you from having to register your site with the search engine every time you make a change.

- ✔ **Try to develop linking strategies that entice links from other Web sites.** These enticements are sometimes called *link bait* strategies and basically involve you creating your own content as sites to get linked to more sites. Web sites with interesting information or articles tend to get linked to more than those without – thus increasing your ranking. This tactic will help you to accumulate large numbers of *backlinks* – links that are made to your site, as opposed to links that you make to other sites.

✔ **Join a *Web ring* that is relevant to your business.** These rings are groups of sites that have all linked to each other to form a ring. When someone visits a site in the ring they're offered links to relevant content from others in the ring.

✔ **Enhance your online PR through writing interesting articles.** These can then be offered to other sites in exchange for a link back to your own site being placed with the article.

This list just covers some basic principles. You also need to take a whole host of other things into consideration, such as keeping any text you want to be read outside of pictures – that is as part of the HTML, not as part of the graphic itself – and making sure that each page carries at least one static text link to make it easily readable. Spiders find it easier to read static links as they are the basic format used by most pages. So if you have put links inside pictures it may not spot them.

If you want an exhaustive look at white hat practices, try these links for the major engines' suggestions:

✔ http://www.google.com/support/webmasters/bin/ answer.py?answer=35769

✔ http://search.msn.com/docs/siteowner.aspx?t=SEARCH_ WEBMASTER_REF_GuidelinesforOptimizingSite.htm

✔ http://help.yahoo.com/help/us/ysearch/deletions/ deletions-05.html

Black hat practices

Spamdexing, a mixture of spamming and indexing, is the practice of deliberately creating Web pages which will be indexed by search engines in order to increase the chance of a Web site or page being placed close to the beginning of search engine results, or to influence the category to which the page is assigned. Spamdexing is the big no-no in SEO, and falls into two categories, *content spam* or *link spam:*

✔ **Content spam:** This type of black hat practice is intended to alter the search engine spider's view of the Web site so that it is different from what the user will encounter when they click through on the search results. All the techniques aim to boost the site's ranking in the results lists.

   • **Keyword stuffing:** Hidden, random text on a Web page to raise the keyword density or ratio of keywords to other words on the page. These pages are usually used to try to sell advertising by tricking search engines into sending searches there.

- **Gateway, doorway, or cloaking pages:** Particularly sneaky, these are low quality, hastily built Web pages that are stuffed with very similar keywords. These pages will then rank highly in the search results and will then have a link on them to the destination site.

- **Hidden or invisible text:** This tactic is the act of disguising keywords and phrases by making them the same colour as the background, using a tiny font size or hiding them somewhere else on the page or in the HTML. Doing so makes the site seem more relevant to the search engine spider, when in fact it will be less relevant to the user.

- **Scraper sites:** Scraper sites are in fact not sites, but programs designed to 'scrape' content from search engine results pages and Web sites, dumping it on a site that will then probably be filled with unrelated adverts. The content is designed to fool the spiders and attract users to the ads.

- **Meta tag stuffing:** This practice is the act of 'stuffing' keywords in the meta tags, so repeating them over and over and often using unrelated words to the page to fool the spiders. Unscrupulous site owners use misleading keywords to attract users to their sites, usually so they can serve up advertising

✔ **Link spam:** Link spam is specifically targeted at search engines' Web page ranking systems. These systems are partly based on the quality and quantity of links from other similar quality Web sites to the destination site.

- **Hidden links:** The act of hiding links where they won't be found by Web surfers, but where they will be found by spiders, in order to increase the Web page ranking.

- **Link farms:** These farms are created by designing a group of Web pages that all link to each other over and over and over. This makes the pages seem that they are more popular than they really are as the number of links that a site has, has an effect on its search ranking. This practice is also carried out with blogs.

- **Spam in blogs:** With weblogs, or *blogs* becoming more popular online, they've been targeted by black hatters who place random comments that are placed in the comments section of blogs that carry links to the spammer's Web site. These placements are usually found on any site that offers the chance to comment, has a visitors' book, or operates a forum or blog. This practice has even become automated with computers posting links all over the Internet.

- **Google bombing:** This tactic involves a large number of sites combining to link to one site and drive it to the top of the search listings. Doing so works due to the nature of Google's search algorithm, but is usually only used for malicious non-commercial purposes such as the famous use of a Google Bomb to promote a joke 'File Not Found' page that was returned top of the list when searching for the phrase 'Weapons of Mass Destruction' on Google.

If you follow the rules given out by the search engines and the white hat rules that we outline, you should have no problem creating a site that is visible to search engines and useful for users. But, to use a Star Wars reference: 'Do not underestimate the power of the dark side.' The draw of the quick fix that black hat practices offers can be alluring, but remember it was Luke saved the galaxy in the end, so following the righteous path is better. May the SEO force be with you!

Using an Expert

SEO is a complicated process and you may need to have quite a bit of experience in dealing with its subtle nuances. Well, luckily help is at hand. SEO agencies have sprung up all over the UK to feed the growing market for specialist SEO skills as search becomes big business.

Deciding whether you need to outsource

As with outsourcing any work to an agency, you need to go through the correct processes to ensure that the agency you choose fits well with your business and will be able to offer you all the services that you require. As search engine marketing covers a very wide set of skills you may want to shop around before you decide on a search partner. One thing to take into account is that hiring an agency that can handle both your SEO and also your paid search needs – the two together are often called *search engine marketing* (SEM) – can be beneficial. A number of agencies can offer you this service. The bigger media agencies that offer paid search services will most likely offer SEO services as well, but it won't be them carrying out the work; they'll use their own SEO partner to do it. This practice isn't a big issue, but obviously any degree of separation between client and contractor is less desirable than none at all.

So do you need to hire an SEO agency? Well, if you feel comfortable with everything covered so far in this chapter, then you're probably well equipped and educated enough in the market to manage your SEO strategy alone. But for the majority of people an agency or at least some individual expertise is required to implement an SEO strategy.

If you decide that you do not have the skills to take on the project yourself, you need to have a look at the market to find the best agencies. Don't be afraid to ask contacts or other industry peers as some of the best agency appointments come about as a direct result of personal recommendation.

Choosing an SEO expert

Here is a basic checklist to mark off against any agency that you're thinking of employing. Although not exhaustive, this list should be enough to point you in the right direction and weed out some of the more undesirable agencies and SEO 'professionals' operating out there:

- ✔ **Use the major search engines and search under the terms 'Search Engine Optimisation' and 'SEO'.** The agencies that come up top have obviously got their act together and are worth a look.

- ✔ **Check out potential suppliers' Web sites for work they've done.** Find out which clients they've worked for and any case studies and recommendations that the suppliers have. Any decent agency worth their salt will carry information on previous projects and you could even ask for recommendations based on the agency's client list.

- ✔ **Request a site review free of charge.** Decent agencies should provide these reviews free of charge. Site reviews show you how well the supplier operates and are an interesting gauge if you get a few of them to compare.

- ✔ **Work out what the supplier is really about.** Remember that in this instance we're talking about SEO, not paid search, so if agencies spend a lot of time talking about AdWords or other paid services they may not have the expertise that you want in SEO.

- ✔ **Set your price.** Insist on a set price for the work and set some targets to achieve as well. Setting up a payment on results model may even be possible.

- ✔ **Ask questions about the agencies' white hat and black hat practices (outlined in the 'Do's and don'ts of SEO' section, earlier in this chapter).** Ensure that you're not going to be working with an unethical company.

✔ **Make sure that the agency explains to you exactly what work needs doing.** Don't let the agency bamboozle you; you're paying them, so make sure they explain things satisfactorily to you.

✔ **Beware anyone who offers to get you to number one in the Google rankings.** Wild promises won't be true, certainly not by white hat practices only and without massive investment.

✔ **Protect yourself legally.** Get the agency to sign up to a money back guarantee or a document indemnifying your brand from damage.

✔ **Ask the agency how it will work with your other marketing efforts.** Any decent agency will want to know the whole marketing picture and really understand your company to achieve best results.

Following these rules should ensure that you don't end up employing the John Wayne of the SEO world. You can even ask for meetings in the agency's office, to make sure they actually have one. Following all these precautions may sound a bit drastic, and we don't want to put you off carrying out SEO, which can be massively beneficial to your digital marketing efforts, but you must be aware of all the pitfalls as well.

When SEO all goes wrong

For a perfect example of the power of SEO when it goes wrong, look no further than what happened to www.BMW.de when its SEO agency broke the rules over the use of doorway pages.

A doorway page, a fake front door to the Web site that is stuffed full of keywords that are relevant to the site but do not reflect the content of the page, was being used by the car company's SEO agency to fool the search engine spiders. The Google spiders read the hidden content and gave the page a ranking accordingly. However, when a human comes along to visit the page he is immediately re-directed to another Web page and see something that doesn't relate to the content that the page was ranked on.

This tactic is a black hat practice and is frowned upon by Google, which exacted swift and chilling retribution. Google served what is known as the 'Google Death Penalty' on www.BMW.de,

deleting its listing entirely and sending its PageRank back to the lowest possible value, 0. As a result, a search for 'BMW Germany', which before de-listing would have brought up the page at the top of the search results, would after removal from the index show no sign of www.BMW.de at all.

This issue has now been resolved and the BMW Germany site is back on the Google index, but the lasting brand damage that can be done through unethical SEO can last for a long time. Now if you search for BMW Germany on Google you're not given the www.BMW.de site at the top of the listings, but a Web page that talks about the SEO incident instead (see Figure 8-1). The story on the site comes out higher than www.BMW.de for the 'BMW Germany' keyword search as it has more links to it. This story provides a stark warning for anyone thinking of taking the black hat path.

Chapter 9

Understanding the Power of Google

. . . .

. . . .

*G*etting started in digital marketing and not knowing about Google is like driving a car without a steering wheel. You will get started, but you'll have trouble controlling the car. You can't be seriously involved with digital marketing without knowing about a company which has been responsible for shaping the Internet as we know it today.

Not content with revolutionising search as we know it and becoming the default search engine for most people using the Web, Google has launched a host of services which you wouldn't typically associate with a search engine. We explore some of these services in detail later in the chapter, but first let's look at the reasons behind this diversification.

Planning for World Domination

Google offers advertisers a wealth of opportunities, but its main two services are AdWords and AdSense.

> ✔ **AdWords:** AdWords is an advertising system that allows advertisers to place their adverts next to the results returned by search engines. It operates on a keyword bidding basis, which means that advertisers bid for the rights to certain popular search keywords, such as 'restaurant' or 'shoe-shops' with the winner of the bidding war gaining the top position in the paid listings when the phrase is searched for by users. Paid listings are found on the right-hand side of the results page under the heading 'Sponsored Links'.

✔ **AdSense for Advertisers:** AdSense gives advertisers the opportunity to place their adverts on partner Web sites to accompany contextually relevant content. It operates in the same way as AdWords and is usually linked so that you can choose to display your ads through AdSense as well when you sign up for AdWords. Again, the ads are shown in a special area on the Web site, usually found on the right-hand side.

✔ **AdSense for Publishers:** AdSense allows Web publishers to make money out of their existing content by allowing Google to place relevant adverts on their Web pages – in this case Google and the publishing site share the revenues for every ad that is clicked on by a user.

If Google wants to stay ahead of the competition then it has to diversify beyond search. Although search is a very valuable business, being in a position to offer Web services to the same customers that are searching is potentially even more valuable – especially when considering that with each service potentially comes additional advertising revenue. So, whilst Google is very much focused on search, the company is also seeking to establish itself as a Web site that provides a range of personalised services (also known as a portal) more like Yahoo! and MSN to help build closer ties with its customers. For this reason, Google in the last few years has launched e-mail – its *Gmail* service – and an instant messaging and telephony service, Google Chat. Google has not only sought to develop communication tools, the company also has Microsoft's domination of software in its sights, with the launch of both a spreadsheet and word processing tool.

For an idea of just how broad Google's offer is, go to www.google.com, click 'More' and then visit Google Labs. On this page you can see just what Google has been up to – and you can be one of the first to try out its new Web-based tools, software, and services.

Just within search, Google offers image search, news search, book search, and blog search tools as well as a host of search advertising products that it sells to advertisers and which we will discuss in much greater detail later in this chapter. But away from search, Google has numerous tools and programs, which the authors of this book are constantly trying out, so make sure that you check them out too.

As well as trying to build closer links with its customers, Google is also mindful that it has to be at the heart of the Internet's innovation, which is why it has its own blog-publishing tool – www.blogger.com – which is now the most popular on the Web. Google's determination to be at the heart of innovation means that the company's constantly launching new services to try and change the way people use the Web, for example with its Desktop Search tool. And where it can't or doesn't launch a new tool or service, then Google buys one and brings it within the Google family if it feels it will benefit its customers. Google really is a superpower within its own right – not bad for a company that was set up just a few years ago within the confines of Stanford University!

Google: A potted history

Google was first conceived by two US university friends, Sergey Brin and Larry Page, in 1995. They claimed that the search engine they developed to scour the Web was more powerful than any existing search engines.

Brin and Page approached a number of the major Internet portals to back their project, which at this point was called BackRub, but were told that 'our customers aren't interested in search'. So instead, they managed to secure nearly US$1 million in funding from friends and family, a number of venture capital firms and technology giant Sun Microsystems. Google got its name a few months later. Google (a play on the word googol) refers to the number represented by the numeral 1 followed by 100 zeros. Google's use of the term reflects the company's mission to organise the immense, seemingly infinite, amount of information available on the Web.

In September 1998, Google opened its first office in a friend's garage.

The next major milestone was the introduction of the AdWords service by Google in 2000. Despite the Internet industry being hit on all sides by the downturn, Google made the conscious decision to build a new revenue model to offer keyword targeted advertising to advertisers wanting to target consumers whilst they were searching. The decision marked a landmark not only for Google but also for the online advertising scene, which was struggling to sustain itself. By the end of 2000, Google was handling well over 100 million search queries a day and in 2004, it finally launched its long-awaited *Initial Public Offering* (IPO) on the NASDAQ, the online stock exchange. Google was seeking to raise nearly $4 billion, which then helped it go on a frantic acquisition spree as it sought to bolster its business to keep the competition guessing.

Since then, the search engine has grown enormously, and is now regarded not only as the search engine of choice for hundreds of millions of people around the world but also for some of the world's biggest Internet companies, including AOL.

Google and the Small Advertiser

Deciding to try out online advertising can be daunting if you're a small business and don't have the budgets of British Airways or Vodafone. If you're a local business, you may well be thinking 'why should I spend my limited marketing budget on advertising on Google', a worldwide search engine, that seems to have no relevance to your business whatsoever? However, if you look more closely at Google it is more friendly to small advertisers than you may imagine, and you don't need to be Amazon or Marks & Spencer to benefit from its search advertising services, which are as we write changing the entire advertising industry.

Google is built on a very solid technical foundation and this means that for an advertiser a myriad of options is always available to control and target an AdWords or AdSense campaign so that you can get maximum benefit from your marketing spend.

As an example of tailoring their service for small businesses, Google's AdWords system is self-controlled by the advertiser and gives you the opportunity to control your ads so that they only appear to people who are searching on your keywords in a particular area, say within 25 miles of your business. Other options include the ability to get your business information overlaid onto Google Maps (see Figure 9-1), so people can both see where your business is in a locality as well as see what you offer.

These options make Google a good bet for small businesses as well as still offering a great way to reach the maximum number of people.

In the new digital age you also don't need to be constrained to a locality just because you're a small business. Online retail means that your shop-front can be global – as long as you have your logistics organised behind the scenes. For Web businesses, Google's advertising services are a perfect fit as they offer maximum reach within the UK and abroad to Internet users.

Advertisers can really take what they want from Google and leave the rest – a selection of advertising opportunities for every business.

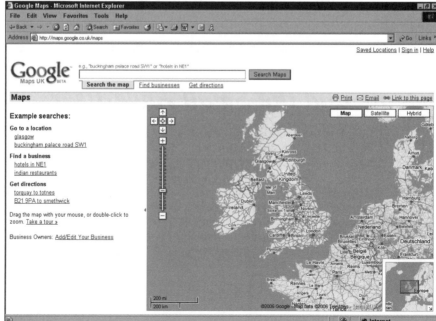

Figure 9-1:
Google
Maps
showing
local
business
listings
marked
on a map.

Why Should You Advertise on Google?

According to industry measurement service Hitwise, Google is used for 77 per cent of all searches conducted in the UK and in the US it has 60 per cent of the search market.

You simply cannot ignore these figures as they represent your customers. Not working with Google is the equivalent of setting up your shop in a dark alley when the bustling high street with all the customers is just round the corner.

Google's search competitors in the UK – Yahoo!, MSN, and Ask – all consistently score less than 10 per cent of the search market each. Now, we're not saying that this situation won't change – indeed online debate exists as to whether Google's dominance in the market is assailable or not – but these statistics show that the lion's share of traffic is going through the Google Web site. This fact doesn't necessarily mean that Google's advertising services such as AdWords are better than anyone else's, but you have to get in front of the consumers in the first place and Google is clearly the place to do that.

Google's competitors are beginning to take up the challenge. MSN has a new paid search proposition through Microsoft adCenter and Yahoo! Search Marketing is no slouch either, but if you look at the cold hard facts Google powers around ten times more searches in the UK than its nearest competitor.

If you haven't done so already, check out the services offered by Yahoo! Search Marketing and MSN through Microsoft adCenter. We're focusing mostly on Google in this book due to its dominance in the market, but the other propositions can work just as well for you, so take a look:

- ✔ adcenter.microsoft.com/Default.aspx
- ✔ searchmarketing.yahoo.com/en_GB

Quite why Google has managed to build up such a commanding lead in the search engine market is hard to say. The first search engine to use the spider or crawler based technology was called WebCrawler and was launched in 1994, the same year that Lycos appeared. This first search engine spawned a raft of others, including Inktomi, Excite, and AltaVista, but not until 1995 did Larry and Sergey come together to create Google. So the success of Google isn't due to first-mover advantage. Consumer perception has probably played some part in its success – Google is renowned for being a fun and funky company that fitted well with the early dotcom hype (although in recent years it has been accused of becoming too corporate and controlling, and sometimes has a difficult relationship with the press). The acid test for a search engine, however, is that it works well; Google returns relevant results to the user and that is why more and more people are using it.

This relevancy is another reason why you need to be advertising on Google. Online advertising is all about targeting the consumer at the right time. Google has built its dominance in the search market through its technology and now you can use it to reach your consumers.

Getting the Best Out of Google

An entire industry has sprung up around Google and if you go to Amazon and search for 'Google AdWords' you get back a whole list of reading material that promises to improve your use of AdWords and make you more money through the search giant. You can even read about Google in the *For Dummies* series: Check out *Google For Dummies* by Brad Hill (Wiley).

The good news is that you don't have to buy a load of books to find out about Google. If you're a beginner, then the search engine itself has a lot of online information that you can read through, a series of quizzes to see how well you understand their services, and even an educational programme that you can enrol on so that you can become a qualified Google advertising professional.

Using AdWords

Google has pages and pages of information about how to effectively use its AdWords advertising system – as this service is the company's main source of income – and to try and make it easier for you we pick out some of the basic principles on how to get the most out of AdWords.

- ✔ **Set goals.** As with any advertising you should set out some clear goals before you begin. Decide what your aim is and set some hard and fast targets against them. You may want to increase sales by 20 per cent or increase traffic volumes by 50 per cent. After you've set your goals you'll find it easier to manage your campaign to meet them.

- ✔ **Choose your keywords wisely.** The basis of AdWords is your keyword selection. We talk in Chapter 10 about how you should choose your keywords and offer some tools to help you. Remember to use plurals and synonyms for each of your keywords to ensure that you get the best possible results. After you've chosen your keywords Google offers Broad, Phrase, Exact, and Negative matching options that will all target your ads depending upon the exact phrase that the searcher has used. For example, Broad matching your keywords *running shoes* brings up your ads no matter where the words *running* or *shoes* appear in the search query, whilst Exact matching only brings up the ad if the searcher searches for that exact phrase. Now that you have your list of keywords and your targeting matches, you can group your keywords. In

AdWords you group your keyword by thematic *ad groups,* which trigger the same text when searched on so that the right ads appear when searches are made on relevant keywords.

✔ **Be creative.** Honesty is your best policy. The AdWords system is designed to return the most relevant ads to the search. So if the system's working properly and you've chosen your keyword strategy correctly, you should be advertising to someone who already wants your products. If you keep your copy honest and to the point you'll get the best results. Google offers a tool that inserts your keywords into ad text. The tool allows the user to create one advert and then have different keywords inserted into it depending on what keyword has been searched on. For example, you can be bidding on both 'diamonds' and 'rubies'. Your ad text could read 'Best Quality . . . '. The space left will be filled automatically by either 'Diamonds' or 'Rubies' depending on which term has been searched for. It saves you having to write different ads for every search term you sponsor. This tactic works well as it catches the user's eye and makes the ad look more relevant. Also try to include a call to action, getting the user to click on your ad. Above all, remember to follow Google's AdWords guidelines, which give you the do's and don'ts of what you should write: `adwords.google.com/select/guidelines.html`.

✔ **Think like a customer.** If as a customer you click on a link to buy running shoes and you land on the homepage of a sports shop promoting tennis rackets and footballs, you probably won't bother to search around for the shoes section. Make sure that the links from your ads direct the user to the information that they want to find and not just to your generic homepage.

✔ **Measure your success.** Use Google's and third-party tracking tools to monitor the success of your campaign. Remember, you have set identifiable goals and you should be able to see if you are meeting them or not. In 2005 Google made its analytics package – Google Analytics – free of charge. Using this package enables you to track how many people are clicking on your AdWords and other paid search ads, what ads they are responding to best, and what they are looking at when they come through to your Web site. To track users on your site you simply paste some code from the system onto each of your Web pages and the AdWords analysis tool allows you to track the *return on investment* (ROI) of your campaigns. Check out `www.google.com/analytics` for the package.

✔ **Try and try again.** If you haven't managed to meet your goals the first time, don't panic; you're now about to embark on the biggest part of paid search advertising – *optimisation.* Through your measurement process you should be able to see which tactics are working and which aren't. Optimisation is about experimenting and tweaking your campaign to get the best out of it. Try changing your ad copy, or the matching options on your keywords, or refine the keywords themselves. All these modifications can have an effect on the result of your campaign.

Take a look at Google's own advice on how to get the best out of AdWords at `adwords.google.com/support` and the company blog on the subject: `adwords.blogspot.com`.

Using AdSense

AdSense is Google's contextual advertising system. This means that your AdWords adverts are placed across a network of *publisher sites* – the business Web sites on which ads can appear – that have signed up to receive ads and are delivered depending on the nature of the content on the site and its relevance to your advert. You sign up to the AdSense service through your AdWords account. The AdSense programme is aimed at the publisher market and can be an effective way of making money from unused space on your site or to make money from your site if you're a content producer. Here are few tips on how to get the best out of AdSense as a publisher.

- **Be attractive.** No, we don't mean put lovely pictures of yourself all over your site. Just make sure that your Web site looks good to users, so it will look an attractive proposition to advertisers. By operating a clean and easily navigated Web site you'll get the best return from standard AdSense ads as your users will be more likely to click on the ads, but you'll also attract additional interest from advertisers. Within the AdSense system advertisers can choose to bid for placement on certain sites on a *cost per thousand* (CPM) basis rather than on a cost per click (CPC) basis. CPM means a set amount is paid for 1,000 *impressions* – the term given each time an advert is served up to a user. This element of choice means that if your site looks good, you'll attract more advertisers and get paid for every impression, not for every click on an ad, which is more beneficial to you.

- **Offer variety.** Google works with its AdSense publishers to develop as many different advertising formats as possible, including text, image, and video. If your site is capable of offering a full range of advertising options potential advertisers will look more favourably on it. The more options you can offer, the more advertisers will compete for the placements in the auction, so the more money you'll earn.

- **Try all the options.** Google has developed a range of different advertising options for AdSense. Alongside the straight text and more complicated image and video ads, Google has also developed:

    - **Link units:** These ad units display a list of topics relevant to the content on your Web site. When the user clicks on a topic they see a page of relevant AdWords results.

- **Referrals:** You can add buttons to your site to refer users to AdSense publishers.

- **AdSense for Search:** This option offers users of your site the ability to search using Google from within your site and results are given alongside ads – which can earn you revenue.

For more information about AdSense and how you can use it as a publisher, check out Google's AdSense help centre: `www.google.com/support/adsense`.

Also take a wander through the AdSense blog: `adsense.blogspot.com`.

Google Advertising Professionals Programme

The AdWords system has become such a part of the daily life of digital marketers that Google has launched an online educational programme to award qualifications to individuals and businesses in the use of their advertising platform.

The programme is designed to promote the use of AdWords within Google's framework and is seen as a badge of honour by those within the industry and a mark that you have a certain level of expertise with paid search marketing. An Advertising Professionals Programme qualification can be useful in demonstrating to employers that you understand and can manage AdWords campaigns and can be attained at a company level to allow agencies that manage client pay-per-click campaigns to demonstrate their quality.

In order to become a Qualified Individual in the Google Advertising Professionals Programme you need to:

- Sign up, then accept Google's rules of use for the programme, which include behaving in a professional manner post qualification and operating in accordance with the Google rules for AdWords.

- Manage at least one AdWords account, either yours or a client's, in the AdWords

My Client Centre – the control tool for handling multiple AdWords accounts.

- Build and maintain at least £500 (or the local currency equivalent) total spend in your My Client Centre account during the 90-day period.

- Pass a final Google Advertising Professional Exam to qualify for the right to use the qualification in conjunction with your work.

To achieve the company qualification you have to employ at least two qualified individuals in the programme and the individuals must be qualified under the main company registered My Client Centre account. Then you must build and maintain at least £52,000 total spend per quarter for the company's My Client Centre account.

You can find details of the Google Advertising Professionals Programme at `adwords.google.co.uk/support/select/professionals/` and at `adwords.google.co.uk/support/select/professionals/`. See Figure 9-2 for the homepage.

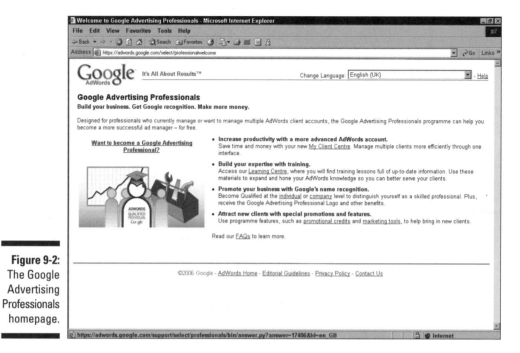

Figure 9-2:
The Google
Advertising
Professionals
homepage.

When Google Bites Back

You may think that nothing can go wrong when you use anything that Google has created for the advertiser or publisher. The company has certainly been very successful in growing its business and raising its profile in the short time that it has been around – but a flip-side to Google exists. We are not scaremongering, but we do want to show you what can happen if things go wrong.

Although Google's trademark policy means, in the UK, that you're safer in terms of competitors bidding on your trademarked terms, the policy in both territories is that you have to make a complaint to Google about the practice before they investigate. (For more details, see the sidebar 'Google versus GEICO'.)

Other issues covered elsewhere in this book can affect how you use paid search on Google and how you are ranked. These include *Google bombs,* which we cover in Chapter 8 and *click fraud,* which we examine in more detail in Chapter 11.

Google versus GEICO

Google and US insurance giant GEICO came to blows in recent years about the use of trademarked keywords in AdWords.

The original complaint was made in May 2004, with GEICO saying that the search engine was selling its trademark keywords to competitors who could then use the ads to direct traffic to their Web sites. According to the suit, the practice caused consumer confusion, in violation of the Lanham Act, the primary federal law covering trademark registration and protection.

A very long and lengthy legal battle ensued and eventually the warring parties settled out of court. The case received widespread interest from the search engine and digital marketing community and now Google operates two separate trademark policies with regard to AdWords, one for inside the US and Canada and one for outside the US and Canada. The crucial difference is that in the US and Canada Google only investigates the use of the trademarked terms inside the ad text, but outside the US and Canada it investigates trademarked terms in both the ad text and the keyword trigger.

Of these issues, *click fraud* is the most prevalent and occurs when a competitor deliberately clicks on adverts you have placed in order to cost you money. Click fraud can also happen when a publisher deliberately clicks on links on their own page to generate revenue for himself through AdSense. Google has taken people to court over this issue and has developed technology that can identify when click fraud is taking place, but it is still a problem and is proving very hard for companies to eliminate. Click fraud can happen on any service that offers a pay-per-click remuneration model – Google is just the biggest player in the market and so attracts the most attention.

Despite these issues, Google still represents one of the most important areas of digital marketing in the search field and if you're serious about being a digital marketer you need to use Google's services.

Chapter 10

Getting to Grips with Paid Search

• •

• •

*S*earch engines are becoming the *de facto* place where people go for information; sad as it is to see encyclopaedias being put out of business, they simply can't compete with the amount of knowledge online. You can use this to your advantage by getting to know the wonders of paid search.

Put simply, *paid search* is the service that is offered by search engines such as Google, Yahoo!, and MSN, enabling a business to advertise next to search results that have been requested by a user.

The system works on an auction basis using *keyword bidding,* meaning that a business can bid on relevant keywords that are entered into the search engine by users. The keywords that a user searches on determine what results they are shown. If you can find out what your potential customers are searching for, you can make sure that you are prominent in the paid listings by bidding on those keywords.

What Is Paid Search?

Paid listings are nearly always found on the right-hand side of search results pages and are often marked out separately from the natural or free results which make up the main bulk of the page – see Figure 10-1. They comprise a link to your site and a small ad blurb underneath that can describe what your company offers or highlight a special promotion. Writing these ads in the small amount of space you have is a skill in itself!

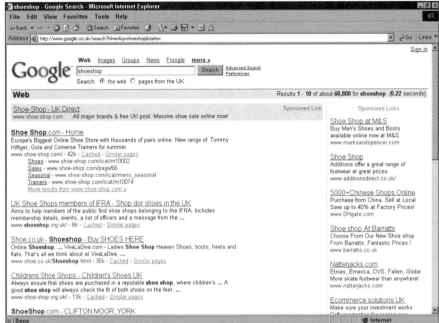

Figure 10-1:
Results
page from
Google
showing
natural and
paid search
results.

The difference between paid listings and natural listings is that you can't buy your way to the top of the natural listings. The top spot can only be achieved by building a good Web site, generating lots of links, and most probably employing a reputable *Search Engine Optimisation* (SEO) agency: See Chapter 8 for more on these. One of the benefits of paid listings is that you can jump the queue and go to the top of the paid listings by outbidding competitors on your chosen keywords. Doing so can be very useful if you want to get instant traffic to your Web site, say if you're running a specific campaign or special offer but don't have the time to undergo extensive SEO, which will take much longer. When a user sees your ad and clicks the link, they are then delivered to your homepage, or a page that you have specified they are sent to if you're using paid search for a specific campaign.

Another benefit of paid search is that if you choose your keywords wisely – we help you with this later in the chapter – you are advertising to consumers who are already interested in the product or service you offer. These consumers have made the effort to look for information on your chosen keywords through the search engine. The effectiveness of this advertising medium and the success that it brings to advertisers are the main reasons why the UK paid search industry was reckoned to be worth over £750 million in 2005 and why it has accounted for much of the growth of Internet advertising over the last few years.

A good test to see whether you should be doing any paid search marketing is to type in keywords relevant to your business and see who is listed there. If lots of your competitors are coming up then you need to do some paid search work otherwise your customer will never find you!

Every time that a user clicks on one of your competitor's ads you're losing a potential customer. In a worst case scenario, even though you've followed all the rules in Chapter 8 and made sure that your Web site is optimised for search engines and has a good natural listings rating, a competitor can still come in and steal potential business by having a good paid search strategy that places them at the top of the paid listings. Bidding on other companies' keywords is rife – although you can't always bid on competitor trademarks, as we explain later in this chapter – and if nothing else you should protect your SEO investment by carrying out some limited paid search marketing.

We explain more about the keyword bidding process later in this chapter, but it is worth bearing in mind that paid search is not a technique that can be set up and just left to run – it is in a constant state of flux. Competitors can *up-weight* their bids on certain keywords around promotions or products – increase the amount that they are willing to pay for each click on an ad as part of the auction based bidding system – or simply try and price other competitors out of the market. So if you decide to undertake paid search marketing, make sure that someone within your company or your agency is keeping an eye on your keyword bids to make sure that they're working as hard as they can for you.

Keyword bidding can become complicated if you decide to use paid search on more than one search engine. Unfortunately each search engine has its own system and interface for paid search, meaning that if you bid across a wide range of keywords and across a number of search engines the process can become very time consuming and complicated. If this happens, then you may consider using a search marketing agency – check out the section 'Deciding between in-house or agency', later in this chapter.

Paid Search Options

After you make the decision to carry out paid search marketing, the next thing you have to do is make some decisions about how and where you will direct your effort. The main decisions you need to make involve how many search engines you will use, and which ones.

Picking a search engine

In the UK, the big three search engines are Google, Yahoo!, and MSN. Of these, Google has by far the biggest reach. Figures from research company Hitwise in June 2006 showed that Google powered 77 per cent of UK Internet searches, with Yahoo! and MSN each powering 7 per cent. Each search engine is considered to have slightly different demographics, however, so thinking about who your customers are and where they may be searching for products and services is worthwhile.

Each search engine has information about its audience and reading about each one to see if you should be using their paid search services is useful. For example, if your business sells stairlifts for the elderly, then Yahoo!'s audience of young, affluent, and upmarket users – 46 per cent are 16–34 years old, 64 per cent are economically classed as ABC1 and 15 per cent earn £30k+ a year – may not be your best target market; if you sell MP3 players, though, Yahoo! seems a perfect fit.

Check out these pages for more information on users and search engine demographics:

- uk.media.yahoo.com/yahooaudience/yahooaudienceprofile/index.html

- advertising.msn.com/home/audienceprofile

Google has an almost unassailable lead in the search market in the UK at present, so if you're going to carry out any search marketing you'll be a fool not to use Google's service, AdWords. Not using this service means you'll miss out on 75 per cent of the entire market.

The other big search players, Yahoo! and MSN, each have their own systems that you can use to conduct paid search marketing. Yahoo!'s offering is called Yahoo! Search Marketing and MSN's is accessed through the Microsoft adCenter, which allows you to advertise across all of Microsoft's Web businesses including the search service.

Although the array of services may seem daunting at first, each company offers in-depth tutorials into paid search marketing and how their particular tools can be used.

For a brief introduction to each search engine, visit these sites:

- **Yahoo! Search Marketing:** searchmarketing.yahoo.com/en_GB/srch/index.php

- **Microsoft adCenter:** www.advertising.msn.co.uk/MSNKeyWords/default.aspx?pageid=902

- **Google:** www.adwords.google.com/select/Login

Choosing local or global search

After you've decided which engines you are going to list with, you should also consider whether your business needs to be listed on a local or a global basis.

Although casting your net as wide as possible sounds like a good idea, bear in mind the cost that will be associated with doing so. Yes, you'll get more traffic delivered to your Web site, but in terms of your budget, going global makes paid search marketing a lot more expensive. You have to bid against other companies in every country, as pay-per-click systems are based on geographical areas. This makes sense, as most businesses are limited by geographical area – for example, M&S would not want to bid against US companies for words such as 'underwear' as they don't sell in the US. So if you are a multi-regional company then you will be competing against different companies in each country and so it will be more expensive.

Think about the products or services that your company offers. Are they applicable to overseas users? If so, are you set up to accept payment from foreign countries? Do you have the logistical capabilities to ship your product to a foreign country? If the answer to many or all of these questions is no, then we strongly advise that you limit your paid search advertising to your local market. Although the Internet opens up the entire world to your services, you don't necessarily want to advertise to everyone. If you wouldn't take out a radio and press ad in China for your cuddly British Bulldog toys, then advertising to China online is a waste of time.

If you have a product or service that is available in more than one territory, then consider the option of advertising in more than one territory. Each search engine can offer you this service but bear in mind a few things before you begin. The bid values in different markets may be very different to the UK; minimum bids may be higher, which you need to take into consideration when setting out your budget. You must also comply with the editorial rules in each market, so you may have to rewrite your ad copy for each territory. You also need to understand consumer behaviour in different markets; just sticking up an ad won't do the trick if you don't understand consumer purchasing behaviour and online use in different territories.

The key to effective advertising is being informed. Each engine can give you more specific details on what countries you can advertise in and what rules to follow.

Deciding between in-house or agency

After you've chosen which engine to go with, the next big decision you have to make is whether to carry out your paid search in-house or to outsource to a specialist search marketing agency.

Pros and cons exist for both in-house and agency paid search. Carrying out paid search in-house means you have more control over what is happening, but you may not necessarily have expert skills. Employing a specialist agency may cost you more money than handling paid search in-house, but the agency may make your market budget work harder for you and so save you money in the long run. Also, dealing with paid search in-house means that you'll have to build relationships with the teams employed by the search engines, but the agency will already have developed these.

Tossing the pros and cons backwards and forwards, we come to the conclusion that deciding between in-house or agency paid search really boils down to just one consideration: If you don't carry out much paid search marketing then you can comfortably handle the process in-house. But, if you perform lots of paid search marketing, do you really have the skills and resources to handle it in-house? If not, then outsource.

Bear in mind that if you want to handle your paid search in-house you will be paying upwards of £20,000 a year for someone to look after it for you. If you are carrying out minimal paid search you can add it to someone else's job, but if your paid search is more extensive, you should think about whether it is more cost effective to hire someone to handle it in-house, or to outsource paid search to a third party.

If you decide to handle paid search in-house, you need to get at least a couple of people up to speed with the ins and outs of paid search marketing. Unlike many other marketing disciplines that you may have undertaken, paid search is a fast moving and constantly changing medium and unless you're on the ball you will lose out to the competition. Settle on two people, in case one leaves or is unable to carry out their duties. Having two staff with paid search skills ensures that you have continuity in your search marketing.

The people you put in place to handle search marketing should liaise with your other marketing people to ensure that they know exactly what marketing is taking place and can change the paid search strategy accordingly.

Keeping your search marketing staff up-to-date is important, because users' searches are often impacted by other marketing channels. For example, if a user sees a TV, press, or billboard ad for a detergent, they may not remember anything more than the name or the tag line of the ad. One of the first places they'll look for more information is through a search engine. If your paid search team knows that ads are out carrying these tag lines they can up-weight on those search terms and catch customers who have seen the ads when they search. See the section 'Integrating paid search with other channels', later in the chapter, for more on this technique.

Keep your paid search team aware of your marketing plans, make sure that they're taking advice and learning from the search engines' free resources, and ensure that they're aware of developments in the paid search market – such as new products and techniques.

If your paid search needs are extensive and you decide to use an agency to carry out your search marketing, choose wisely. Since the explosion of paid search marketing a few years ago, hundreds of small agencies have sprung up in the UK alone to provide services to the industry. Not all of these agencies are good and not all of them are competent. Some agencies can really make a difference to your paid search marketing, though.

A good starting point is looking at some resources online to get a feel for a few different agencies. You can try the Search Engine Marketing Professional Organization (`www.sempo.org`), a US-based organisation that has international, including UK, membership. Another good resource is `www.Semlist.com`, which gives a list of companies that offer paid listing management.

A few others worth checking out include:

- ✔ `www.bigmouthmedia.com`
- ✔ `www.searchlatitude.com`
- ✔ `www.spannerworks.com`
- ✔ `www.ambergreeninternetmarketing.com`
- ✔ `www.thesearchworks.com`

To help you choose your shortlist of agencies, the most important things to be looking for are:

- ✔ **Dedication to your account:** Make sure that your business will be high on the priority list of the agency.

- ✔ **Client list and case studies:** Check out what the agency has done in the past and how that work's regarded.

- ✔ **Memberships and associations:** Affiliations to trade associations such as Search Marketing Association UK, or the Search Engine Marketing Professional Organisation (SEMPO) indicate that the agency has good working relationships with the key search players.

- ✔ **Press cuttings:** Look at the cuttings the agency has on its site and also check out its profile online. Try a few searches on the Google News site and see what comes up.

After you've checked out the basics, you can move on with your shortlist and chat to your chosen agencies about what they can offer you and how they will work with you to get the most out of your paid search.

Discovering How to Bid on Keywords

With paid search, the devil is in the detail and the detail in paid search's case is in keyword bidding. Each search engine has its own services to guide you through the bidding process, but before you get to this stage you must first of all decide on what keywords are best suited to your business.

A few basic rules exist when it comes to choosing your keywords for your paid search marketing. The first rule is to ensure that the words that you decide upon match the products or services that you offer. This detail may sound obvious, but if you trick users into clicking through to your site from an ad, you are losing money, because they'll only be disappointed when they get there. So keep your keywords simple and truthful. The second rule is be careful not to bid on other people's trademarks – we go into this in depth in the section 'Looking out for trademark pitfalls', later in this chapter – as doing so can get you into trouble.

Start by brainstorming with employees to find out what people most associate with your business, and the words which are most commonly associated with your products. After you have your list – don't worry if it looks long at the moment – you can whittle it down to the keywords that you think are most relevant. At this point you may discover that although a certain word is most relevant to your Web site, it is also the most relevant word to thousands of other sites. Under the auction system that search engines use, you may want to shy away from these very popular keywords unless you have very deep pockets.

A good tip if you're using Google is to use the keyword matching options, which can improve results and lower potential costs. Using the service you can *broadmatch* your keyword phrases, meaning that if you use the phrase *running shoes* your ads will appear when a user's query contains *running* and *shoes,* in any order, and possibly along with other terms. You can also enter your keyword in quotation marks, as in *'running shoes',* and your ad will appear when a user searches on the phrase *running shoes,* in this order, and possibly with other terms in the query, but not when the words are out of order. You can even use a negative keyword match, which means that if your keyword is *running shoes* you can add a negative keyword such as *blue* so your ad will not appear when a user searches on *blue running shoes.*

After you find your main keywords you can get help from sources online that will give you more keywords that are not directly linked to your company's products or services, but can still be usefully linked.

Try out these sites for a start:

- ✔ www.wordtracker.com
- ✔ adwords.google.com/select/KeywordToolExternal
- ✔ inventory.overture.com/d/searchinventory/suggestion

Now that you've decided to carry out paid search marketing, selected your search engines to use, decided whether to handle the process in-house or through an agency, and selected your keywords, you're ready to start bidding on keywords.

For ease of use we explain the Google AdWords sign-up process as it covers the majority of the UK market at present.

1. **Go to www.google.co.uk/ads and click on the AdWords link on the top left of the page.** The landing page will give you a description of the AdWords service, how it works, the costs involved, and some case studies to look through.

2. **After you're satisfied that AdWords is the right option for you, click the Sign Up Now link at the bottom of the page.**

3. **You'll be given the option of signing up for either the Starter or the Standard Edition.** If you're new to paid search, choosing the Starter edition is best until you're more confident – don't worry, you can upgrade at any time. Check the Starter edition box and click *Continue* to begin creating your ad.

4. **Enter your Web site URL in the box provided.**

5. **Enter the text of your ad.** Information is provided to help you create this text, if needed. After you enter the text in the box provided, a sample of your ad shows up on the left so that you can see what it looks like.

6. **Enter your keywords in the box provided.** Again, tips are provided at this step to help you out.

7. **Choose your currency and set your budget.** This detail is handy as you now know that you can't spend more than this amount initially on your ad. When you have completed all these details, you can choose whether or not to receive information in the future from Google and click the *Continue* button to get to the next stage.

8. **If you already use Google services, such as Google Mail, you'll already have an account and can enter in the details.** If not, then you'll have to sign up before proceeding.

9. **After you sign up or log in, click the *Continue* button.** You should now see a congratulations page.

10. **Sign in to your AdWords account to provide billing information and to activate the account.**

11. **Fill in the account info section.** Simply select your location, choose your form of payment – you can pay by bank transfer or credit card – agree to the terms and conditions, and provide your billing information.

Congratulations, you are now a paid search advertiser!

Optimising your campaign

After you've managed the sign-up process you'll be given access to your account control panel, which enables you to control your paid search campaign. In this section you can add keywords, manage the cost of how much you pay per click, and change the locality of where and who sees your ads.

Optimising a paid search campaign is possibly more important than setting one up in the first place; the optimisation determines how effective your paid search budget will be.

You can optimise your campaign in a number of different ways, with both the agencies and the search engines offering their own optimisation services and technologies.

Google allows you to optimise your campaign from your AdWords account, allowing you to choose daily budgets, delete, pause or resume campaigns, and even schedule your AdWords campaign so that only at certain times and places will your ads be seen. Every search engine has its own optimisation tools and, broadly, they all let you do the same things – such as control your prices, keywords, and distribution.

If you're using more than one search engine but handling your search marketing in-house, one of the best ways to optimise your campaign is to go through a third party that has developed software that can manage all your paid search campaigns through one interface. One of these third parties is BidBuddy, provided by search agency The Search Works.

BidBuddy is a good example of how search agencies have taken the *Application Programming Interfaces* (APIs) provided by search engines in order to create tools that can work across different search networks. These tools can talk to all the search engines in their own language, rather than you having to have separate log-ins to control your paid search on each engine. See Figure 10-2.

As an example of these types of tools, BidBuddy gives you access to all the major search engines from one log-in; the ability to use timed bid strategies so you can manage your bidding at peak times; automated tracking of consumer activity; budget management and reporting; campaign projection tools so you can see how your campaign is likely to do and what its return on investment will be; the ability to manage all your keywords across all the different engines you use; and a keyword generation tool to help you target customers.

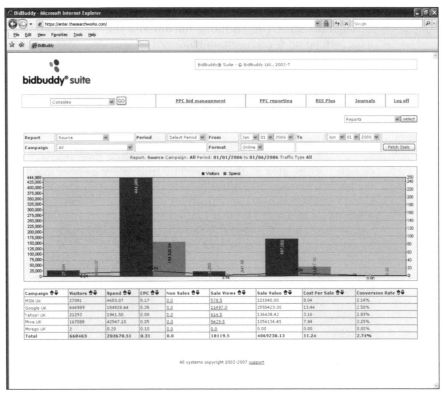

Figure 10-2: The BidBuddy interface.

These tools are handy as they save you both time and the hassle of trying to manage all your different accounts in-house. They also give you links to the expertise of the agency without necessarily having to hand over your entire paid search strategy to them. As a hybrid between in-house or going to an agency, using these tools is a good compromise.

When you optimise your paid search campaigns you'll begin to see what strategies work best for you. No right or wrong way exists to optimise as every business is different and has different customers. Luckily, paid search is a very versatile medium and you'll discover very quickly what works and what doesn't. If an optimisation strategy doesn't work, you can easily change it. The best advice we can give you is to keep your strategy simple to start with. Think about your customers and their behaviour. Chapter 3 describes how to find out about your customers to inform your marketing plan – refer to this chapter to find out how to discover some basic information on your target audience. Use the data from your marketing plan along with information from your Web site analysis to inform your paid search strategy. Armed with this information and the optimisation tools at your disposal, either through the search engines or a third party, you are well on your way to a successful paid search campaign.

Looking out for trademark pitfalls

When choosing keywords for your paid search marketing campaign you need to avoid bidding on other people's trademarks.

Google investigates matters raised by trademark owners in relation to trademark infringement through search. The search engine's Terms and Conditions with advertisers prohibit intellectual property infringement by advertisers and make it clear that advertisers are responsible for the keywords they choose to generate advertisements and the text that they choose to use in those advertisements.

In practice, these Terms and Conditions mean you can't bid on a rival's trademark on Google.

For example, if you've broadmatched *running shoes* on Google and someone searches on *Nike running shoes,* sees your ad, and clicks through, you've done nothing wrong as your keywords are *running shoes*. If your keywords are *Nike running shoes,* though, you're in trouble and your ad will be taken down – not to mention what Nike's lawyers will do to you!

In March 2006, Yahoo! adopted the same policy as Google in the wake of a number of lawsuits in the US and Europe over trademark issues involving search engines that carried ads for third parties that were using trademarked terms as keywords. So even if you think that stealing a competitor's traffic by using their company name or products as your keywords is a good idea, think again: You could be the one who ends up out of pocket.

Integrating Paid Search with Other Channels

After your paid search campaign is up and running and you've got to grips with optimisation, you can go to the next level by integrating your paid search campaigns with other marketing channels.

What this means is that your other marketing channels can now receive a boost from paid search as it picks up with the consumer further down the marketing lifecycle.

Here is an example: You sell cars and a consumer is interested in buying a car. They have done some research online; possibly they have even seen an ad of yours in the paid or natural listings. One evening they're sitting in a cinema waiting for a film to start and view your cinema ad for your latest model. They like the look of this model, but can't do anything about it as they're currently sitting in the dark. So they watch the film. Later, when they're driving home, they hear a radio ad for the car but only catch the tag line – 'the faster, the better'. When the consumer gets home, they want to find out more about the car, but can't remember its name; just the tag line comes to mind. So they go online, type 'the faster, the better' into a search engine and if you've integrated your paid search into the rest of your marketing, hey presto! Your ad comes out top of the paid listings. The consumer can now get the info they want and possibly even buy the car or arrange a test drive. Without integrating the paid search into the rest of your marketing you'd have lost that potential lead. The consumer would have had nowhere to go for the information, or worse still, could have ended up at the site of a competitor who is a bit more Web savvy when it comes to paid search.

That story is just a simple example of how easy it is to integrate paid search into your wider marketing mix. In order to make this strategy work, ensure that your paid search team or agency is fully up-to-date with your marketing department so your marketing efforts can pull hard together rather than sending consumers to rival businesses.

Uplift is the practice of getting more out of your existing marketing channels by using digital to increase their effectiveness and vice versa. As well as making other marketing channels work harder, search can also get a serious lift from other channels. The perfect example of this situation is the US TV event of the year, the Superbowl. Superbowl XL, held in Detroit in February 2006, had the eyes of the nation glued to their screens. Traditionally, this event provides a great opportunity for new adverts to be aired during half-time, and media prices skyrocket.

Interestingly, not only TV viewing figures rocketed. For the same event Yahoo! reported that consumer searches on the phrase 'Super Bowl XL Commercials' increased by roughly 800 per cent on the day after the game was played and advertisers including Cadillac, Honda, and Dove all bid on the phrase and took advantage of the resulting increased search traffic from potential customers who had seen the ads and wanted to see them again. Amusingly, other search terms that rocketed around the event were Appetizer Recipes – up 336 per cent, Chicken Wings – up 97 per cent, and Salsa Recipes – up a spicy 76 per cent.

Although amusing, this Superbowl anecdote has a serious point: It demonstrates perfectly the spikes of traffic found online that are created offline by other channels and events. The phenomenon was recorded by US search agency Reprise Media, who created a table to show those brands that had succeeded, and those that had failed the digital challenge – see Figure 10-3.

To reach its full potential, your paid search marketing strategy has to be integrated into the wider marketing mix.

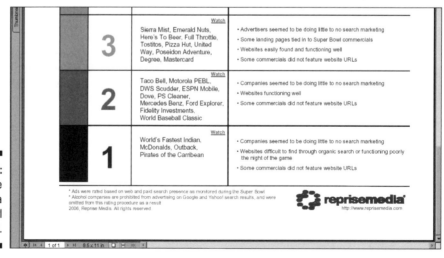

Figure 10-3: Reprise Media Superbowl XL scorecard.

Chapter 11

Checking Out Affiliate Marketing

· ·

· ·

*A*ffiliate marketing is as old as the hills and is just another way of saying *finder's fees.* Finder's fees are commissions that are paid to companies when they deliver customers to another company. For example, when a third party call centre signs up another customer for a mobile phone company they would be paid a finder's fee or commission by the mobile phone company.

Affiliate marketing programmes work by rewarding Web sites that deliver users to other Web sites, usually when the users click on an advert for the destination site on the affiliate's Web page. Affiliate programmes are usually used by online retailers who pay the referring Web site a fee for every con-sumer who completes a certain function, such as purchasing something or signing up for something. Although early affiliate deals were rewarded on a *click basis,* so every click that went through to the destination was paid for, this system has changed in recent years and it nearly always operates on a performance-based remuneration model.

The clicks are traced by the affiliate marketing network administrator which can either be a third party such as Google in the case of AdSense or the company that is running the affiliate marketing programme, that is, the destination site for the advertising. The clicks are tracked using online site traffic software that can tell the where traffic has come from as it enters the destination site and where it goes to when it leaves. Payment for the affiliate that is providing the traffic to the site will be billed on a per lead basis, so they will get a set amount for every person that they deliver to the Web site from the advertising on their site. This is commonly called *pay per click* as the advertiser pays for every click made on the advert.

Getting Others to Do the Work For You

Carried out correctly, affiliate marketing can be a remarkably effective method for advertisers to get people to their site to buy things or to get more people to view their site so they can charge advertisers more, as more people will view their adverts. Like paid search (see Chapter 10 for more), its payment by results nature makes it very Web friendly and means that advertisers are not afraid to get involved, as they only pay when they get results. Payment by results works well on the Web, because you can track every part of the process through software, something that is impossible for other media. You cannot tell exactly how many people have seen your newspaper advert or even your TV advert, but you can see exactly how many people have clicked on an advert online, so you can justify the cost of your marketing effort better than in any other channel. Web publishers – anyone who operates a content-based Web site – are keen on affiliate programmes as they can use up unsold advertising space – or *inventory* – on their sites and make money from advertising to help pay for the production of their content.

The idea of getting other Web sites to do your work for you is very appealing, but affiliate marketing can also be a very tricky beast and must be carried out within set guidelines otherwise it may do as much harm as good.

Affiliate marketing has a bit of a stain on its character in the UK. In the early days of the Web in the UK, affiliates were merciless *spammers* (that is, they generated huge amounts of unsolicited marketing mail aimed at customer inboxes), creating a lot of negative feeling towards them. In recent years this practice has reduced substantially: Now the problem is that affiliates have become big *spamdexers* – that is, they often use unethical SEO techniques to boost fake pages to the top of search engines hoping that users will then click on the links from these sites to the advertiser's page. See Chapter 8 for more on such 'black hat' Search Engine Optimisation (SEO) practices.

Other things to look out for when starting out on an affiliate marketing programme include managing your affiliates so that they treat your brand and company image in the correct way. Poor quality advertising or false advertising that leads people to your site will result in you losing business. Hopefully, poor quality advertising, or advertising that is not relevant to the destination Web site, will not be used for an affiliate campaign as the mechanics of affiliate marketing mean that an affiliate does not get paid until the consumer has completed whatever he was supposed to be doing. Unfortunately, poor quality and poorly targeted advertising is used all too frequently as the volumes of adverts involved in affiliate marketing can be very high.

Also look out for affiliates if you allow them to bid on keywords in paid search as part of your affiliate programme. Letting affiliates bid seems very attractive, as the affiliate sites can bid on keywords that you do not have to bother with, and you still get to see the results in the end. However, if your affiliates start to bid on keywords that you bid on directly, you will be bidding against yourself and paying a higher rate for that keyword. We cover these issues in the 'Avoiding Affiliate Marketing Dangers' section, later in this chapter, but they are worth bearing in mind whenever you are making decisions about how to carry out affiliate marketing.

You can 'go to market' in lots of ways with affiliate marketing, just as you can with SEO and paid search. You can decide to operate your own affiliate networks – groups of Web sites that work to drive traffic to your Web site – building up Web sites and keeping a tight rein on what they are doing. You can choose to create your own ads that are given to Web sites to use, give them brand guidelines from which to make their own, or you can use an agency to create your ads. Using an existing affiliate network set up by a third party is also possible. These types of service are widely available and we highlight a few later in this chapter.

Whichever route you decide to take, bear in mind that an affiliate programme is not something that you can set up and leave running on its own. Affiliate marketing requires constant service to ensure that it is running smoothly and delivering the results that you expect from it.

Deciding where to go

So how do you get started with affiliate marketing? Well, unless you're a big company with a lot of time and resources to spare that will allow you to develop your own programme, consider joining an existing affiliate network.

A number of affiliate networks exist in the UK and all have different affiliate member Web sites and focuses, so matching your business to the network that can deliver you the best results is important.

To begin with, here is a list of a few – in no particular order – of the bigger networks active in the UK today:

- www.tradedoubler.co.uk
- www.affiliatefuture.co.uk
- www.dgmaffiliates.com
- www.affiliatewindow.com
- www.buy.at
- www.paidonresults.com
- www.webgains.com
- www.linkshare.com/uk
- www.uk.cj.com/?setlang=UK

We won't go through every option that every affiliate network offers you, but as an example of how different networks can deliver different results the DGM affiliate network covers the travel, finance, shopping, telecom, and automotive sectors and the Trade Doubler network is used by companies including Dell and Dominos Pizza. So a lot of scope exists for shopping around, although almost all networks have strengths and weaknesses in different areas.

Every network is also likely to show you the three arms of its business on its homepage (see Figure 11-1), which are:

- ✔ Advertisers/merchants
- ✔ Publishers/affiliates
- ✔ Agencies

Work out which one you are, either advertiser or publisher, or if you are using an agency to handle all your affiliate marketing, before you decide to go hunting for a network. You may find that as well as using affiliates to drive traffic to your site, you may want to join a programme yourself as a publisher and make some money!

Figure 11-1:
Homepage
of affiliate
network
operator
DGM
affiliates.

Asking the right questions

Picking your way through the different affiliate network offerings can be a bit of a minefield, but when you are engaging any agency for outsourced work you should try to get as much information about them as possible.

Use the following checklist to select an agency, but remember that this list should only be used to whittle down your selection of networks to a few; the ultimate decision rests with you. These questions simply help you to identify which networks will be of more use than others.

- ✔ **Ask the network about their expertise in your chosen sector.** Ask them to back it up with examples and case studies if possible.

- ✔ **Get your potential affiliates to show you a client list.** They should be willing to show you any testimonials that they have.

- ✔ **Ask them about the size and breadth of their network.** Is it only UK based? What are the demographics? Online is the realm of data and if they want your business they will give you some to get you interested.

- ✔ **Check out the top ranking affiliate networks from a search engine results page on the keywords 'affiliate marketing'.** Search is a key part of affiliate marketing and this may say a lot about the network.

- ✔ **Talk about pricing and costs.** You are better off knowing what you are dealing with at the outset.

- ✔ **Come into the process with your eyes wide open.** These guys want to sell you the affiliate marketing dream, so don't get carried away with the hype; if it sounds too good to be true, it probably is.

- ✔ **Ask them what support and services they offer to advertisers and merchants.** Some networks will provide comprehensive support to ensure that affiliate marketing programmes are working effectively; on others, you may be left to fend for yourself.

- ✔ **Find out which networks your competitors use.** Being in the same network as a competitor can drive up the price of your affiliate marketing as your competitor may offer a better commission deal to publishers than you do, meaning publishers will try harder for your competitor than you, thus forcing you into a bidding war.

- ✔ **Ask your potential affiliates how they will protect your brand in the programme.** Your brand is your online currency and dodgy publisher practices can tarnish your image.

- ✔ **Find out what measurement technology the network uses to track clicks to your site.**

- ✔ **Discover what the payment basis is for publishers.**

If you have gone through this checking process you'll know that you have done your homework and less chance exists of something going wrong when you begin using affiliate marketing.

Understanding Google AdSense and MIVA

Both MIVA and AdSense syndicate advertising across networks of publisher sites and match the ads to relevant content. So if you're on a Web site of a publisher signed up to the AdSense programme and you read about motorbikes, the ad space features adverts from AdSense about motorbike shops, mechanics, and other related topics.

MIVA uses the same basic principle of matching ads to relevant content (see Figure 11-2) but is subtly different to AdSense.

Figure 11-2:
MIVA ads
on a page
of relevant
content.

Some people wouldn't call either AdSense or MIVA affiliate advertising programmes because they're both based on a pay-per-click measurement, whereas genuine affiliate programmes are based on lead generation. MIVA does have some other options, however, and Google is launching new services – which we cover later in this chapter – meaning they only deliver traffic to Web sites and the publisher is paid for that click.

For the purposes of this book, though, we've decided to include AdSense and MIVA here as affiliate marketing is their most natural home within digital marketing.

Google AdSense

AdSense is a contextual advertising programme from Google that allows Web publishers to earn a portion of the advertising revenue for placing Google sponsored links on their sites. As soon as publishers sign up to the system, Google places adverts on their Web sites relevant to their content. When each advert is clicked by a user who wants to visit the advertiser's site, the publisher gets a cut of the money that has been paid by the advertiser to Google for the service.

The main benefit of Google AdSense is that it is one of the biggest services in the market, so it has massive reach to bring in traffic. The downside of using AdSense is that you're paying for traffic, which does not guarantee sales and may amount to paying for nothing.

Google's AdSense seems to be a good bet for publishers as they simply get paid for every click, but this situation has led in recent years to questions over *click fraud* – where a publisher continually clicks ads on his own site to generate himself revenue or when a competitor continually clicks on a rival's advert to cost that rival revenue. The benefit of AdSense for the advertiser is not as compelling as in genuine affiliate marketing, where you only pay when the user completes a certain action.

Advertisers sign up to the service through an existing AdWords account, which we show you how to obtain in Chapter 10. After the advertiser has signed up, AdSense uses Google's search capabilities to serve their ads onto a network of Web sites based on the content within the publisher's Web site, and also dependent on other factors such as the user location – so if you're in the UK you are not served adverts about US companies that are not relevant to you, even if they are relevant to the content.

The service offers benefits for publishers because a relationship with the advertiser isn't necessary, and few worries over content and brand issues exist because the ads take a similar form to search engine paid results, which are simple and recognisable to everyone online. Another major benefit is that Google is superb at technology and all the AdSense ads pass through filters to determine how closely they match the content on the page, theoretically giving you the best chance of receiving traffic.

You can try AdSense for a while and if it doesn't work for you, then you haven't lost out too much. Take a good look at the service before you decide whether or not to proceed with it.

For more info go to: www.google.com/ads.

MIVA

MIVA is a collaboration between a number of different companies that have been involved in the Web business for many years, including FindWhat.com, Espotting Media, Miva Corporation, Comet Systems, and B&B Advertising.

The collaboration now specialises in online advertising and marketing. MIVA boasts that it delivers over 2,000 business leads to advertisers every 60 seconds and, like the Google AdSense programme, it runs a network of sites that take contextual advertising based on the content of the site.

Like AdSense, the process for setting up your ads on MIVA is very simple.

1. **Set up your MIVA advertiser account.**

2. **Choose the keywords you want to bid on.**

3. **Set your bid amount – how much you want to pay for each keyword.**

4. **Write the title link and description that you want to appear on the advert.** MIVA then matches your advert and keywords to partner content sites and also to relevant partner search engine results.

Both MIVA and Google also offer keyword-related search services so that you can add search functionality to your site as a publisher and generate commission every time that a user uses the search and clicks on a sponsored advert.

In addition to the pay-per-click model that both MIVA and AdSense operate, MIVA has pioneered a new service called pay-per-call. Pay-per-call allows an advertiser to bid on keywords and create tailored ads for their business and instead of the user clicking through to a Web site, they can call the advertiser on the displayed number. The addition of this service was designed to open non-Web businesses to the potential of search online.

MIVA has also recently pioneered *TXT//AD,* a service allowing you to advertise on the outgoing *Short Message Service* (SMS) message sent when a user of directory service 118118 requests a number. The ads can be targeted depending on what services have been requested.

For more info on MIVA go to www.miva.com/uk/index.asp.

Controlling Your Affiliate Marketing

To ensure that your affiliate marketing programme works for you, you must control it. If you decide to go with a network or use either Google's AdSense or MIVA's services, which we're sure 99 per cent of you will, then your chosen supplier will give you a campaign management tool. This tool is your friend and you should get to know it intimately. Don't take it out for wine and a fancy dinner, but do spend a lot of time getting to know the different functions that are available as a campaign management tool will save you time and money. The basic functions allow you to set bid amounts, wording of your campaign, and the frequency with which your ads are distributed. We can't possibly go into all the different functions that these interfaces provide, but asking your affiliate partner about the services that they can offer in this area is a very good idea.

Google has handy analytical software – formerly called Urchin and now rather dully called Google Analytics – which you can use to analyse nearly every aspect of your site, including affiliate ads and paid search. So if you use AdWords, check it out – this software's free to all Google account holders.

Control of your affiliates is not just the responsibility of the networks that you join; you also need to monitor the situation – after all, your money is being spent. Many networks encourage communication between advertisers and affiliates, while others try to keep the two separate sides apart. The more you can motivate your affiliates to work for you, the more return you'll see from your affiliate marketing pound. Affiliate network operator DGM says that some of its most successful affiliate programmes are the ones where the advertiser has got involved themselves, such as BT. If an affiliate programme is good enough for BT, it should be good enough for you.

Agency creative and brand guidelines

One way that you can lose control of your affiliate marketing is in the *creative executions* – how your adverts are put together and what they look like – that you use as adverts. If you use a creative agency to develop your adverts, you must decide if the agency communicates with the affiliates, or whether you use the agency for its creative skills and then handle the communication yourself. If you use an agency to handle all your affiliate marketing they'll have their own relationship set up with the network or affiliates. Drawing up brand guidelines about how your logo, company name, and so on should be treated is vital. Brand guidelines ensure consistency in the eyes of the public when they see your advertising. Adverts for the same company where the logos are different sizes or colours look totally unprofessional and will make consumers worry about the quality of your services.

Some companies have branding guidelines that are incredibly detailed in terms of what you can and can't do with a logo, as well as all the fonts and colours used in any advertising and the spatial relationships between logo and anything around it. For all but the smallest companies, some form of brand guidelines are very useful.

Gaining a measure of success

At the business end of affiliate marketing you can judge whether your programme has been a success or not by matching the results – sales, sign-ups, or whatever it may be – against the targets that you set yourself. All the tools that you've been given by your various agencies and networks or the ones you've been using through AdSense or MIVA will tell you whether or not your campaign has been a success.

If you've met your targets, then work out how you can improve the programme or tailor it to meet other specific targets. If it has not been as successful as you would've liked, ask yourself why? Analyse the data you have on the campaign and try to work out where you may have gone wrong or where you can improve. Maybe you need to tweak details such as the location of where your ads are viewed, or the wording of your ads, or the use of different pictures or graphics in your advert.

Remember, data rules online and now you've been through your first affiliate marketing campaign you should be armed to the teeth with information and ready to do even better next time.

Avoiding Affiliate Marketing Dangers

Once you decide upon whether to create your own network, outsource to a network, or use services such as those offered by Google's AdSense or MIVA, you then have the small matter of launching and controlling your affiliate marketing programme to consider.

When embarking upon an affiliate networking programme, set targets that you want to achieve. A campaign that has targets helps publishers and advertisers to work together. Affiliate marketing can be a little bit like Chinese whispers. As you are not fully in control of the marketing process yourself, you cannot be sure that everything is going how you want it to. The clearer your objectives are at the beginning – such as generating a certain number of click throughs, attaining as certain number of sales, or getting users to complete a certain number of actions – the easier your success will be to gauge and generally the more successful you will be.

If your programme has been well thought out and well set up, you shouldn't have too much to do as its smooth running will benefit all involved. Only when room is left for error can things go wrong.

When troubles do arise they are more often to do with miscommunication than with serious foul play and the better you know and can talk to your affiliates and the network operator, the less likely this is to happen. When bad behaviour does occur, however, it can be expensive.

Click fraud

Click fraud shouldn't affect you if you are operating your affiliate network on a *cost per action* (CPA) basis. This problem is most common in services such as paid search and AdSense, which is a type of affiliate programme that remunerates publishers purely on the basis of the number of clicks. Click fraud occurs when a publisher deliberately clicks the ads on his own site, generating himself revenue. It can also happen when a rival advertiser clicks on your ad to cost you money. Click fraud is still rife, but some major cases of people being prosecuted for it may mean the situation will improve.

Spamdexing

Spamdexing is a problem for affiliate marketers. Spam used to be the preferred weapon of the affiliate marketer who was from the wrong side of the tracks, clogging inboxes with ad links for people to click. As consumer behaviour has changed and more people now use search engines to find information, Spamdexers in the affiliate market have realised that they can trick people into clicking their ad links by fooling the search engines into thinking that their fake page is relevant to the user. Spamdexing is an ongoing problem and if one of your affiliates indulges in this practice, it can leave the consumer with a nasty taste in their mouth about your brand.

Keyword bidding

Search is often also operated on an affiliate basis, with affiliate partners allowed to bid on keywords surrounding the main brand keywords of the advertiser. If you undertake this type of affiliate marketing you must set very strict guidelines on what affiliates can and cannot bid on. If you don't control your affiliates, they'll start bidding on your own keywords and you'll effectively be driving up your keyword price by bidding against yourself.

All these issues should be avoided if you've struck a deal with your affiliate partner to provide commission on a CPA basis rather than a cost per click basis as it is much harder for the rogue affiliates to make money this way.

Part IV
Even More Digital Marketing

'You've just logged into a blog
from who!?!'

In this part . . .

Spreading your marketing message around the Internet can go far beyond your Web site, e-mail, and search. Use this part to learn how to work effectively with online communities and bloggers to develop and measure the effectiveness of an online advertising campaign, and prepare Internet public relations efforts. Finally, use this part to get an insight into the future of the Web.

Chapter 12

Controlling the Message with Online Advertising

*I*f you want to make a die-hard, traditional marketer nervous, then suggest advertising on the Internet. For although print and broadcast advertising are well-developed advertising mediums, online advertising is still viewed as the Wild West. Even getting two online experts to agree on the same terminology can be a challenge.

Online advertising, however, allows you to maintain control of the marketing message, especially as the online advertiser's armoury is much more than just the humble banner ad. So keep these three key questions in mind when planning online advertising: What do you want to accomplish? What ad formats are appropriate? How do you know when the campaign has been a success?

Working Out Your Goals

Every campaign should begin with a clear set of goals. Two typical types of goal for Internet advertising are:

✔ **Building brand awareness:** Raising the visibility of your product or service for brand purposes, introducing a new item, and/or reinforcing your offline advertising efforts. Awareness is crucial in the selling process; many customers won't buy from you until they've heard of you a few times.

The 'branding is advertising' trap

Advertising agencies will often approach companies and say, 'We can handle all your branding needs.' They can't. Branding isn't advertising alone and increasingly in the digital age, it goes far beyond traditional media and is much more about using the medium to engage the consumer.

Good advertising may be the outward reflection of a well-thought-out brand idea, but building a brand means building a customer's emotional connection to a product, service, or company. *Brand attributes* – what qualities make up a

brand – are built by a combination of customer service, public relations, sales process, packaging, pricing, and the product or service itself. Advertising a logo or company name is not, by itself, 'branding', any more than buying a swimming costume is 'swimming'.

Online advertising should play an increasing role in your branding effort, but it shouldn't be the sum total of your branding effort. Online's main strength is to enhance and bolster your brand activity being run across other media.

✔ **Acquisition:** Encouraging user action such as clicking the ad, visiting a Web site, purchasing an item, or filling out a survey. Acquisition is great because it is much easier to measure than awareness. Also, any acquisition-focused efforts will have some impact on brand awareness as well.

Be as detailed as possible when setting the goals for your campaign – but also be realistic. Do you want to increase orders on your Web site by 5 per cent? Boost recall of your company logo amongst your target audience? Increase the average add-on sale to your core product by £10 per order?

By being specific, you make measuring how well your campaign has done easier. By being realistic, you set achievable expectations and can more easily determine the appropriate amount to invest in an advertising campaign.

If you have trouble coming up with clearly defined, measurable goals, beware. You may have fallen into one of the two dangerous Internet advertising traps:

✔ **Me-too mentality:** Your competition or colleagues are doing it, so it seems as though you should too. As your (and our) mother said: 'If your friends all jumped off a building, would you too?'

✔ **One size does not fit all:** If you try to meet too many goals with one campaign you may end up meeting none of them at all, which is why you need to have your goals clearly defined.

Finding the Right Format

Now that you've decided what you want to accomplish, what are the most appropriate advertising formats to get you there? The most popular – and established – formats are banner ads, site sponsorship, e-mail newsletter ads, and search engine keywords.

Banner ads

Banner ads are the ubiquitous rectangular advertisements that run across the top or bottom of the most heavily trafficked Web pages. As one of the oldest forms of Internet advertising, banner ads are also one of the few with some standards. The Internet Advertising Bureau (`www.iabuk.net`) recognises a standard ad banner as 468 pixels wide by 60 pixels high, as shown in Figure 12-1. This space isn't much – filling only about 10 per cent of the screen area on a typical Web page – but provides enough for some text and graphics, often including simple animations. *Rich media* banner ads also exist that include HTML graphics. Generally recognised alternatives to horizontal, 468×60 banners are:

- ✔ Taller *vertical banners.*
- ✔ Smaller *buttons.*
- ✔ *Message plus units* (MPUs), which take the form of square adverts that usually occur in the middle of ordinary page content and involve text and graphics.
- ✔ *Overlays,* which are whole page ads, often animated, that take over the screen for a brief time.
- ✔ Full-screen *interstitials* – Web pages displayed before an expected content page. The user has to click somewhere on the screen to move on to the content.

Banners have fallen out of favour among some digital marketers because average *click-through rates* (CTR) – the percentage of users who actually click an ad – have dropped from 2 to 3 per cent a few years ago to 0.5 per cent or less now. However, average banner click-through rates aren't as important as several other factors:

- ✔ The *conversion rate* (the percentage of people who click through and take an action you're encouraging)
- ✔ How well a Web site your ads are on reaches your target audience (a better match usually means a better click-through rate)
- ✔ The quality of the ad graphics and copy (known as ad *creative*)
- ✔ The quality of the Web site the ad banner clicks through to (a bad or confusing destination Web site can destroy the conversion rate)

Also, banner ads that aren't clicked on still put your product name in front of a large number of people, much as TV and radio ads do. Debate continues between advertisers and online advertising networks as to how much this effect is worth. You need to work out for yourself whether this 'side effect' of banner advertising has value to you within a specific ad campaign.

Banner space can be purchased either from individual Web sites or more commonly through ad networks such as 24/7 Real Media, AdLINK, and ValueClick, which represent a number of sites.

Site sponsorships

Site sponsorships are a major step up from banner ads, in terms of commitment, and involve a brand sponsoring the content of the site.

As sponsorships are not integrated into site editorial content, they're not standardised in terms of duration or level of presence. But expect to commit to a sponsorship from one month to a year at a flat rate and expect to pay a high price. Sponsorships are most effective when the site's editorial content (and/or target audience) and your product or service are closely aligned: Toyota sponsoring ITV's F1 Web site, for example.

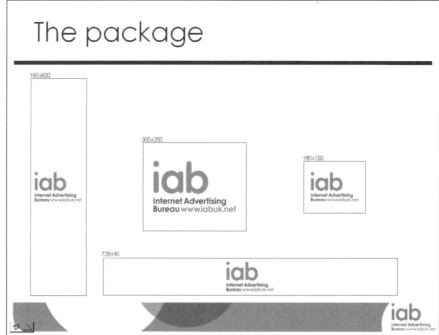

Figure 12-1: The standard banner sizes (as prescribed by the IAB).

If you're new to online advertising, don't make sponsorship of a site your first foray into online ads. Sponsorship deals, from site to site, can be very different and can be a significant commitment in terms of contract length and budget. Starting with banner advertising is a better idea. Typically, sponsorship packages include a package of banner and other online ads. If you get your feet wet with banner advertising first, you'll see what works before you dive completely into sponsorship of a site.

E-mail lists

E-mail discussion lists and newsletters give you access to some of the most targeted audiences, because – unlike a Web site, which attracts all kinds of people – e-mail list readers identify themselves to the newsletter publisher when they opt in to receive information.

Advertising is either in the form of short text ads of four to eight lines each, or in the format of an HTML newsletter that allows graphic ads much like banners. The key mechanism for delivering customers to you is a link to your Web site in the ad (see Figure 12-2 for a typical HTML newsletter from www.lastminute.com).

Integrating online and offline marketing

If you're doing any *offline* (non-Internet) advertising, then the key is to integrate your online and offline campaigns. Use any graphics, tag lines, offers, or other elements in your online ads to reinforce your other advertising and get the most out of your marketing budget. Apparently, seven exposures to an ad are needed to get a customer's attention, so in this multi-channel age, why not make sure that your Internet ads support that statistical goal?

For example, insurance company Norwich Union, owned by Aviva, has bought the keywords 'Quote Me Happy' from Google UK. The phrase features in all their advertising campaigns because customers were searching for the phrase online expecting to find Norwich Union. Using the same phrase helped them close the loop between their offline and online marketing effort.

The one exception to following an integrated approach is when you're testing a new logo, tag line, offer, or other concept. In this situation, your activity on the Web can serve as an ideal test bed as long as you choose online ad formats that reflect your business's overall target audience.

Figure 12-2:
A www.
last
minute.
com
newsletter.

Search engine keywords

Search engines like Google and Yahoo! auction keywords to the highest bidder, allowing you to target specific searches on the service. For example, if you sell football boots, you would want to buy the words 'football' and 'boots' to secure the best ranking. Keyword auctioning is now a multimillion pound industry but it doesn't stop companies from trying to bid for keywords – so being specific is crucial.

Keywords are sold on a click-through basis, but even if your ad is not clicked on, it can still deliver brand awareness.

For more on the vehicles of traditional advertising, see *Marketing For Dummies* by Craig Smith and Alexander Hiam (Wiley). This book covers print, radio, TV, and outdoor ads – all of which can mesh with your Internet ad efforts.

Clinching the Deal

The three most important words to remember when buying online advertising are *clinching the deal.*

Online inventory, more than in any other media, is elastic. You can only cram so many 30-second spots into an hour of TV, or column inches of advertising into a newspaper. But when owners of a Web site decide that they want more ad inventory, they can just make a Web page longer or add more Web pages – for significantly less cost than a print publication faces when printing and distributing more pages.

No hard and fast statistics exist on the amount of unsold ad inventory in the UK but according to the IAB, around 85–90 per cent of online ad spend goes to the top 20 sites such as Yahoo! and MSN. This situation means that a lot of unsold inventory exists on other sites, so Web site publishers try to maximise the value of this by joining ad networks such as 24/7 Real Media. Advertising on major sites or with niche players who have a very specific audience can be expensive, but ad networks will charge you anything down to about 50p for 1,000 banners on their network of sites. Even so, there will usually have to be a total bottom limit of about £500 for a campaign to make it worth their while.

A few words about words

To appear in the know in online advertising, you've got to speak the lingo (or, at least, realise that a language is being spoken). Some terms you'll come across include:

✔ **Cost Per Thousand (CPM):** The amount it costs to buy 1,000 ad impressions. CPMs can range from 50p for non-specialist inventory to upwards of £100 for highly targeted sites and e-mail newsletters, meaning that each respective impression costs 10p. CPM is the most common way to price online advertising. (Why 'M' for 'thousand'? 'M' is the equivalent Roman numeral.)

✔ **Cost Per Click (CPC):** What an advertiser pays the site or e-mail newsletter for every individual click on his or her ad. CPC is generally disliked by those selling the ads because they get paid only if the ad performs, and ad sellers (accurately) point out that CPC compensation is dependent on factors out of their control – the quality of the ad creative and of the Web site the ad clicks through to. But CPC is a good deal for you – the advertiser.

✔ **Impression:** One of the fuzziest words in the online advertising lexicon. When you're buying CPM, you're buying per 1,000 ad impressions. On the surface, it seems that the definition should be clear: An impression is counted when someone sees the ad, right? But how and when that count is made is the subject of significant advertising industry debate. Is it counted when the ad is requested from the server? Is it counted when the ad's completely delivered to the final pixel? As you may expect, media agencies like to count impressions when they're requested from the ad server (even if the viewer clicks away before the ad loads) and ad buyers like to count them when they're fully delivered. Make sure that you know what you're paying for – the difference between the two counting methods can be 10 to 20 per cent.

Size matters

When you're planning to buy online advertising, remember these two words in addition to 'everything is negotiable': Size matters.

The size of the deal, and the size of your company, matter a great deal to the media agency or Web site you're buying from. Basically, if you're a small fry, you pay top whack for poor placement. If you're a big fish, you can cut a much better deal.

What if you truly are a small fry? Follow the example of the pufferfish: Appear bigger than you really are. Conduct yourself professionally; especially, don't appear over-eager. Talk about your growth plans and the size of your target market, and describe the planned campaign as a 'first step' toward possible future business.

But don't get so caught up in your own hype that you spend more than you can afford. Do negotiate as if you were a much bigger business – which, if you do everything right, you soon will be.

Never buy an ad based on *hits*. A hit is simply a request to a Web server for an element on a Web page. That request could be for a graphic, a text block, or a button and is a largely useless measure of the popularity of a Web site. Far better is to buy ads based on *page views* (the number of full pages that are actually served up by the site) or *unique visitors* (the number of individuals who come to a site). The site should be able to provide those statistics; ideally, the source of the numbers should be a neutral, third-party Web site measurement firm.

The purchase process

To prepare to buy an online advertising campaign, start at the Web site on which you're interested in placing ads. For an e-mail list, go to the list's home Web site or send an e-mail to the list moderator asking for advertiser information. Look or ask for a *media kit,* which contains current ad pricing on a *rate card,* with rates usually listed as cost per thousand (CPM) impressions, as shown in Figure 12-3. Then politely ignore it.

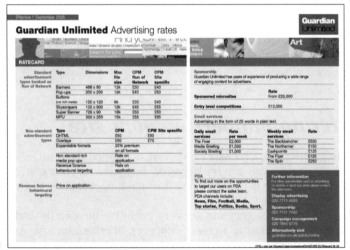

Figure 12-3:
A typical
rate card.

Rate cards have become one of the most popular works of fiction published online. Rarely are significant campaigns ever bought based on rate card rates. But the key word is *significant,* as rate cards give you an indication of prices and a good starting point for bargaining.

Structuring an online campaign based on a hybrid payment model is also possible – balancing a lower CPM with a modest CPC of, say, 10p per click-through, for example. This model offers the publisher the carrot of higher revenues if the campaign is a success, but ensures you're not out of pocket if things go wrong. Alternatively, if you have a product, service, or Web site audience of interest to the site or e-mail list with which you want to advertise, you can structure some or all of the transaction as a *barter or contra* deal. But be careful: Generally, bartering occurs at the rate card price, so make sure to adjust the value of what you're bartering with to make sure you get value for money.

Bartering banners on your site

If you're looking to keep costs down, but still get some more exposure and traffic to your site, you can try bartering ad space on your site for advertising on others. Bartering is usually done through link or banner exchanges.

These bartering arrangements are very primitive but can be useful as a first step to online advertising. Beware, however: In return for space on your site you may get to place banners across the network, but the quality of banner that will be shown isn't guaranteed. Poor placement of your ad or a shoddy campaign can sometimes do more harm than good.

When to call in a professional

If you're uncomfortable negotiating media buying, you need advice on setting ad campaign goals, don't know what a realistic budget is, or don't know how to create effective ads, an agency can help. Interactive ad agencies have sprung up everywhere and this area's now big business. Agencies and individual ad consultants excel at:

- ✔ **Cutting the deal:** They've done this before and are likely to be on top of the shifting sands of what's currently 'standard' practice in a still non-standard industry.

- ✔ **Getting the best rates:** Agencies may already have placed ads with the sites you're targeting. Their existing relationship – and knowledge of how far to push – can be an asset.

- ✔ **Creating killer creative:** An ad campaign is no better than its worst creative – that is, graphics and ad copy – either on the ad or on the destination Web page. Agencies either have in-house creative teams or can recommend freelancers.

- ✔ **Test, test, test:** A good agency knows how to rotate and test which ads get the best response, helping ensure that only ads that pull the best are the ones that are running.

If you're a small or medium-sized company, look for an agency of similar size. Odds are that you'll get more attention from the principals, and the cost structure will come without the large agency overhead. You can find interactive agencies through referrals on discussion groups, advertising e-mail lists, or from colleagues. Or simply find an online ad campaign you like and e-mail the advertiser about the agency it used.

Don't try online ad creative yourself, unless you already have experience doing it. The combination of skills – short, punchy copywriting, tiny yet effective graphic creation, and banner sizing and looping – are best left to people who do it for a living. A creative firm can also handle all the technical details of ads, such as knowing the maximum file size a site will allow, and acceptable colour palettes. Do understand what your goals and your advertising call to action are. But leave implementation to either a freelancer or an agency with experience in creating interactive ads so that your company looks good.

Still tempted to create your online ads yourself? You can find a number of freeware and shareware ad banner creation tools online. But remember that just as desktop publishing software was once credited with giving anyone the power to create incredibly ugly newsletters, many of the banner creation tools have done the same for interactive ads. So your ads will look basic and you will fail to stand out against your competition.

Measure by Measure

Ultimately, you'll want to know whether your ad campaign was a success. One simple and effective way to determine your success is to calculate the *Cost Per Action (CPA)*.

Say you buy 1 million ad impressions at £10 CPM. The ads had a click-through rate of 2 per cent and a subsequent conversion rate of, say, people filling out a form for more info, of 10 per cent. (You should have been tracking all these stats, or had your agency track them, throughout the campaign.)

1. **Calculate your CPA by taking the total cost of the ad campaign and dividing it by the number of customers who took the desired action.**

2. **Calculate the total cost of the campaign, by multiplying (1,000,000 impressions/1,000) by ($10 cost per thousand) for a total cost of $10,000.**

3. **Calculate how many people took direct action, by multiplying (1,000,000 impressions) by (0.02 click-through rate) by (0.10 conversion rate) to make a total of 2,000 total actions.** (Alternatively, you can track total actions directly on your Web site, if you feel that you can identify their source.)

4. **Calculate the final CPA.** Five pounds each in this example: $10,000 total cost divided by 2,000 desired actions.

With any luck, the value of each desired action was $5 or more. (If the desired action was to buy a $99 magazine subscription, you've done well; if it was to fill out a form for more information leading to a $4.50 purchase, you've overspent.)

CPA is most useful in determining the effectiveness of ad campaigns focused on generating a clear-cut action, such as completing a sale, filling out an online registration form, or attracting visitors to a Web page. However, measuring CPA to determine the effectiveness of your campaign does have flaws. Customers can easily see your ad, not click through, but return to your site later and complete the action – so remember to look at the total number of actions, as well as those that have come direct from your advertising, before deciding whether your campaign has been a success or not.

Using CPA to determine the effectiveness of an awareness-focused campaign isn't possible. These campaigns are much harder to measure, as TV adverts have been proving for years. For these campaigns, surveys on your Web site or pop-up window surveys on Web sites where you placed your ads may be more useful. An interactive agency may be able to help you with measuring the success of an awareness-orientated campaign using specifically designed tools.

No online ad campaign should be considered complete until you close the loop that begins with goals and ends with measurement.

Chapter 13

Spreading the Word with Internet PR

In This Chapter

▶ Targeting Internet public relations efforts

▶ Planning an Internet PR campaign

▶ Getting your press releases distributed

▶ Tracking your press release coverage

Despite the high-tech communications made possible by the Internet, one of the best ways to market a product online is through word of mouth and buzz marketing.

The primary marketing tactic for generating word-of-mouth buzz is *public relations* (PR), which is the ongoing management of a company's public image and how it's perceived by the wider public.

Whereas advertising gives you control over the message you want to convey, public relations gives you the unique power to influence. But unlike traditional PR, online PR provides a direct channel to your target audiences without always having to use the filter of the media.

In this chapter, we focus on how to understand and take advantage of the differences between Internet public relations and traditional PR. For a basic understanding of public relations in general, see *Marketing For Dummies,* by Craig Smith and Alexander Hiam (Wiley).

Whom Do You Want to Influence?

Public relations is primarily about relationships: Between your company and reporters and between the reporters and their audiences. And the first step in successful Internet PR is knowing which relationships you want to cultivate and which channels you're going to use to do that.

Targeting the right contacts

When you've targeted an audience for your product or service (Chapter 2 tells you how), you next need to determine the digital media these customers rely on for their information. Are they trade industry sites? Internet-only publications and trade magazine Web sites? Specific discussion groups or random blogs?

Next, work out who decides what editorial content goes into each of these media vehicles. Check publication Web site 'Contact Us' pages, and get the names of message board moderators and bloggers. Build a list of the key contacts you develop, or several lists if your products or services have multiple distinct audiences, particularly if they're niche products.

Finding the right Internet media contacts can require a fair amount of research. For Internet-only publications, check directories like those in the News & Media category of Yahoo!; for blogs search Technorati (www.technorati.com) or BritBlog (www.britblog.com); and for trade magazines, check out a directory like the bradgroup (www.intellagencia.com) or speak to contacts within your industry.

Make sure you set your sights on realistic coverage goals. If you're the manufacturer of hiking boots, odds are you won't be profiled in *Management Today* – unless your CEO is a celebrity. But you may be profiled in outdoor and adventure specialist publications and on their Web sites.

 Keep in mind that print publications that cover your industry or appeal to your customers are more than likely to have Internet editions – and in many cases, those Internet versions have additional content not found in the offline version. For example, both FT.com (www.ft.com), the online version of the *Financial Times,* and media industry trade site MediaGuardian (www.mediaguardian.co.uk) feature significant amounts of content that you can't find in their print editions. These Web versions may have news desks that are separate from their print or broadcast counterparts, with a separate list of contacts.

Conversely, realise that some Web publications can't be influenced directly. Sites that rely on getting all their editorial content from sources outside the site itself have no editorial departments of their own to influence. In order to reach them, you have to know what their sources of editorial content are. These sources may be:

✔ **PR wire services:** For example, PR Newswire or BusinessWire

✔ **News wire services:** Such as Press Association or Reuters

✔ **Specialised content sites:** Including, say, ZDNet for tech news

Don't forget that your company's PR efforts may have more target audiences than the general marketing audiences for your products or services. Two common additional targets are analysts who follow your industry and the financial and investment press. Make a list for the online constituencies of each of these as well.

Using the right touch

After you develop a list of contacts, start your approach slowly. Indiscriminately blasting out a press release via e-mail to your new contact lists is probably the best way of alienating reporters and analysts – because you're creating spam! When researching editorial contacts, pay attention to how the contacts like to be approached – e-mail, telephone, fax, or not at all. Respect these wishes. Check if these contacts are happy to receive attachments; lots of journalists aren't and will just delete all e-mails with attachments. Having your well-crafted release deleted the minute it enters an inbox is the last thing you want to happen.

If you're not sure of the best approach, ask. Most reporters don't mind a very brief (one- or two-sentence) e-mail in which you introduce yourself, confirm that they cover what you think they do, and enquire as to how they would prefer to be contacted in future.

Fee-based Internet resources exist for finding editorial contacts and their preferences. Two of the best known are Gorkana (www.gorkana.com), shown in Figure 13-1, and MediaDisk (www.romeike.com/mediadisk).

The best place to start, though, is on the Web sites of publications that you already know reach your target audiences. No substitute exists for first-hand research and relationship building.

Make sure you're aware of the media outlet's news cycle. Sites with print monthly, weekly, and daily counterparts have different deadline structures, as do broadcast media and Web-only news sites. Not every Web site is updated daily; the ones that are can be pretty hungry for new comments and breaking news, so plan accordingly.

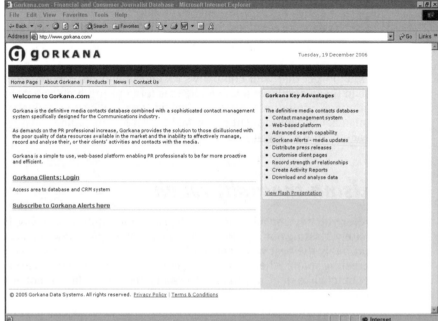

Figure 13-1:
Gorkana
provides
journalist
contacts
and prefer-
ences.

Planning an Internet PR Campaign

When you know whom you want to influence, you're ready to determine what you want to tell them.

As with any marketing tactic, your Internet public relations effort has to start with a plan. Effective public relations is not just about grinding out reams of press releases. Good public relations is about getting the right messages to the right audiences – which may be conveyed by press releases or by other means.

This PR rule is even more true of Internet PR because of the speed at which a message can travel and be posted on news Web sites, public relations Web sites, in blogs, and in discussion groups, sometimes with biting commentary.

In creating your Internet PR plan, determine what messages are important to your company and interesting to the press, how often you want to convey those messages, and whether you have the time and expertise to do it all yourself.

Messages are key

Before communicating with the press, ask yourself: What are your three key messages? In press communications you may be tempted to spew every tiny detail about your company. But face facts: Reporters, like anyone else, are busy people. Think about a unique aspect of your product or service that makes a difference to your target audience. Are you the fastest, the cheapest, the first? And why should anyone care? Consider the classic feature/benefit split.

Then take those messages and simplify, simplify, simplify. Unlike in advertising, in PR you can't influence how the message will be interpreted and filtered. The simpler and cleaner the messages, the more likely they'll be to survive the media grinder. Realise that your message, no matter how pretty, will be reworded and possibly re-interpreted. So, the message should be 'the first widget that gets computer screens squeaky clean', and not 'the first robust, scalable technology platform that utilises industry standard architecture to polish monitor surfaces to 98.6 per cent of their factory-manufactured tolerance'.

After you identify your key messages, repeat them in all your communications. And communicate only three messages, maximum. Anything else will get lost in translation because reporters have only so much space and time.

Excuse me, did you say something?

Your key messages are constants that permeate your news communications. But in order to make news, you can't just repeat your messages; you have to have a *news hook* – information that is likely to arouse a journalist's interest. And nowhere is that more important than on the Internet, where timeliness is crucial.

Typical times to contact the press – online or off – are when significant company news exists in the eyes of your target audiences. Such news includes new strategic relationships, new products, executive-level personnel changes, and so on.

But you can't leave news to chance, because you want your company and products to appear in the news regularly. Your PR plan should indicate how often, on average, you want to contact each news media target audience (see the 'Whom Do You Want to Influence?' section, earlier in this chapter) with company news.

Having a plan doesn't mean that you must slavishly stick to this schedule, but it gives you something to shoot for in terms of resources and budgeting: 'Contact industry analysts each quarter by e-mail', or 'Pitch key editors on a feature story every six months', or 'Distribute company press release every three weeks' may be targets.

Using Internet marketing means that you can have many more meaningful, casual contacts with members of the news media by using e-mail. You can politely e-mail a reporter who does an industry round-up (and didn't include your company) with a brief introduction, for example. The key to any of these casual contacts is to keep them brief.

PR agency or not?

You can do an awful lot of PR work yourself. But in some instances, hiring an outside public relations agency, PR freelancer, or marketing consultant to handle your PR makes sense. You can use outside help:

- ✔ To assist with messaging and planning when you can't get enough objective distance from your own products and services
- ✔ To ensure rapid turnaround of incoming press enquiries by e-mail or telephone; same day is a must, with a one-hour response the ideal
- ✔ To develop press lists from databases of contacts they have built from previous work or from specialised databases to which they have access
- ✔ To leverage their existing relationships with members of the press and knowledge of how media outlets like to be approached
- ✔ To write releases and other press materials, both online and offline, if you don't have the ability or time to do it well yourself

Do you need one of the many new agencies that 'specialise' in Internet PR? Probably not. As with everything from books to news, the Internet has rapidly become just another distribution channel and medium for press information. As more reporters have gone online, the PR professionals have followed.

But if all you get when you mention blogs, e-mail newsletters, communities, and forums are blank looks, go elsewhere.

PR planning by pixel

If you need help doing public relations planning, a number of discussion groups, trade magazines, and Web sites may be of help.

Consider looking at the different industry body Web sites. The best-known bodies in the UK are the Chartered Institute of Public Relations (www.ipr.org.uk), the Public Relations Consultants Association (www.prca.org.uk), and, globally, the International Public Relations Association (www.ipra.org).

Preaching to the choir

One of your most important audiences for PR is the employees in your company. Make sure that you distribute all press releases to everyone in your company so that all employees kept up-to-date. Do the distribution in a timely manner; the press release should go out on company e-mail or the company Intranet no later than when the release is distributed to the news media. That timeliness prevents the morale-killing phenomenon of reading about your company's latest news online or in the paper before the company tells its employees about it.

And make doubly sure to tell everyone about press mentions; such mentions can create the kind of morale boost that money can't buy.

Getting Your Release Distributed

Although PR is much more than just distributing press releases, the press release is still the primary communications medium. And putting it on paper has rapidly diminished in impact and importance as reporters have turned to the Internet for research.

Ready for release

When writing your press release, keep the following Internet-inspired changes in mind:

- ✔ **Keep it short.** The equivalent of a page to page-and-a-half of printed text is more than enough. Take into account that your release may be posted, verbatim, on blogs and message boards. Brevity is the basis of good online communication.

- ✔ **Provide links to more information.** These can be links to a news area on your Web site for background too detailed for a press release or for downloading high-resolution product photographs and company logos.

- ✔ **Include URLs and e-mail addresses for your company.** The *boilerplate* at the end of the release should include where you're located, your URL, and a brief description of the firm. Don't forget press contact info – telephone numbers, e-mail addresses, and a physical address. If you expect the release to be controversial or of wide interest, include the mobile number or even home phone number of the primary PR contact for your company.

Don't include anything in your press release that can't be reproduced as plain text – no special characters such as the trademark symbol (use '(TM)' in plain text instead), and no embedded graphics or HTML tags. Any non-text elements can get garbled in transmission and mess up your whole message. If something doesn't work in plain text e-mail, it shouldn't be in your press release.

Putting it on the wire

To get the release to reporters, you can (and should) maintain an in-house press e-mail distribution list. But press-release distribution services, or PR wire services, will broadly circulate your release to reporters and editors. Most such services charge a fee, which can range from fifty to several hundred pounds, depending on factors such as the PR wire service you've chosen, desired geographic reach, and press-release length. Following are examples of the different types of PR wire services:

✔ **BusinessWire** (www.businesswire.com) and **PR Newswire** (www.pr newswire.com), as shown in Figure 13-2, are the two mainstays of traditional PR wire services. They are routinely scanned by major on- and offline news organisations as well as industry analysts for story leads, and they charge based on which of their targeted topic and geographic media lists you select.

✔ **Sourcewire** (www.sourcewire.com) is a technology newswire, which is used by some of the UK's biggest tech companies and is also accessed by staff and freelance journalists.

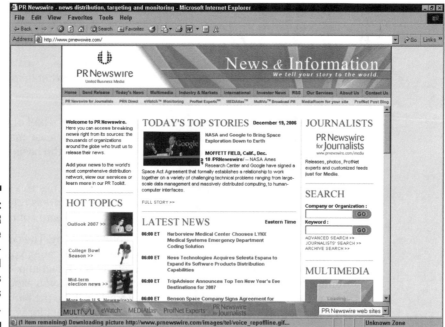

Figure 13-2:
PR
Newswire
both dis-
tributes and
displays
press
releases.

Stupid PR tricks

Do you want to know how to make a journalist into an enemy without any thought or effort? Don't put any thought or effort into your PR. You can irritate journalists in several ways with lazy PR moves unique to the Internet:

✔ **Blindly add journalists to e-mail press release distribution lists without asking.** This tactic is especially annoying if a journalist makes a one-time request or asks to receive limited information – for example, about a trade show in which your company is exhibiting – and you add him or her to your permanent PR distribution.

✔ **Include a press release as an attachment to an e-mail message.** Not only may you wrongly be assuming that the journalist has the right software handy to read the attachment (questionable if he or she is on the road and reading e-mail from a Web interface) but also quite a few journalists simply bin any attachments because they can harbour viruses – yes, even innocent-seeming Microsoft Word documents can contain them.

✔ **Attach graphics or full press kits to an e-mail message.** You may have a high-speed connection and not notice the transmission time, but not everyone does; journalists can be working from home with a narrowband connection. Plus, any attachment carries the threat of a virus.

✔ **Go on and on.** If you can't catch a journalist's attention in the first paragraph, you've lost him or her. No one likes to wade through paragraph after paragraph of self-congratulatory prose to see whether you'll ever make your point.

Many more 'don'ts' exist, but these are among the most universally despised.

BusinessWire, PR Newswire, and other major PR wire services feed their press releases raw to hundreds of other Web sites that then reproduce them verbatim – and these releases are also available for viewing on the originating PR wire service site. Distribution points include such large sites as Yahoo! and MSN, and online syndicators like newsnow.co.uk. When you write your press release, keep this direct audience in mind: They could be customers reading about you in your own words. But the primary audience is still the analysts, reporters, and editors you hope to influence.

Tracking Your Release

Measuring public relations impact is hard enough in the offline world; on the Internet, the task is reminiscent of the phrase, 'Things are never so bad that they can't get worse'. Whereas print and broadcast made it at least possible to count column inches and placement (where in a newscast or magazine a story was slotted), few accepted parallels exist online.

However, if you can't easily measure your PR impact, you can at least monitor it. As in most things marketing, two methods are available: Do it yourself or pay someone else.

Monitoring PR on your own is as simple as visiting specialised search engines that track news sources, using a content aggregator service such as www.blog lines.com or www.newsgator.com and/or setting up *clipping services* on a variety of sites.

Using these methods, you can track not only your own news coverage but also that of your competitors – providing a nice, fast tool for gauging comparative coverage and analysing your competition. Here is a list of services you should consider trying out:

- **Content aggregators:** A buzzword of the new Web movement, Web 2.0, content aggregators constantly check your favourite sites for updates and then feed you those updates through your browser. The best known are probably Bloglines (www.bloglines.com) and Newsgator (www.newsgator.com).

- **Clipping services:** These are available on a number of sites, including Google Alert, which can be customised based on your subject or companies of interest, and is available either free or by subscription, with farther options or enhancements. Other subscription alert services are available from the financial press, including the *Financial Times,* which offers an alert service through www.ft.com.

    These services clip incoming news items and press releases for phrases, keywords, or categories of interest, and many alert you of a successful result by e-mail – although these are becoming less useful online with the advent of content aggregators.

- **PR wire services:** BusinessWire and PR Newswire both sell customised electronic feeds of their press releases, sliced by industry category or keyword, to non-journalists.

A press release of yours posted by others on a blog or message board gives you a great opportunity to see how that online community reacts to the news.

If you can afford it, you can use even more powerful publication search engines such as Dow Jones and Reuters' Factiva (www.factiva.com) and Lexis-Nexis (www.lexis-nexis.com). But you'll pay for the privilege – on some databases, for both the news story you retrieve and the initial search to find it.

Chapter 14

The Emergence of Web 2.0

. . . .

. . . .

Web 2.0 is the name digital specialists are using to categorise the second boom in the popularity and usage of the Internet – both for consumers and big business.

When the first dotcom bubble burst in early 2000, pessimism abounded about the long-term future of both the Internet and the impact it was having on our lives. Big business became anti-Web and a lot of the big dotcom projects were either mothballed, went bust, or were left to carry on with very little financial backing. A few notable exceptions existed, such as Amazon and eBay, which, having built up flourishing businesses, were able to ride the storm. The big companies had their fingers badly burnt – some watched £100 million valuations turn into £1 valuations overnight – and lost interest in the Web. Consumers, however, had well and truly caught the Web bug and carried on not only using it, but using it more and more. With the advent of broadband, consumer take-up of the Internet has exploded, with most of the country now 'wired', and accessing the Web at least once a day, at work or at home. Web 2.0 is intended to signify this constant reliance on the Internet and the fact that thanks to broadband, the Web's now a much more useful and engaging place.

Grasping the Basics of Web 2.0

The early phases of Internet development – retrospectively named Web 1.0 – were all about its 'wow' factor: Web 2.0 is all about its 'lifestyle' factor as the Web becomes a vital part of all of our lives. Our explanation of Web 2.0 concerns the lifestyle angle anyway but as with all things Internet-related, what it actually means is a topic of hot debate, one which you can follow on the Web site of the company that claims to have been the first to use the term: www.oreillynet.com/pub/a/oreilly/tim/news/2005/09/30/ what-is-web-20.html.

Undoubtedly, the advent of Web 2.0, in 2005, has led to a reawakening of interest in the Web from big business. Digital is 'cool' again and companies now demand to know how to use the Web to best connect with their customers.

Perhaps the best example of the world's biggest companies once again investing heavily in the Web as they try and play catch up is the case of MySpace, which we cover in more detail in the 'Understanding the MySpace Generation' section, later in this chapter.

Originally set up as a chat room for college kids in the US to communicate with each other, MySpace (see Figure 14-1) has become a global phenomenon and has created a whole new buzz phrase – *social networking*. MySpace's rise to global fame was cemented when Rupert Murdoch's News Corporation bought it in 2005 for £318 million. In the UK alone, it has over 3.5 million users.

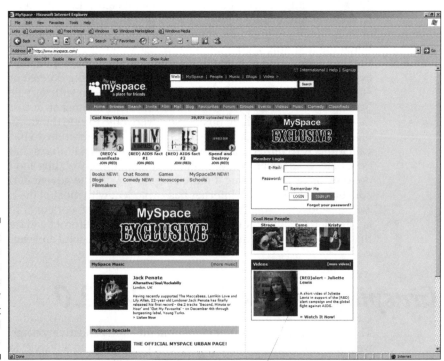

Figure 14-1: The MySpace homepage is a gateway to a vast virtual community.

MySpace's formula for success was very simple: Build an easy-to-use site, which its users could personalise and in which they could add their own areas; launch it with a *viral* and buzz marketing campaign – depending on users to pass on the marketing material by e-mail – and then encourage all its users to tell all their friends about it, thus building one of the world's biggest virtual communities.

Web 2.0 has three key factors relating to how people use the Internet: community, communication, and content:

- **Community:** The community aspect of Web 2.0 is all about using the Web to manage your social and professional networks and expressing your likes and dislikes via Web sites – just as hundreds of thousands of people are doing with MySpace.

- **Communication:** People have been using the Internet to communicate since the very early days of the Web, but now broadband is enabling more advanced communication and participation through video messaging via Instant Messenger and telephone calls over the Internet with services such as Skype.

- **Content:** Again, content is not new to the Web but now a number of content-based services exist that encourage the individual to self-publish. Numerous video sharing sites are available, such as www.youtube.com. These sites have sought to harness user-generated content by asking people to send in videos of themselves doing funny – and some not so funny – things, which other people then send on in their thousands.

Web publishing tools are also launching en-masse to help even the least technology-literate person not only write content for the Web but even build their own Web log – or *blog*. Blogging has opened up Web publishing to the masses.

Understanding Blogging

Blogging is a way of recording thoughts, collecting links, and sharing ideas with other people via a very simple Web site. In effect, blogs are online journals for individuals or organisations and currently a blogging craze is sweeping the world, with millions of people writing blogs on a daily basis. In April 2006, more than 35 million blogs existed around the world, with a new one being launched every second according to the blogging search engine, technorati (www.technorati.com).

According to `blogger.com`, which is owned by Google,

> A blog is a personal diary. A daily pulpit. A collaborative space. A political soapbox. A breaking-news outlet. A collection of links. Your own private thoughts. Memos to the world.

Blogging is now massively popular in the UK, providing some of the best-known political blogs, such as Guido Fawkes at `5thnovember.blogspot.com`, or the daily musings of a Saville Row Taylor, `www.englishcut.com`.

Everyone's blogging, from David Cameron to London Underground tube drivers. Even the authors of this book are blogging, documenting the changing digital world and how both business and consumers are reacting to it. You can check these blogs out at:

- ✔ `accidentalobserver.blogspot.com`
- ✔ `theinteractivezone.blogspot.com`

As blogging is often done on an anonymous basis, it has become a whistle-blower's paradise and an easy source of stories for journalists, who are turning to the *blogosphere* – as the blogging world is known – in droves.

Blogs can also turn their authors into mini-celebrities. Guido Fawkes – although remaining anonymous – is now a journalists' and politicians' daily must-read.

Getting started in the blogosphere

Blogging is very simple and after you get started, you can update your blog as often as you like. Bear in mind, though, that if you want people to keep coming back to look at your blog you need to keep it up to date, interesting, and relevant. Boring blogs are a turn-off.

Lots of blogging tools exist to help you get started but perhaps the best-known are Blogger.com, Wordpress, and Typepad. As Blogger is perhaps the best-known, we use this tool as the example (see Figure 14-2). If you want to use another tool though, just do a quick search on Google and you'll be presented with a multitude of options.

Not all blogging tools are free. Blogger is, but others aren't and will charge you a monthly or annual subscription. Because moving your blog from one tool to another isn't easy, make your decision carefully.

Figure 14-2:
The Blogger
homepage
provides
an easy
guide to
publishing
your blog
online.

Getting started with Blogger is a simple three-step process:

1. **Type in www.blogger.com to your browser and click on the button 'Create your blog now'.** Page one will ask you to choose a user name, a password, to give your e-mail address, and to accept its terms of service.

2. **Click 'Next' and you'll be asked to give a name to your blog – for example, 'Accidental Observer'.** Choose the Web address (for example, accidentalobserver.blogspot.com).

3. **Click 'Next' for the last time and choose your template.** You have lots of different colours, or *skins* as they're known, to choose from. After you choose your template you're ready to blog and have become the world's latest blogger!

To actually write a post, you need to access your *dashboard,* which includes basic word editing tools and also gives you the ability to upload images into your blog. From there you just type what you want and then click 'Publish' to make it go live. The beauty of blogs is that you can make them as simple or as complicated as you like and can add pictures, video, and music all at the touch of a button. Hundreds of thousands of people use Blogger to publish blogs, so if you want any tips or hints use the message boards and help sections to get going.

Getting your blog seen

With so many blogs being launched, taking some basic steps to ensure that people can find yours is important. Firstly, make sure that what you're writing about is likely to be interesting to someone out there. Your content can range from gardening tips to disclosing complicated scientific formulae. The key to a successful blog is that someone somewhere wants to read it. Secondly, when asked by Blogger during the set-up, make sure that your blog is visible to Google and other search engines. Finally, and perhaps most importantly, to keep people coming back and to attract new visitors, keep updating your site. And don't be afraid to self-promote your blog to your friends or colleagues or by advertising it at the bottom of your e-mail or by linking to it from a Web site – if you already have one. Just taking some basic steps like these means you'll have traffic from day one. But as with all things, if you leave the blog and don't update it, people won't come and check it out.

Maintaining a company blog

Blogging mania isn't limited to individuals. A number of the biggest companies in the UK are now using blogs to communicate with their customers – with varying degrees of success – including Guinness, Honda, and BT. These blogs are known as corporate blogs. The Guinness blog (www.guinnessblog.co.uk) is perhaps the most engaging of these because the content's written by the black stuff's marketing team and gives Guinness fans a behind-the-scenes look into how the blog is produced and how the adverts are made. As more and more companies are starting to view blogging as a crucial communications tool, you need to follow a few guidelines to ensure that your company gets the most out of blogging.

- ✔ Be open and honest. Hiding the truth on the Internet is impossible and if you try and mislead consumers via your blog you'll get heavily criticised, or *flamed* as the experience is known in blogland.

- ✔ Keep your blog up to date, relevant, and interesting.

- ✔ Be clear what the aims of your blog are from the outset and stick to them.

- ✔ Do let bloggers comment on what you write and make sure that you don't overreact if and when they post anything negative about your company.

- ✔ If negative posts do appear, react in a balanced, open, and honest way. Blogs are a very useful way of 'getting your point of view across'.

- ✔ Avoid 'corporate speak'.

- ✔ Don't try and sell to your customers. Blogs should be about commentary and observations, not product details or hard sell.

- ✔ Make sure that only one or two people are blogging on behalf of the company otherwise the content becomes confused and inconsistent.

When it all goes Bang . . .

Last year, the oven cleaning brand Cillit Bang ran a disastrous campaign. Its PR agency Cohn & Wolfe created a blog for the brand's fictional frontman Barry Scott. 'Barry' then posted comments on other people's blogs, leaving a link to the Cillit Bang Web site. The blogs chosen included one on which the writer had recounted the emotional story of how he had just met up with his father for the first time in 30 years. When the link to Cillit Bang was discovered, it caused outrage among the blogger community, and Cohn & Wolfe and Cillit Bang were forced to apologise.

Bloggers hate being sold to, and react badly to companies that try and do that – especially by subversive means. See the sidebar 'When it all goes Bang . . . ' for an example of how such subversive blogging can backfire.

Mastering Podcasting

Unless you've been living on a different planet recently then you'll have heard of *podcasting*. Podcasting is a way of subscribing to and receiving popular content such as radio shows from the Internet and then either playing them on your computer or on your iPod. Like blogging, podcasting is becoming a craze and is hugely popular amongst Net-savvy teenagers.

Podcasting is being mentioned everywhere, and is fast establishing itself as the best way of getting either audio or visual content from the Web.

Comedian Ricky Gervais's podcast has been downloaded more than 5 million times and is the most popular one in the UK. Other popular podcasts include those made by Radio 1 DJs like Chris Moyles and Scott Mills and the Baddiel and Skinner podcast during the World Cup in Germany in 2006.

If you download podcasts and a subscription option is offered, take it – your computer will then automatically check for updates and download the latest podcasts if you're already subscribed.

Podcast files on a computer are exactly the same as digital music files, normally MP3 format, and can be transferred and played on most players. Video podcasts are also starting to be introduced by companies such as Apple, which has just launched a film download service.

Podcasting is not quite as simple as blogging and does require some level of expertise if you want to use it. Some companies now offer their AGM or annual results via podcasts online, but the main use for the medium continues to be entertainment.

If you want to get involved in podcasting, check out this site, which gives you some tips on how to get started: `podcasts.yahoo.com/publish`.

Networking with the MySpace Generation

If you have teenage kids then you probably know about MySpace – the Web site that has revolutionised the way people (children and students in particular) use the Internet (see Figure 14-3). MySpace is made up of millions of profiles crafted by individuals to tell the rest of the world about themselves. Some profiles are very basic while others have obviously taken hours to design. MySpace is so big that a whole new cottage industry has sprung up giving MySpace users the tools to redesign and build their own profiles. Just do a quick search on Google and you'll see how many Web sites are selling MySpace materials. MySpace has also become a unique marketing tool for unsigned bands, with one band in particular, The Arctic Monkeys, now famous for having used it to get people to listen to their music and talk about them.

No chapter on Web 2.0 is complete without a look at MySpace, as not only has it had a major impact on how people use the Internet but it has also helped to develop a whole new type of Web site – a social network – of which hundreds are launching all the time. The MySpace generation are typically aged between about 12 and 24. They're spending less time watching TV and a lot more time surfing the Internet and sites like MySpace. A recent UK government survey found that over 70 per cent of this age group visit and use social networks, while a third are bloggers or run their own message boards.

MySpace is actually a whole new group of Web sites, which young people regularly visit and share with their mates. If you want to develop digital marketing, you need to know about these sites. They include `www.youtube.com`, detailed earlier in this chapter; `www.bebo.com`, another social network, which is competing with `www.myspace.com` but has more of a UK audience because you have to sign up based on what school you go to; `www.flickr.com`, where you can host and share photos; and `http://del.icio.us/`, which enables you to store all your favourite bits of Web content and access them from any computer or device. All these sites have the basic Web 2.0 principles at their heart – community, communication, and content – and are fast becoming some of the most popular Web sites in the world.

From a marketing perspective, knowing how to take advantage of the Web 2.0 opportunity is very difficult and some companies are doing it better than others.

A lot of companies are looking at how to build communities for their customers – again, some more successfully than others.

The marketing advantages for tapping into a community are pretty clear. You get a ready made, extremely active audience who are aged primarily between 16 and 24 – that dream age group for all marketers. In theory, you can use communities like MySpace to build your own branded environments letting the site's users come and see what you have to offer through your community. But the reality is very different. Only brands that have a right to be in the community (for example, music acts or films) can really make community work because let's be honest, as a consumer you are much more likely to go to the Web site of your favourite band than you are to a soap powder community! However, advertisers can and do add value, normally where they offer members of the community something they can't get elsewhere (for example, behind-the-scenes clips of the film or interviews with the band). This sort of added-value marketing is becoming increasingly popular and is known as *engagement marketing*.

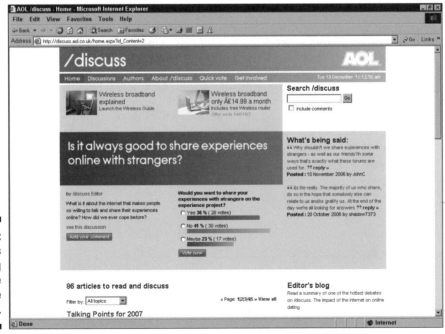

Figure 14-3:
AOL took its advertising into the online community.

When the community talks back

AOL UK is one company that has built a thriving community site based around its advertising. At the start of 2006, AOL launched an advertising campaign asking the question, 'Is the Internet a good or a bad thing?'. The campaign was intended to get UK consumers to see AOL in a different light and at its heart was `www.aol.co.uk/ discuss`, a Web site where consumers could debate the points raised in the ads and respond to issue-based articles written by celebrities and public figures, including Piers Morgan, Alastair Campbell, and Mariella Frostrup. Since the campaign launched, the site has had nearly 1 million visitors and is receiving hundreds of posts a month – proof of how a company can build a successful community.

Content is another area that brands are looking to exploit through the creation of their own films or viral clips – video clips that can be forwarded to friends for their amusement, which are then distributed through Web sites such as YouTube (`www.youtube.com`).

Nike has been particularly successful using this tactic, distributing clips of some of the footballers it backs, including Ronaldinho, across the video-sharing sites. These have then been accessed by hundreds of thousands of people.

If you want to take advantage of the change in how people are using the Internet, talking to the experts before trying to launch your own community or viral is worthwhile. Anything which is hastily done can reflect badly on your brand and can even annoy your customers. So, if you have one, speak to your digital agency and ask them what they think the opportunities are; if you don't have an agency, speak to a digital consultant who knows what works online and what doesn't.

Part V
The Part of Tens

'And whether the world likes it or not, <u>everything</u> will be digital within ten years.'

In this part . . .

Summing up many of the most important points of this book is embarrassingly easy, but crucial – especially for marketing people who often like to see important points in the form of a quick list. We do so with two chapters outlining the ten advantages and ten disadvantages of Internet marketing. (The rest of the book has the details to help you make your Internet marketing presence really work.) Our last chapter points out useful *offline* marketing resources that will help you do your best marketing online, offline, or both.

Chapter 15

Ten Advantages of Digital Marketing

Digital marketing still accounts for only a fraction of marketing budgets for most companies. Despite all the hype and attention that surrounds the Internet, working out how to use it properly for marketing, selling, customer service, and more is still very difficult. You may well need some ammunition to help convince others that you should be spending more time, and more of your company's money, on digital marketing.

Following are ten of the most important advantages of digital marketing – some of which we also look at in a different light in Chapter 16, 'Ten Disadvantages of Digital Marketing'.

Digital Marketing Has Low Barriers to Entry

Low barriers to entry are a great advantage of digital marketing. You can begin building an effective online marketing presence with tools such as a basic business Web site (Chapter 5), a search marketing strategy (Chapters 8, 9, and 10), or setting your PR approach by focusing on message boards and blogs (Chapter 14) for a few hundred pounds and a small investment of time.

Much useful Internet marketing work is done on the cheap. If your initial work is successful, you can use your experience to justify building a larger, albeit more expensive, online marketing presence. For this reason, always have one eye on the cost justification for your digital marketing expenditure.

Digital Marketing Is Informational Marketing

Many people see marketing as a less than completely scientific or honourable art, and see marketers as people who are willing to stretch or even invent facts to make a sale. Obviously, this perception doesn't lend itself to using marketing to build an enduring or engaging relationship with customers and potential customers.

Digital marketing has evolved in such a way that it avoids some of the disadvantages inherent in popular negative perceptions of offline marketing. Online marketing has become more *informational marketing*, that is, a style of marketing in which you build a reasonable case for your product as the best, and for you and your company as trustworthy partners with the buyer in the purchase process. In digital marketing, core marketing skills, such as finding and clearly stating the user benefits of product features, are valued over other disciplines such as fast-talking salesmanship. Increasingly through the digital medium, marketing is becoming less about delivering an advertising message and more about creating one-off brand experiences or environments with which your customers interact.

To find the write tone, if you'll excuse the pun, look at sponsored *advertorial* ('advertising' + 'editorial') sections in business magazines like *The Economist*. The goal in advertorials is to deliver solid information, the content of which is just as true as anything in the magazine's articles, but written from the advertiser's point of view and selected to help build the case for purchasing the advertiser's product.

If over the years you've been instilled with a tendency when writing to express yourself in breathless superlatives, as have many marketing people, you need to change your style on the Internet – even in e-mail. Find someone who knows the online world and ask for a frank evaluation of the straightforwardness and clarity of your writing. On the Internet, words equal clutter and only the bare minimum of words that add value are needed!

If editing isn't your thing – or if you're a great editor of anyone except yourself – you may want to hire a copy editor to check your copy for you before posting. One place to look for editors and other professionals who are willing to work on an hourly basis is www.freelanceuk.com.

The Online World Enables You to Respond Rapidly

The ability to respond quickly – in many cases instantly, off the top of one's head – distinguishes the best marketers from the rest in offline marketing. Rapid response is even more vital online – it enables you to build a one-to-one relationship with your customers and potential customers and gives people the impression they're getting factual information rather than a carefully crafted sales pitch. Marketers who aren't afraid to risk occasional criticism of timely, honest responses – for instance, mentioning a competitor's products as well as one's own in answering a question on a message board or a blog, as described in Chapter 14 – can do a lot to advance the interests of their companies on the Internet.

The Internet World Highlights Marketing's Role

One key reason that marketing in general is viewed as important is the link that it helps to establish among products, customers, and sales. In the digital world, this link gives Internet marketing an advantage over offline marketing in that Internet marketing is both immediate and obvious.

- ✔ The Internet, as an information dissemination tool, is by nature a marketing tool when used in a commercial setting.
- ✔ The Internet is seen as exciting and of great interest to many people, including those outside the marketing function.

Therefore, marketing will inevitably be highlighted and, hopefully, prioritised by your company when you have a Web presence as the rest of the company will inevitably be interested in its capabilities.

Tactical efforts, such as redesigning Web pages for easier navigation, as well as strategic efforts, such as incorporating online sales into your site, are most often left in the hands of the marketing department. Marketing is highlighted in the Internet world to such an extent that its importance in the rest of a company's efforts is brought to the forefront as well. The increased focus that the Internet confers on the importance of marketing may make it easier for people you work with to understand the importance of marketing input in other areas, such as product planning and distribution.

Keep track of your accomplishments in digital marketing; they may impress a recruiting manager or a potential client or customer down the road. A portfolio with your online marketing work alongside offline marketing work shows off your marketing versatility and your ability to stay on top of the latest consumer marketing trends.

Internet Innovations Are Marketing Opportunities

The digital world is built on rapid change and continues to evolve at breakneck speed. These changes are good for you as a marketer, because each change brings you new ways to communicate with your customers and to reach them at a time when other brands are not.

Although the precursor networks to today's Internet existed more than 30 years ago, services such as the early newsgroups, online services, the World Wide Web, and wireless access have arrived steadily over time (some in just the last few years). The Web itself is changing rapidly as new standards and tools appear with dizzying rapidity. Each time new standards, tools, or technologies are introduced in the online world, examine them for opportunities to better communicate with your customers and potential customers. Take a look at Chapter 14 about Web 2.0 for more on new developments.

The Internet Makes Research Easier

The online world is a tremendous resource for all kinds of research, as we describe in Chapter 2. Want to know what users are saying about your product? Scan message boards and blogs for comments and then send e-mails, asking for details, to a few of the people who spoke out. Want to see what your competitors are planning? Check their Web sites and relevant message boards; you're likely to get valuable information such as their past press releases and upcoming events schedules. Sometimes secrets such as product release dates are hinted at, or even blurted out, by less-than-careful insiders. This divulgence of insider information is particularly the case on some blogs, which have become very useful at accessing the latest information about your competition.

Not only is online research informative, the information's easy to share with others and is freely available for others to verify – unlike things people may say to you over the phone or in person, though that kind of information remains valuable as well. Use online information to help convince others whenever you see a need for action.

Although this fact is becoming less of an issue, as valuable as it is, online research is currently hampered by so many people, even in the relatively well-connected UK market, not yet being on the Internet. Another obstacle is the lack of information on many companies' Web sites. However, as the amount of information on company Web sites grows, online research is getting easier and more valuable.

The Online World Forgives Mistakes

Compared to other marketing and publishing media, the online world is relatively forgiving of mistakes. If you make a typographical error in an e-mail or a Web posting, few people are likely to care; getting a factually accurate and helpful response up quickly is more important than waiting for editorial review. Much more embarrassing is making a typographical error on a Web page, and fixing it in a hurry is much more important. But you're still better off than with a printed piece, which you'd just have to throw out – possibly at great expense – if it contained typos.

Factual errors are different but still easier to correct on the Internet than elsewhere. If you make a factual error online, simply post the correct information and an apology for the earlier error, much as a newspaper would publish a correction. People on the Internet seem, in our experience, to appreciate the honesty displayed when an error is corrected in this manner.

 Of course, no one wants to make errors on the Internet. Always use a spell checker when creating Web page content; the better Web page creation tools now include them, though how often they seem to go unused is amazing. For other Internet services, use your best judgement about correcting errors. The larger the number of people who see a given communication, and the more official it is as opposed to being your personal response or opinion, the more important it is that you take the time to spell check and even grammar check the content.

 Although nearly all Web page creation tools and even some e-mail programs have spell checkers, few have grammar checkers, which can catch subtle errors such as using the wrong version of a word when you write. To use a grammar checker on your work, create your text in a full-featured word processing program, spell check it, grammar check it, and then copy and paste it into another tool for use on the Internet. But always remember that spell checkers and grammar checkers are no substitute for a well trained pair of eyes. You should always read through any marketing material for accuracy before publishing.

The Internet World Is Currently English Centric

As the Internet itself began from a network funded by the US military and expanded by further US government funding supported by, among others, then senator and presidential wannabe Al Gore, who also coined the term *information superhighway* (but did not 'invent the Internet', as he may have claimed; this honour goes to Englishman, Tim Berners-Lee). Most of the companies that dominate the creation of hardware, software, and services for the Internet are US-based, and the majority of frequent users are from the Western world. So at this point in its history, the Internet is an English-language dominated medium – although this situation is rapidly changing.

This English-language dominance is a big advantage for UK-based digital marketers. Companies and professionals that operate predominantly in other languages have a large barrier to operating successfully on the Internet. They must either operate only on the small part of the online world that functions in their native tongue, or go through a constant translation process back and forth to English in order to operate in the mainstream of the online world.

Some people predict that the online world will become much more varied in its support for other languages, and no doubt that prediction's true, but the authors of this book suspect that the great bulk of Internet content will continue to be in English for a long time to come. Maybe the tens of millions of people who have other native languages will need to learn English to participate fully on the information superhighway, the same way that they do now in the sciences and some professions. However, the influence of major nations such as China is also starting to be felt and increasingly the balance is shifting.

In the longer term, automatic translation services – the ability for computers to automatically translate one language to another – may make language barriers less relevant. (A good translation service can be found at `www.babelfish.altavista.com`, although a Google search will reveal hundreds more.)

Digital Marketing Removes Geographic Barriers

One of the most exciting but confusing things about the online world is the way in which it removes geographic barriers. In the online world, the challenges consist of getting people interested in what you have to say and helping them find you on the Internet. But reaching someone two time zones away costs no more than trying to reach someone next door. A toy shop based in Bristol can now easily sell to customers in New York or New Delhi.

Of course, operating in this new world requires a considerable amount of work and imagination to decide which tactics make sense and which don't. Should a local hardware shop attempt to go national or international via the Internet? You can get started with an English-only approach, but you also need to decide at what point you need to translate and localise content. Some retailers who've put up a Web storefront have been sadly disappointed by a poor response. Others have been successful beyond their wildest dreams.

You need marketing expertise and considerable self-restraint to use the online world to grow your business without courting disaster. We suggest growing your online presence gradually for just that reason. But if your situation offers a unique opportunity to expand your geographic reach – for instance, if you have a lot of expertise, a lot of money, and a unique product – consider making a bigger initial effort on the Internet; after all, taking a slight risk that works is so much better than not doing it and living to regret your decision!

Web 2.0 Marketing Gets You Closer to Your Customers Than Ever Before

The Web 2.0 revolution, which encompasses blogging, podcasting, and user-generated content applications, allows you to interact with your customers through your marketing in a way that has never been possible before.

Marketing has traditionally been a *push medium,* which means that the advertiser was telling the customer how it was, and that was that. However, Web 2.0 is changing the rules. Now the advertiser may try to tell the consumer what is what, but the customer can answer back and tell the advertiser exactly what they think and what they want. This obviously has some interesting implications for both consumers and advertisers alike and means that customers can become part of the marketing message.

User-generated content in all its forms, whether it is an uploaded video for a competition, a customer review of a product, or simply a comment on a blog, can now have as great an impact as the best laid marketing plan. Customer reviews and referrals are fast becoming the norm online and are carrying as much weight as more traditional marketing efforts. Smart advertisers are taking advantage of this and getting involved in the conversation early on: So should you.

Chapter 16

Ten Disadvantages of Digital Marketing

Digital marketing has tremendous advantages. However, it also has its problems – some of which are the flipside of the good points we describe in Chapter 15. In this chapter, we describe some of the monsters hiding in the digital marketing closet – and show you how to shine a light on them and make them crawl farther back into the corner.

Digital Marketing Is Different

Online marketing is definitely different from offline marketing. It's informational marketing with a vengeance – too much hype and your online readers and Web site visitors may not only turn you off, but turn on you. Online marketing's costs are hard to estimate in advance, and the benefits are not always immediately clear, whereas in offline marketing you have years of past experience to go on. And because of the fast pace of Internet marketing, on any day, a competitor who's one step ahead of you – or makes a lucky bet with the company's money – may get ahead of you.

Not only is digital marketing different from other marketing you've done, each Internet technology has its own kinks and culture. If you aren't already Internet-savvy, you have to catch up; competitors who have more Net experience are much better able to take advantage of the medium than you are. If you don't at least start to get your hands dirty now, you'll fall farther behind. As an example of the different meaning of 'experience' in the digital world, the several years of Internet marketing experience that the authors of this book have, which would qualify us to be competent practitioners in many areas of offline marketing, are enough to make us gurus on the Internet.

What can you do about the problem of falling behind in digital marketing? The solution is information and attitude. On the information side, this book, we humbly submit, is a good starting point for discovering what you need to know to get off to a running start. Experience and other resources, including some described in Chapter 17 and the *Digital Marketing For Dummies* Internet Directory, will do the rest. Attitudinally, the solution can best be summed up in the Latin phrase *carpe diem,* or 'seize the day'. The Internet world is a huge opportunity for marketing; don't ignore the risks and difficulties of working in this new environment, but don't let them keep you from acting, either.

Connection Speeds Can Be Limiting

The march of broadband across the UK has taken a lot longer than many industry watchers expected. For a variety of reasons, from consumer confidence to technical and access issues, ISPs have only recently been able to offer the connection speeds that users anticipated. Broadband has now really taken off and more broadband connections exist in the UK than dial-up 56k modem connections. However, the accessibility of broadband doesn't mean that everyone has joined the technological revolution and if you aim your marketing efforts at only the most Internet savvy audience you'll be missing out on a large chunk of the market.

The solution to reaching both markets is to adopt the KISS principle – Keep It Short and Sweet. Do experiment with multimedia to get your feet wet and liven up your Web site, but use a light touch, and always back up your multimedia information with static text and graphics that deliver the same message. That way, people who surf the Internet with slower connections will still get your message.

Internet Efforts Can Get Expensive

A full-scale Internet marketing effort with a Web site, blogging strategy, online advertising, e-mail campaigns, SEO, and paid search pushes, as described in the earlier chapters of this book, can cost a lot of money. Such an effort for a company with, say, 10 to 100 employees may require employing several people – usually a mix of employees and contractors. Some work on the site full time, others part time. In high-wage areas, the total cost of keeping half a dozen people paid, insured, and housed in offices can be a hefty sum. So be ready to spend some real money if you expand beyond a CYA (Cover Your Arse/Assets) Web and online presence like the one we describe in Chapter 5 of this book.

If you decide you want to go the whole hog, you may encounter a few challenges. The first is that the expenses can sneak up on you – the large expenditures needed for a larger Internet presence can be a shock. The second challenge is that, when all is said and done, not all your target audience is likely to be online where your effort can reach them, as we describe in Chapter 2. You have to plan and budget carefully to make sure that you still have enough money left to reach people offline as well.

The truly big spending, though, comes with online commerce. Carefully plan and budget your expenditures before selling online, and read *Selling Online For Dummies* (Wiley), to get an idea of the processes and expenses involved.

Online Marketing Doesn't Reach Everybody

Your colleagues, the press, the analysts, and the core customers with whom you regularly work are likely to be connected. So you may think that your job of keeping all your customers informed, updated, and happy is done as soon as you put information on your Web site or answer a question on a message board or in a blog. Unfortunately, this situation just isn't so.

To avoid missing a big chunk of your customers, don't shut out people who are offline or have limited online capabilities. Design your online content, especially your Web pages, to be accessible to all. Following World Wide Web Consortium (W3C) guidelines on accessibility, as mentioned in Chapter 5, is a good start. Also, give your customers a contact point in the real world; nothing is more frustrating than wanting to speak to a real person only to be offered the chance to fill in another form. Finally, remember digital marketing is an addition to your traditional marketing strategy, not a replacement for it and it is at its most effective when combined with other marketing channels.

Digital Marketing Efforts Can Be Hard

Measuring the impact of marketing is always difficult, but at least some widely accepted rules exist for what you can reasonably expect in offline media. Also, people in your company get a kick out of seeing and hearing ads on TV and radio. If the decision-makers in your company aren't entirely comfortable with the scale of effort needed to succeed on the Internet, they may not get as much of a thrill from a Web site, let alone a blog posting.

The cost-justification effort is made more difficult by some of the costly processes that you may want to implement in order to make your online presence shine. These processes include:

- **Outsourcing work to consultants and companies that specialise in online work:** Although hiring outside consultants results in extra costs in a form that many financial directors loathe – that is, medium-sized and large cheques written to consultants – outsourcing can save you money in the long run. An outside agency may be able to set up your marketing Web site in a couple of weeks, whereas doing it in-house may take months. (We explain how to use specialists in Chapter 5.)

- **Implementing a central database:** If you choose to launch an e-commerce operation, having robust back-end database systems to store and process information that you collect from customers is vital. A central database is an expensive outlay that you must undertake in advance of 'opening your doors' online and may put off some inside your company who may argue that the expense will outweigh the benefits.

We strongly recommend that you adapt the advice in this book and your own experience into an ongoing effort to actively demonstrate the benefits of your online presence. Possible ways to demonstrate benefits include counting the number of times people click items in your Web site, counting downloads of files that you offer, polling your online visitors about the impact of your Web site on their buying behaviour, and counting responses to special offers that you make on your Web site. Even when no one's asking, keep gathering information about the benefits of your online presence so that you're ready when they do ask.

Making Mistakes Online Is Easy

Any time that you do something new, you're bound to make mistakes. Typos are bad and embarrassing but easy to fix. The real challenge comes when you're put on the spot to answer tough questions – fast.

In the immediacy of the digital world, you're often asked to explain complicated issues online almost to the minute the issues arise – why didn't your company ship a product on time? What are your plans for speeding up deliveries? When are you finally going to start doing customer service properly? If you admit wrongdoing, you may embarrass yourself or others in your company; if you don't admit that you messed up, you can look ignorant, defensive, or clueless.

The approach we take online is to apologise a lot when we do anything that irritates a customer or partner, and always ask for clarification – is there some way you can perform a needed task with the current product? What happened to you when you spoke with our customer service department? The answers to these kinds of questions help you address real problems better and refine your online processes.

When all is said and done, you have to ask others in your company to be tolerant of any mistakes that you and others make online, and you have to be tolerant of the mistakes that others in your company may make. This relatively new medium, the online world, is highly public and demands rapid responses – always a formula for potential embarrassment.

Some of the MySpace generation, as we refer to them in Chapter 14 – mainly people under 30 – have developed the habit of being very informal in sending e-mail, including typing in all lower case and not worrying about typos and punctuation mistakes. Doing so seems to be taken as a sign of 'coolness' and being casual in communications equals being friendly. While a casual style is fine for personal e-mail, in business e-mail you simply have to take the time to compose and check what you write, even for 'laters'-type friendly messages. (By the way, the proper spelling of 'laters' in an e-mail sign-off is 'L8rs'.) People will think that you're an idiot if you're too informal in business e-mails.

You can reduce errors of judgement, as well as typing and other mistakes, by typing an answer and then reading it out loud to yourself. You may be surprised how your own words sound when you read them back to yourself. But whatever you do, mistakes happen – so prepare to be flexible and get better at composing e-mail as you go along.

Guilt by Association

Because of all the negative things in the online world, including pornography, slander, libel, and hateful talk, many people have a bad impression of the Internet. The way that you conduct yourself and how you present your company online can do one of two things. You can reinforce people's negative stereotypes of the Internet, leading them to very quickly form a low opinion of your company, your products, and maybe even your parentage, or you can confound them by making a positive impression, and create a high opinion of your company and your products.

The Internet is bound to face criticism as it grows and develops. If you conduct yourself with class and professionalism online, you and your company can be seen as exceptions, even if the public at large believes that lies, half-truths, and junk are the online rule.

The Uncertain Future of the Digital World

Usually, a fairly high degree of predictability exists between what happens one year and what happens the next. But the entire future of the digital world seems continually up in the air. As a result of this uncertainty, knowing how big a bet to put on your online presence is hard.

Our answer to the rapid rate of change online is to move cautiously but quickly – cautiously in that you shouldn't make large investments at first, but quickly in that you can and should establish a modest, easy-to-use online presence as soon as possible. Doing so means that you can combine the advice you get in this book and elsewhere with your own increasing experience to create an online presence that works best for you and your own unique set of customers.

Digital Marketing Is Still Very New

The Internet is still a baby when comparing it to other advertising media and so because of that there are more people who don't understand it than people who do. This is good news for people like the authors who make it their business to educate brands and agencies about digital marketing but for those of you looking to run your first digital marketing efforts, be warned, it's never simple. As it's so new, the industry is still in the process of setting standards on things like advertising formats and how to measure response rates. The industry is still dominated by jargon and there's plenty of scepticism about just how effective it can be.

The Power of Digital Marketing Can Be Underestimated

As the Internet is the world's first truly viral media, every time you send an e-mail to a friend, colleague, supplier, or even your accountant, there's a danger that this e-mail – as boring as it may be – can be forwarded to anyone else in the world without you knowing. Looking at it from a marketing perspective, this is in theory a massive advantage as now you have a free ready made way of getting your message across to whomever you want. But sometimes it can backfire badly. In December 2006, high street off-licence chain Threshers sent an e-mail voucher offering 40 per cent off alcohol in its shops to hundreds of its suppliers. In the e-mail, Threshers asked the suppliers to pass on the vouchers to 'friends and family'. The suppliers took Threshers at their word and forwarded the e-voucher to millions of people, truly demonstrating the power of viral marketing. Threshers was insistent that it would honour all the vouchers, but you can bet that they were more than overwhelmed by the massive response to their e-mail!

Chapter 17

Ten Offline Marketing Resources

*N*o matter how much the online world grows, most of the world's information will still be printed matter in books and magazines for the foreseeable future. This book's Directory has lots of great online marketing resources; this chapter is the source for some good offline resources. Several marketing classics and other resources listed in this chapter can help you to get a firm grasp of the essentials of marketing in any medium, online or offline.

Paying close attention to offline marketing vehicles such as television ads can help you sharpen and transfer your skills to the online world. As you gain experience in digital marketing, you'll start to look at traditional media – books, magazines, radio, television, and others – in a whole new way.

 All the books recommended in this chapter are available online through Amazon, the online bookseller, at www.amazon.co.uk. (Check the list of books and authors that were also purchased by people who bought the book you're interested in; you may learn even more.)

The Fabled Long Tail

The Long Tail, by *Wired* editor Chris Anderson, has been hailed as the definitive guide to how both technology and the Internet are making the world a much smaller place, revolutionising life as we know it in the process.

The *long tail* is a theory conceived by Anderson to explain what is happening to the global economy now that, thanks to the Internet, almost unlimited choice exists for the consumer.

Crucially for marketers, Anderson believes that the long tail is creating masses of opportunity for both businesses and consumers, with traditional business models being overturned.

Anderson quotes the examples of Amazon and iTunes, which have completely transformed both the music and book publishing industries, and gives an insight into how as marketers you can take advantage of these seismic changes.

Trade Associations

Every profession or industry that we can think of has a trade or professional association, from dentists to decorators to car dealers to computer companies. Many of these associations have marketing sections or groups that exchange marketing information and hold meetings. These associations are great resources for finding out what has and hasn't worked for others online in your industry.

If you're not familiar with all the associations that cover your field – national, regional, and local – talk with a colleague or check one of many directories of associations, available at most library reference desks, ask your peers within your industry, or if all else fails, do a quick Web search through Google.

A number of marketing-specific trade bodies and industry associations exist in the UK, including – crucially – for the online world: The Internet Advertising Bureau (www.iabuk.net), the Marketing Society (www.marketing-society.org.uk), the Institute of Practitioners in Advertising (www.ipa.co.uk), and the Chartered Institute of Marketing (www.cim.co.uk).

Marketing: An Introduction and Marketing For Dummies

Marketing: An Introduction, by Philip Kotler and Gary Armstrong (Prentice Hall), is a marketing textbook that starts by looking at human needs as the basis of marketing – a good thing to think about in analysing your digital marketing efforts – and then covers all the basics of marketing, from market segmentation and public relations to designing new products. Reading all this information with an eye to its application online is a mind-opening experience.

If the textbook approach isn't your cup of tea, an excellent marketing book written in the . . . *For Dummies* style may be more up your alley – if you don't mind our mixing British and American metaphors. *Marketing For Dummies*, by Craig Smith and Alexander Hiam (Wiley), is an excellent introduction to marketing and a valuable companion to this book.

Trade Publications

An invaluable source of trade-specific marketing information is your industry trade publications, whether they're weekly tabloids, monthly magazines, Web sites, or the occasional newsletter. Articles frequently offer marketing tips or profiles of what other companies are doing. Your trade or professional association, or your colleagues, can point you in the right direction but a good starting point is checking out the likes of *Marketing* magazine (`www.brandrepublic.com/magazines/marketing`), which both of the authors regularly write for, *Marketing Week* (`www.mad.co.uk`), or *Campaign* magazine – the advertising agency bible (`www.brandrepublic.com/magazines/campaign`).

Also look at Internet-specific trade publications such as the weekly *New Media Age* (`www.nma.co.uk`) or the monthly *Revolution* (`www.revolutionmagazine.com`). Go to a high-technology-orientated bookshop or the magazine section in a computer superstore, and you may see as many as a dozen such publications. These resources can help you become more familiar with developments happening online.

News Radio

News radio is fairly analogous to the digital world in general and the World Wide Web in particular. Basically, news radio stations are delivering information to attract listeners who then hear the adverts that pay the station bills. You can think of your Web site in the same way: You're attracting people by providing information that interests them and also delivering your sales and marketing messages encouraging them to buy your product. Listen to news radio with an ear to understanding how it mixes many different kinds of information along with ads in a way designed to keep you listening.

The writing style for your Web site may be improved if you borrow from the writing style for news radio – lots of short pieces of information, each capable of standing alone, with nothing extraneous in them.

Any Big Magazine Rack

Imagine a big magazine rack with sewing thread connecting information from one magazine to related information in others. By the time you'd connected all the related pieces, you'd have, well, a web of information links. This idea was part of the thinking behind the creation of the World Wide Web, and you can see it in action today in any bookshop.

Most of the Web is very magazine-like – pages of information mixing text and graphics, the text written in a compact style for easy skimming or scanning, and ads interspersed throughout. (One may argue that the Web has an advantage over magazines in the form of multimedia, but we've never seen a scratch-and-sniff insert on a Web page, so that's at least one 'multi' medium where magazines have an advantage.)

You can pick out magazines you like and then compare them to your Web site. Look for layout and graphic design ideas in the magazine that you can apply to the Web. Find an article you like in a magazine and then compare the writing in it to the writing on your Web site; you may be able to find ways to improve the quality of writing on your Web site by using ideas you get from magazine articles.

Linking is the single biggest difference between the Web and magazines, given that no such thing as a hypertext link exists in print – you have to physically turn the pages to get somewhere else! Look at your Web site for ways to use linking that give your site an edge over magazines.

Permission Marketing

Seth Godin, author of the bestseller *Permission Marketing* (Simon & Schuster), is known as one of the best ambassadors of digital marketing. The surprising thing is that he is not an in-your-face kind of marketer. His thesis is that Internet users have to actively consent to be marketed to or your marketing messages will bounce right off them.

Godin's approach is very much in keeping with what both authors of this book have found to work: Be low-key and invite the user in with information rather than hit them over the head with hyperbole. *Permission Marketing* is a great tool for working out the right way to market on the Internet – or for helping convince your bosses and peers that a low-key approach is the best way to go. His latest book, *All Marketers Are Liars* is also well worth a read!

Television Advertising

What do you do when you have 30 seconds of people's attention – *if* you can entice them not to click a button and surf away from you? TV has faced this problem for decades, and the ways in which it meets (or fails to meet) this challenge are very educational for digital marketers. Think of people giving your online messages their attention 15 – 30 seconds at a time – and realise that if they aren't enthralled at the end of each brief chunk of time, they go somewhere else. Study TV ads and then see whether you can apply the things that do and don't work for you, as a TV viewer, to your own online presence. (But expect people to be a bit surprised when they see you channel-surfing with your remote control to find ads, rather than to avoid them!)

A lot has been written about the death of the TV advertising spot. This process is happening, but very slowly, and at the moment TV isn't going anywhere. So if you're fortunate enough to be able to run TV advertising, consider working together with the Web – using both media together is much more powerful. If you don't have the budget to advertise on it, TV is still a great medium to adapt for the Web!

Direct Marketing – Direct Mail

The annoying little pieces of mail that you receive after you have agreed to being sent 'more information' on a form at some point are sometimes worth looking at. Direct Mail should not be confused with 'door drops' which are the pizza and minicab cards you get through your door, Direct Mail is targeted specifically at you for a reason, is based upon information that you have given to the marketing company at some point and is part of the wider Direct Marketing medium that has a lot in common with online marketing. Direct Marketing specifically targets its audience with a message that is tailored to them. This can be by age, geography, purchasing habits, sex, pretty much any data that has been collected on you at some point.

It is worth taking a look at how companies that use direct marketing to target their audience. Look at the type of words and images that they use on their direct mail and try to understand why they have been used and how they appeal to their target audience, ie. you. Direct marketing's most close ally online is email marketing, the cornerstone of much digital marketing and the same techniques apply to both.

The Immutable Laws

If you ask any marketing professional for two books that you should read about branding and marketing they will undoubtedly point you towards *The 22 Immutable Laws of Marketing* (Al Ries and Jack Trout, Profile Business Publishing) and *The 22 Immutable Laws of Branding* (Al Ries and Laura Ries, Profile Business Publishing).

These books are amongst the most popular published on the subject, with the authors setting out the 22 essential 'Laws' that all businesses need to adhere to if they want to succeed in their marketing and branding efforts. These include the Law of Expansion, the Law of Contraction, the Law of Consistency and the Law of Mortality. And although the co-authors of this book would not normally suggest that you read books with such gimmicky titles, in this case we agree that the best things really do come in pairs.

The *Digital Marketing For Dummies* Internet Directory

'In a previous life, before I became a lemming,
I was a small company without a marketing plan.'

In this directory . . .

Where better to find out more information about Internet marketing than online? This directory gives you a long list of online resources to use for your online marketing effort. We include search engines, technology resources, lists of industry associations, and research companies – all with a description of what you can expect to find at each address.

Surfing the Internet aimlessly for information regarding the marketing of your company, products, or services could result in using up your time, and we all know time is money. Therefore, this section of the book contains a collection of sites to help cut down on the time you spend searching and directs you to the information you need. There are some US sites included, as we feel that as the Web is one big community, some of these can be of use as well, especially as it is a commonly held perception that the US is 18 months ahead of the UK – so we are also giving you a crystal ball!

Here are the main categories in this directory:

- ✔ Advertising
- ✔ Business Owner's Resources
- ✔ Government and Law
- ✔ Marketing
- ✔ News Online
- ✔ Search Engines and Directories
- ✔ Technology Resources
- ✔ Web Tools
- ✔ Miscellaneous

At the end of each category of sites, we include a section titled 'Other Stuff to Check Out.' Here you can find lists of URLs for additional sites that contain information related to the particular category.

Recognising Micons

For each entry, you may see one or more mini icons – micons – which provide a quick graphical reference to the site's characteristics. (No, 'micon' is not a Web site for con artists.) Here is a list of the micons and what each one means.

➔ **Download:** Software is available for downloading at this site.

$ **Fee required:** This site charges an access fee for some or all services.

 Message Board: These sites give you the chance to get involved in the discussion.

🛒 **Shopping:** The site features online shopping opportunities.

✍ **Sign In:** You may be required to register here for some services – such as e-mail lists. This usually means no more than providing your name, address, and e-mail address for demographic purposes.

Advertising

With TV commercials, ads on the Internet, billboards, and the sides of buses, what isn't used for advertising? Each day you are likely to be bombarded with hundreds of different ad messages that are trying to convey something to you. No business can survive unless it gets its message across to its customers. You have to do it, too, so here are a few sites to help get your message to your potential customers.

Brand Channel

www.brandchannel.com

Join the debate about branding: Brand Channel is an offering from global branding consultancy Interbrand. The forum gives you the opportunity to chat with fellow marketers about branding issues that concern you. The site also contains information about careers in branding as well as case studies.

Chinwag

www.chinwag.com

Discussions on this list focus on marketing and advertising: Chinwag is a hub site for a range of different marketing and advertising mailing lists. The areas covered include marketing, design, usability and e-commerce. Signing up to the lists is a good way of keeping up to date with the latest trends in the market You can subscribe by email to any of the forums that take your interest.

The Institute of Practitioners in Advertising

www.ipa.co.uk

$ ✍

Develop best practice guidelines: The Institute of Practitioners in Advertising (IPA) is the trade body and professional institute for 255 leading agencies in the UK's advertising, media and marketing industry covering the following sectors

- ✔ Creative
- ✔ Digital
- ✔ Direct Marketing
- ✔ Healthcare

✔ Media

✔ Outdoor

✔ Sales Promotion

✔ Sponsorship

The IPA Web site carries information about agencies that you may want to use for your marketing, as well as best practice guidelines.

Internet Advertising Bureau

www.iabuk.net

$ ✍

The online advertising industry association: The Internet Advertising Bureau (IAB) is the main trade body for the online advertising industry in the UK. Its resources include access to a knowledge bank of data covering online marketing, and it acts as both a best practice hub and a showcase for the best in online marketing. The IABs Web site carries a lot of links to resources online that can help you to do everything from tracking down an advertising agency to updating you with the latest industry information and news.

Internet Advertising Sales House

www.iash.org.uk

Information about the advertising sales house industry: IASH is the new trade body for the online advertising sales house industry – the people who sell your adspace to advertisers. The organisation's Web site is a good resource for information on this market niche. It also carries a code of conduct that members should adhere to.

Search Engine Watch

www.searchenginewatch.com

👓 ✍

Keep up to date with the fast paced search market: One of the best sites on the Web for keeping up to date with what is happening in paid search. The Web site contains links to a multitude of informational resources on search engine marketing, and also carries message boards on a variety of topics, which are regularly used by search marketers.

Other Stuff to Check Out

www.asa.org.uk

www.nma.co.uk

www.e-consultancy.com

www.ukaop.org.uk

www.dma.org.uk

www.mmagloabl.co.uk

www.mda-mobiledata.org

Business Owner's Resources

Marketing is a crucial part of running a business – but not the only part. There are a tonne of business owner's resources online. Maybe you prefer downloading business letters from the Web and finishing them yourself, as opposed to employing someone else to do it. If you're the do-it-yourself kind of person, these are the sites for you to check out.

Business Link

www.businesslink.gov.uk

✍

Get a helping hand setting up: This Web site provides you with information covering a whole range of business processes that you have to get to grips with when starting your new business. Practical advice is available on employment, marketing, taxes, IT and how to grow your business. The site is a must-view if you are starting your Web business.

Byte Start

www.bytestart.co.uk

Business plans, counseling, and various services for the small business: This portal is operated by small businesspeople for small businesses. The advice given ranges from start up guides to show you how to set up and structure your company to information on what technology hardware you might require for your needs.

Market Research Society

www.mrs.org.uk

Find a market research company: The Market Research Society (MRS) does pretty much what it says on the tin. The Web site gives you the ability to search for your market research requirements from a database of members, and carries a Research Buyers Guide for the UK and Ireland that is very useful if you want to hire a market research company. The online message boards allow you to ask questions and make specific requests of other users.

Other Stuff to Check Out

www.hmrc.gov.uk/startingup
www.bgateway.com
www.companieshouse.gov.uk

Government and Law

The government is a great source of marketing information. All UK government departments have Web sites, which are much more convenient to visit than going to a government office in person or trying to get through on the phone. Legal resources are also a good bet when planning your marketing efforts. Check out the following low-hassle government and legal resources.

Intellectual Property

www.intellectual-property.gov.uk

Protect your assets online: Intellectual property is very important to an online business. You should ensure that you have your intellectual property fully covered when you market online, and you should also ensure that you are not transgressing the intellectual property of others. This site will guide you through the protections and permissions that are involved in intellectual property.

OFT Distance Selling Regulations

http://www.oft.gov.uk/Business/Legal/
   DSR/default.htm

Legal help for e-commerce: If your online business involves e-commerce then you must ensure that you comply with regulations surrounding distance selling. The Web site of the Office of Fair Trading carries a downloadable document that gives you the outline of what you must do to comply with the law.

Small Business Service

www.sbs.gov.uk

Market research from the government: As an agency of the Department of Trade and Industry the small business service carries out consultations with small businesses in the UK with the aim of making the UK an enterprise society, and the best place in the world to start and grow a small business.

Web Accessibility

www.drc-gb.org

Make sure you are within the law when it comes to accessibility: Since the implementation of the Disability Discrimination Act all Web sites should give access to people with disabilities. The DRC Web site will give you clear guidelines on what you should do to stay within the law. For further info you can check out `www.w3.org`.

Other Stuff to Check Out

www.w3.org
www.direct.gov.uk
www.statistics.gov.uk
www.hmrc.gov.uk
www.dti.gov.uk

Marketing

Acquiring demographic information and marketing how-to info has never been this painless! The Web was seemingly *made* for storing statistics and suggestions that you can search and retrieve easily.

The Chartered Institute of Marketing

www.cim.co.uk

$

The UK's main marketing association: The CIM is the main trade body for the marketing sector in the UK. Its online services include online polls, directories of agencies, communities, notice boards and a vast amount of data on the UK market. It is well worth checking out if you are serious about your marketing efforts.

The Direct Marketing Association

www.dma.org.uk

$

Direct marketing practices, regulations, conferences, and seminars: If you're a direct marketer, – and, in a sense, everyone who uses the Internet for marketing is a direct marketer – this site deals with issues that may be useful to you. The site offers guidelines on ethical business practices, online marketing privacy principles, marketing by phone, and a news and events section. Other services include legal advice and best practice guidelines.

The Institute of Direct Marketing
www.theidm.co.uk

$

Using direct marketing effectively: The IDM provides services to the direct marketing industry including interactive marketing expertise, how to create successful email marketing campaigns and the publication of a quarterly magazine entitled 'The Journal of Direct, Data and Digital Marketing Practice' that covers new trends.

Marketing News Sites
www.brandrepublic.com, www.nma.co.uk and www.mad.co.uk

$

Read all about it: There are plenty of online resources that cover the online marketing industry. We have picked out three of the best here for you and you should check them out to monitor the latest trends and find out what companies are doing in the digital marketing field. These sites are also linked to offline magazines that may also be worth checking out. Also check out the blogs, events and directories that these sites offer.

The Marketing Society
www.marketing-society.org.uk

$

Championing marketing and marketers: The Marketing Society is designed to create a network for marketers to discuss current issues in the sector. It holds annual awards ceremonies and events as well as offering an email service called eNuggets which sends out regular information on trends in the industry.

Social Networks for Business
www.ecademy.com and www.linkedin.com

Keep in touch with like-minded professionals: Capitalising on the latest trend in online behaviour, these social networks are aimed solely at the business community and allow you to build up contacts within the marketing world. Such contacts can be very useful, allowing you to ask for help and garner recommendations to meet all of your marketing needs. The services include email alerts when new people want to join your network and profiles on all members, so you can screen out anyone who is not of use to you!

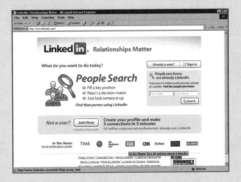

Other Stuff to Check Out
www.warc.com
www.e-consultancy.com
www.netimperative.com
www.zdnet.com
www.clickz.com

News Online

You don't need to go to your local library to get your hands on the latest copy of *The New York Times*, the *Wall Street Journal,* or magazines such as *Time* and *Forbes*. These leading publications – along with many others – are now available on the Web. Best of all, no ink to rub off on your hands!

FT

www.ft.com

$ ⊿

The world's number one business newspaper: The FT has been trailblazing online for many years. Its subscription-based services include email alerts, breaking news, in depth business analysis and specialist columns such as Lex. The breadth of the FT's business coverage is quite outstanding and you should definitely take up the Web site free trial offer and use the service for a while to see if it is of any use to you.

Guardian Unlimited

www.guardian.co.uk

⊿

Best online newspaper: The Guardian is consistently voted as the number one online newspaper in the world. It is worth checking out for its specialist Media Guardian section online and also for the range of services that it offers. It was the first publisher to see real success with podcasting and is ahead of its rivals when it comes to technological innovation. Like the more specialist FT, Guardian Unlimited offers a range of services from alerts to in-depth analysis and best of all is the fact that it is free, although the more specialist sections require you to sign up to them.

Wall Street Journal Online

www.wsj.com

$ ⊿

The first digital newspaper: The WSJ claims the accolade for being the first newspaper to embrace digital and charge for its services online. It operates different editions depending on where you are in the world and offers similar serices to those of The FT. The difference between the specialist newspapers is often in their tone, politics and reporting style – juts as it is in the mainstream press – but it is worth taking up the trials of these products to see if they inform you decision making at all.

Other Stuff to Check Out

www.businessweek.com
www.forbes.com
www.fortune.com
www.reuters.co.uk

Search Engines and Directories

When you don't know where to find something or somebody, these are the sites you turn to. Often searching for a term will make you end up with hundreds, thousands, or even millions of sites targeted to your search. Still, with some practice and patience, you can end up with some worthwhile *hits* (successful searches).

Google

www.google.com

Search overlord: Google.com is among the fastest pure search engines around. The search giant has been constantly developing its services over the past few years and its offering now includes Google Maps, Google Local, Google News, Google Groups, and Google Images to name but a few of the services available. (We cover Google in more detail in Chapter 9). All of these services are underpinned by adWords, Google's pay per click advertising service.

Lycos

www.lycos.co.uk

Directory services: Lycos is not considered to be one of the major search players out on the web, but it does contain a useful directory service that can be used to access business services. There was a time when the Lycos site offered little more than a service to search the Web for information, but since then it has broadened its offering to include free e-mail and site build and hosting services. It still places search on its home page but is not considered to be one of the 'Big Boys' these days.

MSN

www.msn.co.uk

A portal and a search service: MSN, like Yahoo!, is a business that combines both search services and a portal business that is based on advertising. Both MSN and Yahoo! differ from Google in this respect, although all three offer free email service

through MSN Hotmail, Yahoo! Mail and Google Mail respectively. The MSN Search service is commercialised through Microsoft adCenter – Microsoft's service that allows you to buy ads across all MSN and Microsoft online properties. In addition to this, MSN also offers a directory of services and other consumer products such as MSN Messenger.

Yahoo!

www.yahoo.co.uk

Search and Answers: Yahoo! is one of the big search players in the market and was created after two graduate students at Stanford University started cruising the Web and maintained links on their personal Web sites of all the sites they visited. Before long, this hobby became an obsession. Their graduate studies were put on hold, they became full-time Web cruisers, and they soon founded Yahoo!. Yahoo! has commercialised its search service through its pay per click advertising model called Yahoo! Search Marketing. Yahoo!, along with other search engines MSN and Google, cover almost the entire UK search landscape. It has also launched Yahoo! Answers, giving you the chance to put questions to real people for answers, and not just a search technology.

Yell.com

www.yell.com

Yellow Pages on the Web: What you find on this site is a lot more than what you would find in your local phone Yellow Pages directory. Yell.com has utilised the best of the Web to provide an impressive search experience that can cover the whole of the UK, not just your local area. The company has laso made its service available wirelessly through your mobile phone via WAP or text. It is a great resource for finding businesses no matter when or where you are.

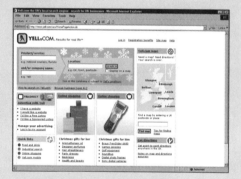

Other Stuff to Check Out

www.ask.com

www.dogpile.com

www.excite.com

www.hotbot.com

www.blinkx.com

Technology Resources

Whether you're in the market for hardware, software, or just some technical advice, you can find plenty of information online.

CNET's Download.com and Shareware.com

www.download.com and www. shareware.com

Collection of free software and shareware: Companies think nothing of paying hundreds of pounds for software; however, the general public have to think twice about it. Before diving into the high street shop and donating a few hundred pounds to its livelihood, drop by these sites to see whether you can find something that will do what you're looking for. Most of what's here is *shareware,* which means that you can try it for free before you buy it. In addition to shareware, the site also carries *freeware,* which is – you guessed it – free software. To find all the freeware on the site, do a search for *freeware.*

Microsoft

www.microsoft.com

Free software, technical information, and business resources: Hardly a day goes by that this company or its founder, Bill Gates, is not in the news. The largest software company in the world – with more than its share of millionaire employees – has a wealth of information on its Web site. Getting lost on this site is easy, but around every corner is useful information. Find free software, online technical support, and lots and lots of other goodies for managing a Web site and getting a business rolling.

Open Source Initiative

www.opensource.org

Open source software: This site gives you access to some of the web's best known software as used and developed by industry giants such as IBM, HP and Apple. The site champions Open Source — a process that makes the source code of software available for all to work on and create new developments, as long as those developments are then put out to the open source community again. It's a bit techie, but if you know what you are doing there are some good links to Web browsers and other software that you may find useful.

Voice over Internet Protocol

www.vonage.com or www.skype.com

'Free' phone calls over the Internet: Although VoIP sounds like an intimidating abbreviation it merely represents one of the more recent technological developments of the Internet age. Basically the technology allows you to make phone calls to other users on the same network for free through your Internet connection. You can also call standard phone lines, although there is a charge for this. This technology will only develop, so it is worth getting up to speed with it now and it could prove a cost effective tool in your marketing armoury, whilst at the same time showing that you are a forward thinking company.

Web based email

www.hotmail.com, www.gmail.com, and mail.yahoo.com

Get a free e-mail account and check e-mail from anywhere: When the Internet revolution took off, everybody wanted an e-mail address. So everybody got one, and then two, and then three addresses. If you're wondering why anybody would need more than one e-mail address, you probably haven't been hit with junk e-mail yet. What you may want to do is have one e-mail address for official business and another one for random, potentially frivolous e-mail (because you never know when you might find something useful in all that junk mail). The former you guard carefully, and the

latter you hand out freely. You can easily get a free e-mail account from MSN Hotmail, Google or Yahoo!. And one of the greatest things about these e-mail accounts is that you can check e-mail from any computer, anywhere, that has access to the Web.

ZDNet

www.zdnet.co.uk

Technical reviews of hardware and software: If you're in the market for a particular piece of hardware or software, visit this site for quality recommendations. ZDNet tests more hardware and software in a month than any one person can use in a year. Their recommendations are unbiased and usually on the money. So before you spend that hard-earned cash on a computer that breaks down every time the clock chimes 12, check out this site. In addition to hardware and software evaluations, you can also find interesting articles on current trends in the computer industry and technical how-tos about using new technology.

Other Stuff to Check Out

www.theregister.co.uk
www.vnunet.com

Web Tools

A tremendous number of great Web tool resources are out there – many are listed elsewhere in this Directory. Unfortunately, some Web tools sites have fallen out of date as technology has shifted. Others have "gone pro," moving out of the reach of beginners, or combined with non-Internet software development sites to create monolithic resources that are hard to find your way around in. Here are a few that are accessible by ordinary people.

Slashdot

www.slashdot.org

What would happen if a bunch of computer geeks who felt absolutely no obligation to the rest of society – except a shared need to bash Microsoft – created a news and information site? You'd get Slashdot. If you want to know what professional software and Web developers think, talk, and dream about, check out Slashdot.

The World Wide Web Consortium site

w3.org

You can track the ongoing deliberations of the World Wide Web Consortium as it builds the technical infrastructure for the Web at w3.org. If you're interested, you can even join one of the committees that contribute to the various aspects of Web infrastructure development. You can also research "from the horse's mouth" exactly what all those HTML tags do (and when they started doing it).

Miscellaneous

Here are some additional research-related sites. They didn't fit into a category listed previously but are sites that may be useful in your Internet marketing endeavors.

About.com.

www.about.com

Helpful information dished out by experts in their fields: About.com's approach to providing information on the Web is unique and refreshing. Like many other sites, this site provides a comprehensive listing of sites or areas of interests. But that's where the similarity ends. Each of the About.com's areas of interests is hosted by a Guide – a person who's an expert in that particular area. So, for example, a Guide who has actually started a business or two and gives a first-hand account of running a business, watching for pitfalls, and taking precautions hosts the Entrepreneur area. And if you'd like to be a Guide you can apply and be able to add .your opinions for the world to see.

Amazon

www.amazon.com

Any marketing book you can ever think of: Never underestimate the power of the written word. If you are looking for further reading about any aspect of online marketing then you must check out what has been written about the subject. Amazon is the best site for this as the reader recommendations can lead you to books that you may not think about searching for yourself.

European Union Resources

http://ec.europa.eu/enterprise/
index_en.htm

Your source of information for business in Europe: As the UK is part of the big melting pot that is Europe we thought that we should point you in the direction of information provided for small and medium sized businesses in Europe. Unfortunately, the EU is not well known for producing easy to explore Web sites, but this site carries links to information about grants and regulations that cover specific industries so may be worth a look. We warn you though, you may have to be a lawyer to understand any of the information that you find!

For Dummies Guides

www.dummies.com

Get simple information on a variety of subjects: What could be better than searching the Dummies Web site for information on your chosen subject. If something is stumping you and you can't figure it out and would like someone to walk through it with you, why not see if Dummies have a book that covers the subject?

Hitwise

www.hitwise.com

$

Even more quality research: Again, this site will require you to cough up if you want the detailed research, however it also releases top-line statistics that can be useful to your business. Check out the Data Centre on the web site to find out the top 10 sites in different categories. Hitwise monitors traffic usage by collecting data directly from the users ISPs, rather than Nielsen//NetRatings, which uses a panel based methodology. It's always best to cover your bases so we recommend you keep an eye on the data coming out of Hitwise as well. Also check out the analysts blogs which are linked from the site to see what the experts are thinking.

Nielsen//NetRatings

www.nielsen-netratings.com

$

Quality Research: You generally have to pay for this research but we felt that it was worth including as it is the premier online research company in the world and its results are generally respected. You can get some basic stats from the site that can be useful to you, such as the size of the UK net audience. Keep an eye on the company's press releases to find out the latest trends.

The UK Patent Office

www.patent.gov.uk

$

Patent and trademark searches,: The UK Patent office is a great place to see what is going on in the world of intellectual property. It has some great links to other sites containing important patent information as well as hosting the UK's database of trademarks – which you have to be registered on to protect your trademark. You can search by company to see who has registered what and when they registered it. This resource can prove very useful when researching for a new product launch or to see what the competition are up to.

Other Stuff to Check Out

www.dilbert.com
www.comscore.com
www.jupiterresearch.com
www.forrester.com

Index

Notes

Notes

FOR DUMMIES®

Do Anything. Just Add Dummies

UK editions

PROPERTY

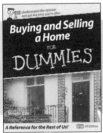

0-7645-7027-7

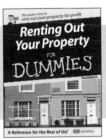

0-470-02921-8

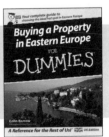

0-7645-7047-1

PERSONAL FINANCE

0-7645-7023-4

0-470-02860-2

0-7645-7039-0

BUSINESS

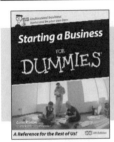

0-7645-7018-8

0-7645-7056-0

0-7645-7026-9

Answering Tough Interview
Questions For Dummies
(0-470-01903-4)

Arthritis For Dummies
(0-470-02582-4)

Being the Best Man
For Dummies
(0-470-02657-X)

British History
For Dummies
(0-470-03536-6)

Building Confidence
For Dummies
(0-470-01669-8)

Buying a Home on a Budget
For Dummies
(0-7645-7035-8)

Children's Health
For Dummies
(0-470-02735-5)

Cognitive Behavioural Therapy
For Dummies
(0-470-01838-0)

Cricket For Dummies
(0-470-03454-8)

CVs For Dummies
(0-7645-7017-X)

Detox For Dummies
(0-470-01908-5)

Diabetes For Dummies
(0-7645-7019-6)

Divorce For Dummies
(0-7645-7030-7)

DJing For Dummies
(0-470-03275-8)

eBay.co.uk For Dummies
(0-7645-7059-5)

European History
For Dummies
(0-7645-7060-9)

Gardening For Dummies
(0-470-01843-7)

Genealogy Online
For Dummies
(0-7645-7061-7)

Golf For Dummies
(0-470-01811-9)

Hypnotherapy For Dummies
(0-470-01930-1)

Irish History For Dummies
(0-7645-7040-4)

Neuro-linguistic Programming
For Dummies
(0-7645-7028-5)

Nutrition For Dummies
(0-7645-7058-7)

Parenting For Dummies
(0-470-02714-2)

Pregnancy For Dummies
(0-7645-7042-0)

Retiring Wealthy For Dummies
(0-470-02632-4)

Rugby Union For Dummies
(0-470-03537-4)

Small Business Employment
Law For Dummies
(0-7645-7052-8)

Starting a Business on
eBay.co.uk For Dummies
(0-470-02666-9)

Su Doku For Dummies
(0-470-01892-5)

The GL Diet For Dummies
(0-470-02753-3)

The Romans For Dummies
(0-470-03077-1)

Thyroid For Dummies
(0-470-03172-7)

UK Law and Your Rights
For Dummies
(0-470-02796-7)

Winning on Betfair
For Dummies
(0-470-02856-4)

FOR DUMMIES®

Do Anything. Just Add Dummies

HOBBIES

0-7645-5232-5

0-7645-6847-7

0-7645-5476-X

Also available:

Art For Dummies
(0-7645-5104-3)
Aromatherapy For Dummies
(0-7645-5171-X)
Bridge For Dummies
(0-471-92426-1)
Card Games For Dummies
(0-7645-9910-0)
Chess For Dummies
(0-7645-8404-9)

Improving Your Memory
For Dummies
(0-7645-5435-2)
Massage For Dummies
(0-7645-5172-8)
Meditation For Dummies
(0-471-77774-9)
Photography For Dummies
(0-7645-4116-1)
Quilting For Dummies
(0-7645-9799-X)

EDUCATION

0-7645-7206-7

0-7645-5581-2

0-7645-5422-0

Also available:

Algebra For Dummies
(0-7645-5325-9)
Algebra II For Dummies
(0-471-77581-9)
Astronomy For Dummies
(0-7645-8465-0)
Buddhism For Dummies
(0-7645-5359-3)
Calculus For Dummies
(0-7645-2498-4)

Forensics For Dummies
(0-7645-5580-4)
Islam For Dummies
(0-7645-5503-0)
Philosophy For Dummies
(0-7645-5153-1)
Religion For Dummies
(0-7645-5264-3)
Trigonometry For Dummies
(0-7645-6903-1)

PETS

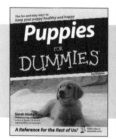

0-470-03717-2

0-7645-8418-9

0-7645-5275-9

Also available:

Labrador Retrievers
For Dummies
(0-7645-5281-3)
Aquariums For Dummies
(0-7645-5156-6)
Birds For Dummies
(0-7645-5139-6)
Dogs For Dummies
(0-7645-5274-0)
Ferrets For Dummies
(0-7645-5259-7)

Golden Retrievers
For Dummies
(0-7645-5267-8)
Horses For Dummies
(0-7645-9797-3)
Jack Russell Terriers
For Dummies
(0-7645-5268-6)
Puppies Raising & Training
Diary For Dummies
(0-7645-0876-8)

FOR DUMMIES®

The easy way to get more done and have more fun

LANGUAGES

Spanish FOR DUMMIES
0-7645-5194-9

French FOR DUMMIES
0-7645-5193-0

Italian FOR DUMMIES
0-7645-5196-5

Also available:

Chinese For Dummies
(0-471-78897-X)

Chinese Phrases
For Dummies
(0-7645-8477-4)

French Phrases For Dummies
(0-7645-7202-4)

German For Dummies
(0-7645-5195-7)

Italian Phrases For Dummies
(0-7645-7203-2)

Japanese For Dummies
(0-7645-5429-8)

Latin For Dummies
(0-7645-5431-X)

Spanish Phrases
For Dummies
(0-7645-7204-0)

Spanish Verbs For Dummies
(0-471-76872-3)

Hebrew For Dummies
(0-7645-5489-1)

MUSIC AND FILM

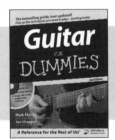

Guitar FOR DUMMIES
0-7645-9904-6

Filmmaking FOR DUMMIES
0-7645-2476-3

Piano FOR DUMMIES
0-7645-5105-1

Also available:

Bass Guitar For Dummies
(0-7645-2487-9)

Blues For Dummies
(0-7645-5080-2)

Classical Music For Dummies
(0-7645-5009-8)

Drums For Dummies
(0-471-79411-2)

Jazz For Dummies
(0-471-76844-8)

Opera For Dummies
(0-7645-5010-1)

Rock Guitar For Dummies
(0-7645-5356-9)

Screenwriting For Dummies
(0-7645-5486-7)

Songwriting For Dummies
(0-7645-5404-2)

Singing For Dummies
(0-7645-2475-5)

HEALTH, SPORTS & FITNESS

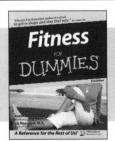

Fitness FOR DUMMIES
0-7645-7851-0

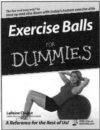

Exercise Balls FOR DUMMIES
0-7645-5623-1

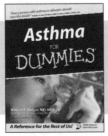

Asthma FOR DUMMIES
0-7645-4233-8

Also available:

Controlling Cholesterol
For Dummies
(0-7645-5440-9)

Dieting For Dummies
(0-7645-4149-8)

High Blood Pressure
For Dummies
(0-7645-5424-7)

Martial Arts For Dummies
(0-7645-5358-5)

Menopause For Dummies
(0-7645-5458-1)

Power Yoga For Dummies
(0-7645-5342-9)

Weight Training
For Dummies
(0-471-76845-6)

Yoga For Dummies
(0-7645-5117-5)

Available wherever books are sold. For more information or to order direct go to www.wiley.com or call 0800 243407 (Non UK call +44 1243 843296)

FOR DUMMIES®

Helping you expand your horizons and achieve your potential

INTERNET

0-7645-8996-2

0-471-77084-1

0-7645-7327-6

Also available:

eBay.co.uk
For Dummies
(0-7645-7059-5)

Dreamweaver 8
For Dummies
(0-7645-9649-7)

Web Design
For Dummies
(0-471-78117-7)

Everyday Internet
All-in-One Desk Reference
For Dummies
(0-7645-8875-3)

Creating Web Pages
All-in-One Desk Reference
For Dummies
(0-7645-4345-8)

DIGITAL MEDIA

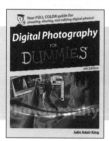

0-7645-9802-3

0-471-74739-4

0-7645-9803-1

Also available:

Digital Photos, Movies, &
Music GigaBook
For Dummies
(0-7645-7414-0)

Photoshop CS2
For Dummies
(0-7645-9571-7)

Podcasting
For Dummies
(0-471-74898-6)

Blogging
For Dummies
(0-471-77084-1)

Digital Photography
All-In-One Desk Reference
For Dummies
(0-7645-7328-4)

Windows XP Digital Music For
Dummies
(0-7645-7599-6)

COMPUTER BASICS

0-7645-8958-X

0-470-05432-8

0-7645-7326-8

Also available:

Office XP 9 in 1
Desk Reference
For Dummies
(0-7645-0819-9)

PCs All-in-One Desk
Reference For Dummies
(0-471-77082-5)

Pocket PC For Dummies
(0-7645-1640-X)

Upgrading & Fixing PCs
For Dummies
(0-7645-1665-5)

Windows XP All-in-One Desk
Reference For Dummies
(0-7645-7463-9)

Macs For Dummies
(0-470-04849-2)
